Vitaly Magidov

VITALY

The MisAdventures of a Ukrainian Orphan

*For orphans around the world and the people
who show them love and care*

Copyright

VITALY
The Misadventures of a Ukrainian Orphan
Vitaly Magidov

ALL RIGHTS ARE RESERVED
Copyright © 2021

All rights reserved. No part of this publication may be reproduced, stored, or transmitted in any form or by any means, electronic, mechanical, photocopying, recording, scanning, or otherwise without written permission from the publisher. It is illegal to copy this book, post it to a website, or distribute it by any other means without permission. The only exception is by a reviewer, who may quote short excerpts in a review.

Cover designed by Jake Naylor
Edited by Linda Forrest

This book is a combination of facts about the author's life and recounts events and conversations to the best of the author's memory. The conversations in the book all come from the author's recollections, though they are not written to represent word-for-word transcripts. Rather, the author has retold them in a way that evokes the feeling and meaning of what was said. While all the stories in this book are true, some dates, places, events, names, and identifying details of individuals have been changed, invented, and altered for literary effect. The reader should not consider this book anything other than a work of literature.

info@vitalybook.com
www.vitalybook.com

Printed in the United States of America

First Printing: Aug 2021
Amazon Kindle, Independent Publishing
Second Printing: Jan 2022
Amazon Kindle, Independent Publishing

ISBN: 9798425943651

Contents

Prologue   iv

I The Beginning

1	Once Upon a Time	3
2	My First Misadventure	7
3	Lullabies in the Rain	15
4	The Buried Secret	20
5	Childish Love	25
6	Bandits	29
7	Octobrists' Summer	34
8	Queen of Spades	42
9	Zarnitsa	54
10	Talent Show	66
11	Botsya's Mother	72
12	Loved Ones Lost	81
13	Chernobyl	87
14	Pan Kotsky	97
15	The Lord's Prayer	103
16	Too Bloody Curious	111
17	My Dear Mommy	119
18	Surprise Visit	128
19	A New Family	137

II Foster Care

20	Bazaar Food	147
21	Seconds	154
22	Bra Dag, Sweden!	163
23	Our New Home	174
24	Playing Games	183
25	New Friends	190
26	The Power of Words	199
27	History Lesson	206
28	My Sweet Sixteen	211
29	Christmas Traditions	220
30	Carol of the Bells	228

III Into Adulthood

31	Much Needed Help	237
32	Family Reunion	241
33	Impossible Dreams	249
34	Vocational School	259
35	My First Job	265
36	Valya's Greed	270
37	Girls	278
38	New Life and Loss	286
39	The One Who Loved	295
40	University	300
41	Searching for Jesus	307
42	The Evils of Alcohol	316
43	Disappointment	322
44	Broken Families	332
45	Choices	341

46 Beginnings Start with Endings   351

Epilogue   359
About the Author   369

Prologue

I AM A LITTLE BOY, running through the fields as fast as I can. I feel myself pursued by some invisible force, as though life itself is chasing me. The race to see my dreams come true consumes me. Still, I find myself distracted by the beautiful sunflowers along the path, tempting me with their promises.

I look back at the field now, trying to see my past, but everything is just a cloudy haze.

The beginning of my life was miserable by any standards. I grew up in an orphanage with life's deck stacked against me. Still, I did my best to enjoy that life and create success where I could. Whenever I walked the streets naively enjoying the day, I always liked to imagine what was behind the faces of strangers passing by, trying to read them as I might read a book. I enjoyed watching a mother walking the street hand-in-hand with her child because I knew it was a priceless commodity to have. I savored the sight of two brothers hugging each other or two lovers holding hands frozen in a moment of endless love. Most of all, I held faith in my parents, silently hoping they would come back for me.

I sought ways to bear the loneliness around me, but it wasn't easy. Being alone in a crowded place is not the kind of solitude that inspires youth. Many of the lonely souls around me—those left by parents who should have naturally given the purest unconditional affection—believed it was their fault for being rejected or left alone.

When I was young, I also thought some parts of me must change for others to love me. There were ways I stayed true to myself, but I also tried to be someone else. There were also people in my life that said they saw signs of greatness in me, that I was a young budding star. I wish these signs were as visible to me as they were to them. Unfortunately, I didn't see what they saw. I felt cursed by gender confusion and sexual attraction that was deemed unacceptable. I tried not to pay attention to what other people thought, but somehow it mattered. I didn't know who to be. So I tried to be like those around me. I tried to conform to the standard, but I was always different, and I often felt guilty for it. No matter what I did, I felt less than average—whatever being average was. I wasn't normal, but I thought I should be. So, I spent years trying to understand what 'normal' was.

Of course, some perspectives of normalcy remained eternal, bred deep in society's roots: enjoy your childhood, be good, don't lie, respect your parents, go to school, finish school, get a job, start your own family, retire and savor the rest of your life. Unfortunately for me, only a minority of the people I knew could live up to that pattern. So I was left trying to reconcile the contradiction.

I struggled for a long time until I finally questioned the standard itself. Who decided what was 'normal' anyway? The definitions of 'normal' are different from person to person. We all have unique beliefs, religions, views, and attitudes because normal depends on individual experiences. Having differences is what makes us normal.

We are all human. So many of our experiences are the same, but we are different from one another too. If only we could find a way to come together and get along with each other, we could see that it is easy to take what we have for granted, to forget we had a childhood spent with doting parents, or that we had opportunities in our lives that others didn't. We may even fail to care about the people who cared for us, regardless of their circumstances, or that even though we might have once felt wrapped up in misery, our lives eventually found love.

When we accept the complete picture of who we are, we can learn to appreciate times of sorrow because we will remember to recognize joy when it strikes us, and it will. I discovered that life is more than just white and black. It is a spectrum full of color, vibrant and versatile for those not bound by the chains of solely striving toward materialistic gains, forgetting about the most valuable and unavailable purchases.

I was lonely as a little boy, but I also understood my life had a purpose. I didn't know the steps I would take to achieve my goals, but I knew I was still alive because I kept moving forward. As long as I was working toward my dreams, I was truly living.

I didn't want to forget about the things that mattered. So, I spent my life searching through books, songs, movies, experiences, and childish experiments, exploring different belief systems and religions in an attempt to unravel the meaning behind my pain and loneliness. In the end, I learned and wish to remind everyone who may be doubting; regardless of the number of days we have in front of us; family, love, and acceptance are the things we all need. I always felt that little in life is more valuable than a simple hug or word of consolation. Even with a million other materialistic values around us, happiness cannot be everlasting without others' love and attention.

I have often wondered how it would be if everyone put their stories on paper, making their lives eternal for others to feel their successes and learn from their mistakes. If we learn from the world's history, why can't we also learn from people's individual stories? Perhaps we would discover that being normal is just one of the ideas we don't need and that judging has no place in any conversation, regardless of how pleasant our surroundings may be.

Now, I seldom reflect upon my history, not because I fear it might haunt me, but because it does not tell me where I am going. Our histories do not tell us who we are. We make ourselves by our choices. I chose not to let the unfortunate circumstances of my past define me.

I did not make peace with what life gave me. Instead, I was inspired to go further, beyond that unbearable state. Overcoming that history, tearing it down, and denying it, I learned to go beyond it. Making goals and striving to achieve them made my life worth living. Studying anything new was the only thing that brought me joy. Finding a way to be better, go further, learn, and later teach others who were willing to learn—that was my way out.

Besides sharing my life experiences, I decided that writing my 'Misadventures' would be an excellent way to draw parallels within cultures and religions. I think we all benefit when we find common ground between us. The best we can do in life is to make every experience count and maybe even help someone else while we do it.

I am not writing to be accepted, nor am I writing to be understood. I am writing to share and show that every life counts, no matter how lonely it may feel. Going back, dreaming, remembering, and recalling, I put my experiences on paper, reviving every moment, breaking loose, telling another story, and ultimately sharing the unique experiences of someone who counts... me.

I

The Beginning

Life is Beautiful! Enjoy every moment of it! Share it with your friends! Focus on the things you have in life and not what you lack!

—Vitaly Magidov

1

Once Upon a Time

Sign at the entrance to Chernivtsi written in Cyrillic - Ukrainian

THE BEGINNING OF NOVEMBER 1979 reflected the air of Communist Russia. It was almost always raining, and the weather influenced my little town of Chernivtsi. On most days, you could only see the bleak gray sky pouring its tears upon the face of the small Ukrainian city. Still, the sun's brightness would sometimes penetrate the clouds and make its way down to earth. The people could feel more than see the light because the sun didn't just pierce the clouds. It also penetrated the windows and the hearts of the people behind them.

Communism dictated its rules to the faithful people of Ukraine then. Still, so gracious were those times when you could buy ice cream for twenty Russian kopeks, or what would be two cents in America today. It was a time when people had respect for each other, and nobody swore or had the thoughts of hurting their neighbor when everybody felt as though they were free, but they weren't, not really. The shadow of socialism still covered their hearts.

Not far from the center of the town lay a petite woman of thirty-eight. She had blond hair, dark brown eyes, and tiny wrinkles that unfairly aged her face. The clouds hung heavy outside her hospital window, spreading as much gloom over her as they did the rest of the town. The first days of November were the worst for her. She was sure she couldn't go on, and she still had to carry the child for who knew how many more days.

Some might argue that the alcohol she consumed every day caused her trouble. It was killing her, but it also saved her. It killed her pain and gave her the strength to endure her suffering. She still had a lot of power. She knew how to fight and win battles, which helped her survive. She knew alcohol might damage the life growing inside her but didn't care. Without her daily dose, there was too much pain. So, she drank. As much as she could, she drank.

She was selfish. There is no doubting that. She would not concern herself with how to get money for food or clothes to wear. She would not think of serving others or how to care for the child she carried. Her only concern was surviving the pain of that day. She would drink, and she would count the minutes until the blessed moment finally arrived—a moment most would still count as the miracle of life. For her, it would be the glorious gift of her freedom.

Peace Hospital silently whispered into the ears of its patients, "sleep, sleep," until the only sound you could hear was the drip of a faucet in the far hall bathroom. Six hours of peaceful bliss were still drifting aimlessly through the corridors when screams suddenly pierced the stillness, bursting with fluorescent light from a single room to flood the otherwise darkened hall. The screams drowned out the doctor and nurses, who were doing everything they could to give this child its very best chance at survival.

The mother lay crying and screaming, begging the doctor for just one drink, "just a little something for the pain... please?!?!"

The doctor ignored her cries, dismissing her sickness to think only of the child.

The nurses responded, begging her, "Please, remain calm. For the sake of your baby."

Her cries continued over their words. She didn't care. She couldn't think of anyone or anything. Her pain was too great. So it was left to the valiant effort of the doctor, nurses, and their overwhelming patience to bring this sweet new life into the world.

"What will you call him?" the nurse asked the exhausted mother as they reached to her with a swaddled baby boy in their arms.

After a moment of deafening silence, she accepted the child, answering, "Vitaly."

I was four kilograms when I was born, and as my name suggests, I was full of life. Though I began on an artificial respirator and didn't grow as fast as the other babies, I gave life everything I had from the very start.

They didn't expect much from me, saying I had some kind of dysfunction in my "Psycho System," but even then, before I was conscious enough to know, I was determined to succeed. I started to walk when I was almost two and had already made tremendous developmental improvements by the time I was three. Life seemed to stack the deck against me, but I was determined to overcome the odds. I wouldn't quit. Maybe I was like my mother that way.

Maybe I learned my courage from the woman that gave me life, but that is all she gave. She walked out of the hospital without me that day. She left, and I stayed with the doctors and nurses until I was a toddler, old enough to attend the young children's home with the other orphans. When I moved to the Detski Dom, or what you might think of as preschool, it was amazing to see so many children there. The hospital nurseries were small. As an adult, I learned that there were over twenty thousand young children in the USSR at that time who did not have parents willing or able to care for them. Those children, like me, lived in children's homes until they were old enough to go to an orphanage.

I was one of about eighty children, thrust into a world where we all needed love. Each of us was different, but with many stories that were the same, getting all we could from just a handful of educators. It seemed we were left to begin our lives with a disadvantage. Still, we all had our chance. In the end, it is what you do when you don't have the advantage that counts.

2

My First Misadventure

Chernivtsi Orphanage on Fastivska Street where I grew up.

SURROUNDED BY THE MAGNIFICENT crown of the Carpathian mountains, Chernivtsi sat atop fertile soil on the upper course of the river Prut. As the cultural, educational, and architectural hub of Ukraine, the city suffered continued attacks by warriors and influxes of refugees as the currents of many nations altered its destiny. Every new conquest changed its history, and its people as various rulers selflessly adapted it to fit their benefit or belief.

A heavy stream of conquerors ravaged the town, but I didn't see scars carved into the cobblestone streets. I saw something more. I loved wandering and wondering who else had passed along the roads I walked. I imagined that those feet were still there, traveling with me, only caught up in another realm, repeating history by trying to fix what is wrong and preserve what is right.

The city is a better place now. It is slowly blooming, finding its way to survive and be free. Some of those currents of the past have stopped, disappeared, or maybe we just forgot them behind the unusual peace empty battlefields left in their place. Chernivtsi was one of those war-torn places that seemed to hold a composure only occasionally disturbed by its chilly wind.

Wherever I have traveled in my life, I have always longed to return and see the sign outside the city entrance, saying "Chernivtsi," but it wasn't always like that, not when I was a boy.

I once heard that Chernivtsi owes its name to the black color of the city walls, built from dark oak layered with its black-colored soil. Like something birthed from the soul of the land itself, a building with the same kind of stoic composure stood on the outermost edge of the town. Surrounded by shy crowns of flowers planted carefully by the little hands of its residents, the Orphanage on Fastivska Street reached toward the fading light of another day. As they worked with discipline cut deep into their thoughts, anyone passing by could hear their voices chanting:

Ravlik Pavlik, vysun rozhki,
   Dam tebe kusok kartoshkii

Esli budet malo, dam kusochek sala

Ravlik Pavlik, show your antenna,
  If you do, I will give you a piece of potato
  If it is not enough, I will give you a piece of fat

My voice stood out from the rest, singing to the snails, hoping to see their antennas. With every rainstorm, they came out, and I joined them. I removed my shoes and thought my shirt was too much to wear. I longed for the awakening touch of moisture falling from the sky, wondering how many other faces it bathed with its crisp refreshment. Rain was one of the things I enjoyed the most. I loved playing or watching television in the playroom I shared with dozens of other curious orphans, but sometimes there were too many children trying too hard to be happy. The rain was something I could enjoy alone.

I was like everyone else on sunny days, trying to squeeze every bit of happiness I could from my environment. No matter how innocent the games, I enjoyed pushing limits and finding ways to test my wit and strength. Our playground was old and well used, but I thought it was magnificent. A steel rocket built for climbing stood glorious next to swings, merry-go-rounds, and teeter-totters. The missile called to me, daring me to abandon my contemplation of the flowing clouds and accept its challenge.

In a few seconds, I was at the top, with my head held high. Taking a deep breath, I puffed out my chest and stood bathed in pride. I reached to touch the sky with one of my hands, but I was cut short. The sound of my friends' voices cut through the rays of sunshine that were selflessly spotlighting my accomplishment.

"Quick, the headmaster is coming!"

Their words released the restless bird waiting in my chest. I felt it flutter and come to life as I saw the headmaster coming toward me.

Then, as if struck with a brick on my head, I reacted. I swallowed the bitter lump growing in my throat and rushed to find a way down from the rocket.

Looking up again, I saw my friends running away from sure detention, but I would not be so lucky. I suddenly slipped and fell to the ground. Uncomfortable warmth rushed through my head, melting the frozen soil beneath me. The earthy smell of dirt and grass joined with the severe vibration of pain, reminding me of bones I seldom considered, bones that were still intact just minutes ago. The warmth I first felt in my head now burst from my wrist, stretching the skin tight as it swelled. Finally, as all these sensations gathered into a single devastating moment, my face twitched in pain, and an uncontrolled scream escaped my lips.

"For God's sake, Vitaly, what were you thinking, climbing up that high?!" The headmaster's voice was a perplexing blend of anger and compassion as he helped me stand. Though he took me by the arm that wasn't injured, I could feel the bones in my wrist trembling in pain and distress. I wanted to cry, but I kept the tears in the corners of my eyes. As we entered the building, we passed my friends all huddled together. I could see them wanting to renounce the guilt of running and bury it deep by their silence. They tried to appear as excluded from the story as my arm was from my body.

The headmaster Vasyl Ivanovych took me to the recovery room we liked to call 'the isolator.' That day, it wasn't a lonely place. Instead, it was full of people who wanted to discover what had happened. The pulsing, hot pain that echoed in my ears like a drumbeat joined their worried voices—making my head spin.

The trauma of the moment, or maybe the pain and hospital-like environment, took me back to growing up in the Peace Hospital nursery, a baby boy, forgotten by his mother. Her name was Evheniya Mikitivna, and she began her life in Russia on a bitingly cold day in 1941.

Born with her, Chernivsti witnessed the birth of a second world war. Tanks rumbled down narrow city streets, drowning out the sounds of her first cries, wiping out her hopes and dreams with them.

I was born thirty-eight years later, in a small hospital painted with the same gray carelessness as the war. I liked to imagine my birthday as a magical day with pleasant expectations hanging above Chernivtsi. Still, I suppose I was just another drop in the sea of humanity, one more soul to explore, love, and suffer, just another crier echoing through the hospital halls hoping to make history.

My mother later told me that I left her womb minutes after a shot of vodka ran through her bloodstream. Neutralizing her pain with alcohol was a deeply established habit. Its roots wrapped around her damaged liver and into the cord that held us together for nine months. I suppose we were never closer than we were at that time. My birth severed that connection, and after a hearty scream, I was breathing the world's air. I did not have the rumbling tanks to overwhelm the sound of my sorrow, but I began my journey crying nonetheless.

The last thing my mother did for me before she left was to name me 'Vitaly,'—with the accent on "a," rather than the "i." Though people often mispronounce it, the meaning is unmistakable. Vitaly means "life" or "the one with a desire to live," and I suppose that my name was, in fact, my destiny. It allowed me to find beauty in even the ugliest of experiences.

I don't think I consciously remembered my beginnings, but I dreamt of what I wanted them to be. But it wasn't night, and I wasn't dreaming. This time trauma enveloped me as I slipped in and out of memories, traveling back and forth between the pain of my origins and the searing agony in my wrist.

"Vitaly.... Vitaly.... Vitaly!" a faint voice called my name from what seemed to be miles away.

My dreamless sleep was interrupted, and I tried to open eyelids that felt heavier than rocks. A silhouette was gently leaning over my body, trying to rouse me from a memory that felt too real to leave.

As the morning sun worked its way through the windows, a golden glow wrapped itself around the silhouette, bathing the angel in a nearly divine halo. A hoarse whisper escaped me, "Mom?"

"Vitaly. Wake up, Vitaly," the clarifying nature of the chilly morning air overtook the warmth of the vision as I recognized the chestnut curls of Tamara Petrivna, a strict but thoughtful teacher at the orphanage. I was glad to see my instructor but also worried about her judgmental reaction. The fear of punishment overtook the dreams of a childhood I never had, chasing the final remnants of who my mother might have been from my mind. Finally, I came back into the moment and the overwhelming pain of my broken wrist.

She saw I was awake, and her fear exploded, becoming the only life in the room. "What did you do to yourself?" she asked, not posing the question to me as much as she was to some elusive power that might one day control my adventurous spirit.

Although I heard her question, I was overwhelmed with the feeling that every answer I could give would be inappropriate or wrong. So I froze like a captured animal, decided not to blink or move, keeping my voice lodged somewhere between my brain and vocal cords.

"What were you thinking? Why would you climb that high, and then of all things, jump from that God-forsaken piece of steel?" She walked in circles in front of my bed, with her eyes nailed to the well-scrubbed floor: She was angry, but I also noticed the worry in her eyes and that her voice occasionally cracked beneath the bitterness and fright.

"You could have gotten out with more than just your arm broken... do you know that? What if you....?" She stopped suddenly, unable to continue. Sighing, she took a moment, looking at the freshly plastered cast binding my wrist. She then continued decisively, "What would we do if you ended up with a broken back or legs? Did you think about that?" I could hear her vocal cords tightening as she fought to control her tears.

After a moment, she continued in an even controlled tone, one painfully void of emotion. For a moment, when she was so upset, she seemed to see me as a mother might see her child. Concern overcame her, but she stifled her affection. She was back again, a teacher speaking to a wayward student. "There is someone outside who would like to see you. I will leave you two alone for a while."

Before she finished saying the words, I knew who it would be. She was talking about Igor, the only other person I could understand without a single word spoken. He entered the room, looking around to gather all of the information he could. Today was his first time seeing the isolator. It wasn't mine.

Tamara Petrivna looked at him, "Please, try not to stay longer than half an hour. Breakfast is about to start." Then, she turned to cast a final glance at me and left the room.

"Hey, Vitaly!" I could hear the guilt nearly burst from him as he nestled himself at the bottom of my wrinkled bedding. "They told me I was supposed to ask you how you feel, but I bet you feel horrible. I'm sorry for not being there."

I suddenly remembered that he wasn't at the playground when I fell from the rocket. I was unable to hide the smile this stirred. I was glad he wasn't one of the deserters who ran to protect themselves and not me. Igor was always there for me. We had a special connection, something more than I had with anyone else in the world. We were linked together like we had known each other all our lives.

I tried to stop his guilt, "You don't need to be sorry. You weren't even there, which is good. Everyone else ran away when they saw the headmaster coming." I was mad. They didn't even care if I was okay, but my curiosity about Igor overtook my worry, "Where were you anyway?"

"I was in the garden, making dens," he said, dropping his head to hide the shame drawn on his face.

I started laughing uncontrollably. "Dens?!?! That sounds cool,"

His laughter soon joined mine, and I knew things would be okay again. "We'll make more dens together when I get out of here. Deal?"

He nodded, "Deal."

We sat silently for a moment as kids sometimes do, waiting for the next thing to say. Before we could come to it, a teacher entered, carrying a breakfast tray. The food at the orphanage wasn't always good, but judging by the growling sound in my stomach, I guessed that anything would taste delicious to me today.

Igor jumped from the bed, looking over the incoming tray, trying to discover what we were having for breakfast. From the look in his eyes, I could see he was hungry too.

He headed toward the door to find some food of his own, but he stopped and turned at the last moment, almost to confirm I would be okay. Then he smiled and said, "See you, Vitaly."

I smiled back. That was all I needed, a smile from Igor and whether I ended up in detention or not; I also knew I would be alright.

3

Lullabies in the Rain

*Kids at the Summer Camp with our Instructor in the front.
I am way on the back corner at the top on the left, hiding.*

AFTER THREE DAYS IN THE ISOLATOR, I returned to my routine, which meant spending more time with Igor and my other friends. However, it also indicated I must return to my chores. I had an endless list of duties, one of which was hand washing my clothes. It was painful with an injury. I can still feel the sting of when the clothes got heavy, all soaked in water and soap. Igor tried to help me, but he also had his clothes to wash, and I didn't want him to get a double round of laundry. So, I pretended not to recognize his attention and worked quickly.

After finishing the laundry, it was time to take a shower. Holding soap was a challenge, but I forgot about the pain as I knew there were rays of sunshine outside my window, inviting me into the open air for a playful afternoon with my friends. I smiled with anticipation as the laughter and screaming of children playing catch, swinging, and enjoying the teeter-totter broke the silence on Fastivska Street.

I would soon be dressed and with them again, deeply involved in games, too busy to notice what anyone else was doing. I loved that time when play was the only chore left on my long list of things to do, but I still found myself distracted, repeatedly glancing at the gate, expecting someone, anyone, to appear and take me home with them. I liked to imagine that someone passing by our building would find the playful screaming enjoyable and decide to enter the world of orphans looking for a child to love. They rarely did. They continued with their lives, not willing to admit the presence of the children they were leaving behind. Still, I dreamed that all of us would have a home of our own one day and that every one of my friends would forget what it meant to be parentless.

As I made my way to the playground, Igor was already waiting for me. I went straight to him, speaking in a mischievous whisper, "How about we start digging?"

He smiled and followed me to the garden. I scrutinized the trees behind us, hoping no one would see us leave, but the only thing following us were more screams and laughter of children lost in their adventures. Finally, we were safe to begin our next experiment.

Leaves covered the ground in the small orchard nestled next to an empty side of the orphanage. Not many children played here as there was nothing but the earth and the garden to entertain them. Enjoying the quiet of nature was something both Igor and I loved. So we could often find places like this where it was just the two of us and everything nature had to offer.

Over the last year, the teachers at the orphanage had guided us through each step of the flower's journey, beginning with the seed. We learned to collect their pistils in the fall and replant them. In spring, we pruned and nurtured the garden's growth by cleaning out the weeds and watering them with buckets of water from the orphanage building. We stood now, surrounded by the earthy fragrance of the garden we had planted. Inhaling the scene around us was sweet and gratifying. The fallen leaves danced with the mild aroma of the flowers, making every one of my senses come to life.

I walked up to lean on a tree, taking a spot I thought was perfect for our work. Igor was crouched in the shadows of the building, bent in search of something. As he came into the light again, I saw he was clumsily carrying scrapped objects he had found. They looked like chunks of brick that had fallen from the orphanage walls and turned out to be perfectly acceptable substitutes for shovels when we started digging the hole for our den.

We were only halfway through making our perfect hiding place when I began to feel random drops of rain land on my forehead. I ignored them, wanting to finish the project we started. As the drops began to multiply, I felt them tangle in my eyebrows before gathering to rest in the corners of my eyes, but I kept digging.

"Do we stop now?" Igor asked.

"No," I laughed, "We just dig faster until the rain starts pouring."

We continued digging, and when Igor thought the den was ready, he jumped in to see if both of us could fit. Igor wasn't as small as I was, but it was perfect. So, we started gathering the already damp leaves, and after we collected a proper pile, we found branches to lay across the top of the hole. After blanketing the sticks with the leaves, we hid inside. Rain drummed atop the stockpile, creating a melody that reminded me of someone I knew. That sound was the closest thing to a lullaby I had heard in a very long time. It took me back to the times when I was too small to sing to myself, a time when nurses probably cradled me, giving me as much motherly love as they had to offer. I didn't know how young I was when my mother abandoned me. So, I closed my eyes and pretended she was there, singing to me through the rain.

The warmth of Igor's body made my imaginings as tangible as they could be, and his silence made me think that maybe he was also trying to recall his mother's voice. We lay together quietly, allowing the rain to be our substitute for the comforting sound of a mother's loving song. I let the memory of a beautiful woman blind me as if this moment was a piece of heaven. I felt it like the sun and the sky, the warm air I was breathing, the earth beneath us, and the bed where I usually slept, cuddling my pillow. I could almost hear her humming a divine melody I had never heard before, making me dizzily intoxicated with the feeling of unconditional love. I lay there knowing that even if the sky fell today, I would be safe, sound, and sleeping peacefully.

After what felt like an eternity spent wrapped in my pleasant trance, I was awakened by Igor's voice telling me that we needed to go. The rain had stopped. Still, the lullaby was playing in my head, mystifying my thoughts with imagined memories of my mother. I tried to hold onto every impression of her, modifying, recreating, and beautifying everything I knew about her. I rewrote the stories I heard, putting her on a throne made of unconditional devotion.

Only later, as I grew, would I see the real woman who was likely lying in the rain-drenched streets, buried in the oblivion of alcohol.

Nevertheless, until that time came, I had a world where I made her mine and where I was hers and where we loved each other. When I wasn't eating, working, or going to school, I spent most days with my head wrapped in a dreamy mist of wishes, hopes, and expectations. Every day I dreamed of falling asleep in her arms, our limbs crossed in one warm unbreakable hug. I held hope until the very last second when they would lock the doors against another day where she didn't come, and I would go to bed, clinging to a pillow wet with tears, pretending it was the giant stuffed bear I always hoped she'd give me.

It was late as we rushed into the building. Tamara Petrivna was already trying to chase the other children into their beds, threatening to call the headmaster if they didn't listen. So, she didn't notice when we came in later than everyone else, still covered in the dirt of our hiding place. I snuck past her, watching her threats successfully work on some of my friends. I never responded well to force, but I knew she was trying her best, so I decided to oblige and head to bed.

Tiny needles coursed through my body, injecting exhaustion into my head and making my eyelids heavy. As I undressed, I was unusually silent, trying to ignore the voices of boys colliding around me and hold tight to the memory of the rain lullaby instead. Mesmerized by thoughts of my pillow and my only other chance to hug and be hugged, I wished I was already out of my wet clothes and drowning my face in the warm comfort of sleep.

As I climbed into bed, clamoring for the same comfort I felt only moments ago in the den, I pulled the blanket over my head and lay on my belly. I was almost entirely covering my pillow—the only thing that separated me from the hard mattress beneath me. Memories of Igor's company clouded the cravings of my dreams as thoughts of my mother faded from my mind, temporarily replaced by the feeling of genuine warmth and safety that only exists when one person touches another.

4

The Buried Secret

My brother Slavik on the very left and sister Nadya at the front right playing in the sand.

I DIDN'T REALIZE THAT MY EYES had closed when I first saw the beautiful woman. I could see she was the kind of woman who knew how to make you feel cherished and loved. In the dream, she was looking at two little boys. One of them wrapped his arms around her, clinging to her love. The boy's skin was blonde and freckled, illuminated by sunlight trying to break through the glass doors that rested behind the woman's eyes.

The woman's skin was as dark as night, holding stars in her chest and showing a thousand moons in her stiff smile. I could see the muscles around her lips trembling as she worked to control the facade of artificial kindness. From behind the woman's eyes, the clinging boy tried to wave, but he was trapped by her as if she was trying to keep him only to herself.

The other boy returned my gaze with lips turned up in a silent grin, glowing like a saint born to rescue the young child. He then took the younger boy's hand and led him from the room, passing through the glass doors. I tried to see where they were going. It was like a portal to another world where a vibrantly green field existed in anticipation of a visit.

The woman watched them. Then, she looked through me, a stiff smile still hanging from the corner of her flawlessly shaped lips. There was no wind. Still, her hair danced, catching bits of sunlight, twisting and waving like a mermaid caught in a raging sea.

I opened my eyes to the endless warmth of my pillow, wanting to bathe myself in the saintly comfort of my dream. I wanted to be in the lush green field, far away from the gray torment of another day at the orphanage, especially this day. But, unfortunately, it was Subotnik—Saturday, which meant there would be even more things to do before I could get back to making dens with Igor.

Shaking the last of the vision still hanging from my eyelashes, I got up, put on clothes, and bolted from the room. I was eager to complete my chores, not just because I wanted to dig with Igor, but because getting busy meant my day would pass quickly. Sunday was knocking at my door with nervous euphoria, and my bones felt as though they were nothing but air. Sundays were the only days I got to have ice cream—one of the best things in life.

Ice cream and our weekly trip to the cinema were the best things we had at the orphanage. There was nothing better to me than the moments when big-screen pictures collided with sweet frozen delights. So, naturally, I rushed right to Tamara Petrivna on Saturday, asking what we needed to do.

As I approached her, she was yelling something about a hole in the ground. The words squeezed past a jaw so tight they made little sense. Her angrily pressed teeth stuck out from her jaw as if she might bite someone. She wasn't just angry about a hole being there. Given that the culprits covered the shelter with fallen leaves, she thought that someone made it as a trap. She never suspected the ditch might be a drum for the rain to play or a sanctuary for the lost.

I stood back, putting on a face that wouldn't expose my guilt, and allowed her to pump out her rage. I tried to escape the fact that Igor and I were the "bandits" she was rebuking and tried not to laugh when I heard the devious plans she imagined were behind our adventure. I stifled my smile and tried to think of something to make things right.

Inhaling air filled with my teacher's screams, I erupted, "I will fix it!" The words burst forth from my mouth before I could stop them.

I waited for her to continue showering screams, but instead, she just stared at me. It felt like an eternity before she snapped coldly, "Very well! You will find a shovel in the garage."

As suddenly as the onslaught had begun, it ended. All that remained was the brisk click of her shoes traveling down an otherwise silent hall.

Knowing exactly where the shovel was, I took off to find it. I didn't want to bury the den, but I had no choice if I wanted my Sunday treasures. Doing something wrong would mean being grounded, which in turn promised that I wouldn't be able to go to the cinema or have ice cream with the rest of the group.

I raced to the small structure behind the main building. Like most garages, ours mainly served for storing tools and old things no one needed. It was an undeniable grave of discarded treasures. I searched for the shovel—displaced from its usual spot by the garage doors—when I unexpectedly stumbled upon a pleasant reward. A small relay engine was sitting by a pile of unwanted aluminum scraps. I moved to the doors, looking to see if anyone was near, then came back in to take the leftovers.

My mind flooded with endless ideas of what I could craft out of the remains I found as I rushed across the backyard, focused on a new use for the den Igor and I created. My heart pounded under the gold mine I carried against my chest. Terrified of being caught, I gently set the scraps in the pit. Then, I covered the treasure with the same leaves we used to bury ourselves beneath the rain.

Returning to the garage, I searched for the shovel, desperately looking to find it before anyone discovered my cache. Eventually, my eyes landed upon it, and relief swelled in my chest. I rushed back to the den, manically scraping dirt from around the hole, to hide my latest prize.

My head swam with ideas and expectations. Making toys was one of my favorite things, but we didn't have much to use. Between classes, writing lessons, meals, and Sunday movies, we didn't have many things to occupy our minds at the orphanage. So, we often visited the junkyard behind our school to find bounty we could use to make new playthings. Our instructors taught us how to sew, knit, and develop our creativity by learning handy activities to help us as adults, but those things weren't the same. They weren't for fun. They were for survival. I can still hear Tamara Petrivna's words to this day, "If I have a hole to patch, there will be no one to mend it for you. You will need to do it yourself." I think that's true for a lot more than sewing.

I often took the things I learned to another level. I would knit clothes for my toys. I also did cross stitch and liked to draw the cartoons I found in wrappers from the bubble gum people would sometimes bring to the orphanage. I found ways to fill the empty times of day, but of all the things I learned to do, those I enjoyed most had to do with electricity. There was something immensely satisfying for me in seeing my creations serve a purpose. When I found the engine, big plans began forming in my mind. I imagined creating something extraordinary from what others thought were scraps.

As I shoveled, I prayed that no one would notice the junk's disappearance, at least not before Sunday had arrived. I took my time making sure I concealed the den, making it appear as if it never existed. By the time I finished, all that remained was freshly tilled soil, and I knew that would dry, blending to match the rest of the dirt. I scattered leaves across the area, mimicking nature as much as possible. In a day or two, no one would imagine it was a place with buried treasure.

I hid it so perfectly, the thought of forgetting the place myself planted a seed of fear in my chest. So, I took a couple of twigs and dug them deep into the ground, leaving only tips to reach for the sky. Then, I stood up and gazed at my handiwork. As I returned to the garage to leave the shovel where it belonged, I thought of how pleased I was with my ingenuity. Two little twigs, invisible to anyone but me, stood guard for me until the day I could come back and reclaim my prize.

5

Childish Love

Children ready to enjoy Summer Camp. Notice the rocket in the back. Just the kind of thing I couldn't wait to climb.

WHEN I RETURNED TO THE ORPHANAGE, it was pulsing with dozens of innocent bodies, each consumed by its current endeavor. Some were sweeping the floor or dusting while others scrubbed common areas. I could tell Subotnik had begun, and I was already waiting for it to end.

Weekdays were already busy for us. Every day, we would wake up and make our beds. Then, we would wash our faces and dress in preparation for our lessons. Our classes began right after breakfast and continued until lunch. After lunch, we had an hour of playing sports and a nap followed by a small snack of milk and cookies or sometimes pie. We would then do homework until dinner. At the end of our busy day, we watched television until it was time again to prepare for sleep. It felt like every day was a long day of exhausting chores and endless lists of things to do, but with our extra duties on Saturday, the sunlight bled out long before we would have time to do anything but clean.

This particular Saturday, I couldn't stop thinking about the nighttime journey of the sun. I couldn't wait for it to rise again and shine its light on my long-expected Sunday. So, the moment I finished my chores, I rushed past the friendly conversations and back to my pillow. Warm notes of red and purple colored the clouds as I stowed the mop and rags and prepared to put another Subotnik behind me.

The other children like to stay up a little longer to talk and play. So, I knew our room would be full of coveted silence. I could fall asleep quickly when it was quiet. So, I rushed to change and climb into bed, but I soon realized I wasn't alone. I noticed the shape of a body lying on my bed, all curled up and trembling quietly.

I approached slowly, wondering who it might be, already believing I knew who it was. Then I saw Igor's head, caressed by the fading light coming through the window. I stopped for a moment. I didn't know what to do. Igor was bigger and stronger than most of us, but tonight he looked small. Still, I understood his pain and inevitably compared it to my own. Emotions buzzed in my head, hysterically bumping into one another as I approached him and laid my hand on one of his arms.

He recoiled with a wet and silent cry and began rocking back and forth, resembling the rhythmic beat of the rain lullaby that comforted us in the den. I stood back, moving to the other side of my bed. I didn't know how to help him. I just wanted to be asleep already, calling to the dreams hanging above my pillow, but I recognized his sorrow. I was drawn to it, almost feeling obligated to make it disappear and frighten it into never coming back again.

Eventually, my instinct took over, and I returned to the bed to lay beside his twitching body. I carefully wrapped my arm around him, silently consoling him, feeling every tear as if it was my face they saturated. I held him until his trembling faded. He relaxed a little, but he wouldn't look into my eyes. Maybe he was like me, fearing loneliness, trusting another person to see, ashamed of being left to face life alone.

We lay together, holding each other as close as we could. I remember feeling overcome with everything Igor was to me. I felt friendship, love, and a stirring of emotion I didn't understand then. I never knew what to think of my feelings for Igor. He wasn't like my other friends. He made me feel special, and he made me feel excited too. My face always flushed when he looked into my eyes. My heart raced, and my body trembled, stirred with an attraction I never felt for anyone else. Still, I didn't feel the same stirrings that night. The heat that usually rushed through my body when I was with him was quiet. We shared only our pain and loneliness. These feelings both of us understood.

We held each other until my eyes collapsed, calling the dream upon me, continuing where I left off the night before. The dark-skinned women stared at the two boys as they ran and played across the sparkling fields of thousand suns. The sky was cloudless, and the grass was still. It is as if the wind had forgotten this place. The boisterous antics of two boys broke the stillness of the otherwise quiet afternoon.

The woman approached them with the same stiff smile on her face and carefully observed their game. Then, she wrapped her arms around their tiny bodies, silently inviting them in with the warm scent of freshly baked food emanating from her apron. She fed them, and their faces were as happy as their mouths were full. They meticulously chewed delicious pieces of honey cake still warm from the oven. They also had almond creme tort, muffins, and chocolate and caramel candies. They smiled, with her smile hanging above them, watching them, never letting the curve of her carefully placed lips disappear. She hugged the children again, and I felt it. I hugged her back, squeezing as tight as possible, trying to grab hold of some of the love I was missing in my own life.

I opened my eyes to discover that I was hugging my pillow again. It was damp with tears. I could tell it was very late as the beds in the dorm were full of motionless bodies dug deep into sleep, only moving enough to breathe, and the moon was still shining. It cast a spotlight on the empty spot where Igor's body was lying when I fell asleep. The only thing that remained—to assure me that he had been there—was a slight depression in the otherwise hard mattress.

I closed my eyes, hoping for the dream to come again, carrying me to Sunday's arrival. As I slipped back into slumber, the last thought I remember having was that of the frozen delight waiting for me on the other side of the moon's visit. I knew the morning was not far away. The sun would soon rise and call me to my next adventure, and Igor would be there to share it with me.

6

Bandits

This playground is typical of what you would still see at many orphanages in Ukraine, but a lot more grass than we had on Fastivska Street.

AFTER A LONG AND complicated night, I woke up covered in sweat. The dorm was empty, and I assumed that everyone was already downstairs emptying their plates. So I rushed to the bathroom to freshen up before breakfast.

As I approached the dining hall, I could hear dozens of forks and blunt knives rattling and jingling in an imperfect symphony of satisfaction. I spotted a seat next to the window and took it without paying attention to who else might be sitting across the table from me. After settling with my food, I turned my head to see Igor sitting next to me. I could see he was embarrassed by the chance he had taken, lying in my bed. He was trying to turn his head away, avoiding my eyes, and pretending to be the part of an argument that our two friends were having right across the table.

I watched him, not saying anything until he released his desperate avoidance and looked back at me. His eyes pleaded with me, asking me not to tell anyone about what had happened. I wouldn't anyway, and I didn't. I assumed that everyone shared feelings like ours, reaching out for a small pinch of something tangible. We spent our days without being hugged, kissed, or put to sleep by a parent reading our favorite bedtime story. No one talked about it openly, but we all knew we needed love.

Everything on Fastivska Street was about being brave and strong, doing what we needed to do to choke down the feelings our young minds couldn't understand. With the menacing presence of the Soviet Union hanging over our heads, each of us found our way to manage. Still, we needed to find connection, lest we become senseless and cold to the world and all its people.

I wanted to let Igor know that no one would ever hear about his sorrow from me, so I acted as if nothing had happened. Then, looking at him decisively, I casually asked, "Which movie do you think we will watch today?"

He stopped chewing his toast with jam and stared at his plate as though something disturbing was resting on it. Then, looking at me, he smiled for just a moment before looking back at his plate to say, "I liked the one we saw last Sunday...even though it seemed a bit odd.

Don't you think?"

"'Kingdom of Crooked Mirrors? Did you think it was strange? I thought it was terrific!"

And with that, we were back to our young little lives. I didn't say anything to Igor, but I thought about how I tried to enter the world behind the mirror once. I stared at my reflection, wondering if I would find a different reality there, just as the character Olya had done in the movie. In my case, I hoped for a better life, but Olya discovered her reflection in the mirror was living in a brainwashed world. In Olya's story, the corrupt people never could face themselves, so they outlawed the mirrors, but for me, I often felt like I lived behind the mirror, waiting for the real me to come and save the day.

"By the way, where were you the other day?" Igor asked, pulling me from my dream. "We were cleaning the entire floor in the dorm, and I didn't see you once." His eyes sparkled as he looked at me. I could see he was trying to read my mind.

As Igor looked at me, I could tell he was feeling a lot better than he did the night before. I was pleased to see him happier. For us, life was about repressing the worst things we felt and grabbing hold of the best moments. Though we were young, we were already so adept at finding the silver linings we probably made it seem simple. Of course, it wasn't, but we were strong, and we made the best of what we could.

My face flushed as I lowered my voice, looking around to see if anyone listened. Then, I responded with barely a whisper, "I forgot to tell you that I had to bury the den."

Igor worked to hold the laughter threatening to burst forth from his belly, "Oh, yes... I heard about Tamara Perdeyevna," he said, trying to continue without laughing. We often called Tamara 'Perdeyevna.' Her middle name was Petrivna, but 'Perdet' in Russian means 'to fart.' So, we translated her name from Tamara Petrivna to Tamara Perdeyevna to make a joke.

"Hilarious!" he said.

Igor's laugh was contagious, enchanting me to join his indulgence. Our laughter wove together in a moment of unified bliss until suddenly, he became sober. Placing his hand on my shoulder, he whispered nervously, "She doesn't think it was us who dug the hole?"

"That's why I wanted to bury the den," I told him. "I ran into her yelling about finding out who did it, and I told her I would fix it. She named us 'bandits!'" I finished, bursting into laughter.

Igor's chest grew proud. I could imagine him thinking about the word 'bandits' with unbreakable might.

Tamara heard us laughing and turned to approach us, wanting to stop the behavior she found to be repulsive and inappropriate, especially at the table. With her head rising from the heights of unquestionable authority, she looked at us, saying, "Looking for detention?"

Our table became an island of silence, standing out from the sea of clinking knives and forks. We were afraid to even think about looking up at her as she towered over us. We knew, if we wanted to go to the cinema and have that long-awaited ice cream, we were to be silent. So, we squirreled away our words and explanations until she was beyond earshot.

I waited to see her focus on someone at the other end of the room before turning to Igor to share the best secret of all, "I buried something in the den."

He looked at me with hunger in his eyes, whispering, "What did you bury? Tell me, please!" His eyes were begging me to share my secret.

"You will see in a couple of days," I replied with a smile that insinuated that my secret was more than precious. It was spectacular, but we would need to save it for another day. Nothing was so special to take away our Sunday.

He understood and dropped the subject as quickly as we did the time we spent together in the dorm. We were still just little boys, and moments only lasted until the next good idea came, and Igor landed on a new one almost before the last faded from his breath, "Want to go play catch before we start getting ready?"

I stood up in approval, moving away from my empty plate. Igor followed me, and we exited the room as Tamara gave us her famously threatening scowl.

The sun was high as we stepped onto the playground. It curiously smirked at us through the clouds, the only one besides us who knew of our hidden treasures. I felt the warmth of it shine on me and could sense the promise of a good day. As Igor and I began tossing the well-worn soccer ball, my smile and plans for our next adventure silently rose to greet our only confidant.

7

Octobrists' Summer

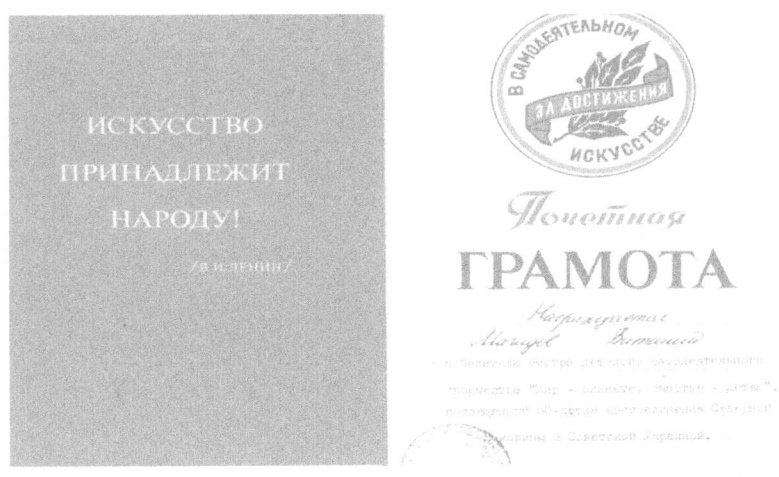

This award was given to me for creativity and participation in the life of the Octobrists' Camp.
On the left it says, "Art belongs to the people." by Lenin.
It also mentions our camp being the 50th Anniversary of Bukovina reuniting with the USSR.

OCTOBRISTS' SUMMER

WHEN I WAS STILL A CHILD IN the land of pioneers and red flags, we lived by a set of absolute, Octobrist values, set by Tsar Nicholas II in October of 1905. Taking recreational summer camps was one of the delightfully effective ways to plant those values into young minds. Though the United Soviet Socialist Republic's (USSR's) motives might have been less than inspired, as kids, we focused on the part of our camp experience that had the word 'fun' in it.

Summer was overflowing with an ever-growing number of summer camps for children, which soon totaled over forty thousand. As budding Octobrists, we all longed to be patriots of the communist party. To be ornamented with a red star pin boasting the face of seven-year-old Ulyanov Lenin, then known as Volodya Ulyanov, and his curly golden locks meant we were spreading the young pioneer spirit and inspiring the nation. We earned the right to wear young Ulyanov's star on our chests when our behaviors depicted what the USSR saw as the spirit of young hopefuls with high potential. We all wanted to be recognized and praised, so we worked hard to be like Ulyanov.

Before entering initiation to become Octobrists, we first learned several handy things. We learned to sew our buttons, tie the knot of the blood-red scarves we would receive one day, and memorized the pioneer oath. A sign hung above the blackboard with the encouraging words of the commitment written on it to help us remember our responsibility. Then, when we were ready, we would recite the promise from memory to join the Communist Youth Organization.

Every morning we read the oath aloud. Our little, insecure voices emerged in a single social symphony:

Octobrists are future pioneers
Octobrists are diligent young men who love school and respect their elders.

Only those who love work are called Octobrists.
Octobrists are honest, courageous, and skillful.
Octobrists are friendly. They read and draw, play and sing, and live happily.

High rise our campfires into the blue night,
  We are pioneers, the children of the workers,
  Near is the time of our best years
  And the pioneers' motto is, 'Always be ready!'

When we knew the oath, it meant we understood our responsibility as a member of the Republic of the Soviet Union. They wrote our lives for us, like pages of a rehearsed book, and celebrated the day when we were ready to prove our commitment to the communist party.

We all knew our day to join Oktyabrenok would come. Thousands of children would line up, standing straight, waiting for initiation to start. Everyone wore black jackets adorned with red stars to show our success. Under the jackets were white shirts unbuttoned at the neck, so our perfectly knotted scarves would be visible, showing off the red order's unique spirit. After the oath, World War II veterans visited us, guided us through moral values, teaching us how to be righteous and noble.

We set off to camp on a pleasant summer morning to begin our excursion. Octobrists' camps were a rare opportunity for children like me to have adventures to remember and cherish. They offered a place for first kisses, slow disco dances, childish loves, and meeting new friends. So our bus was buzzing with excited energy and expectations. I couldn't resist imagining how everyone had a cloud made of wishes floating above their heads.

It wasn't long before we arrived in Boyany, a small town just a few kilometers east of Chernivtsi. The village sat nestled in a small forest not far from the banks of the mighty river Prut. For the next few months, our home was in a valley just off the edge of the trees. The well-worn building radiated warmth and comfort, a perfect backdrop for a field of a thousand knapweeds, daisies, and shy violets; all gathered in competition to become the sun's best treasure. Scents mingled in one divinely forged fragrance that filled my lungs, waking my appetite and inducing a sparkle in my eyes.

After we exited the bus, our instructors sent us to unpack while they organized a late breakfast. The rooms where we would stay were neat and decorated with pleasant minimalism. They furnished each with one closet made of cherry wood and several skillfully placed beds that seemed to fill every corner of the space. I was followed into my room by my friend Lidiya's careful steps. Behind her, I heard the confident gait of Slavik, a chubby boy with messy hair and a cheeky attitude. Slavik was one of my best friends at the orphanage. We were the same age and shared all our classes. So, it was natural for us to share a room.

I threw myself onto one of the beds, diving into its softness, testing how well this pillow could compete with my familiar bedtime companion. Of course, it wasn't everything I expected. Still, I didn't worry about feeling alone. I knew this week would be perfect with my friends so close at hand.

We weren't in the room long before they called us to the kitchen. After a big bowl of porridge complimented with a single cube of something that tasted like butter, we had a couple of hours to do what we pleased. We could go anywhere we wanted, as long as we didn't leave the camp area. Still, most of the children stayed close, joining together to play soccer. Everyone was jumping, kicking, throwing, dribbling, and manipulating the ball in different ways, which—judging by the look on their faces—was an incredibly satisfying thing to do. So, I joined in the fun as well.

At camp, Igor was a leader. He was stronger and faster than the rest of us. So, he was always the soccer team captain. He ran, jumped, and threw the ball quickly and precisely, which sometimes made him think he was right about everything, even if something he was doing was wrong, like kicking a person right in the shin. I liked Igor, and for some strange reason, that made me want to fight him, especially when he was testing me. So, once again, through a disagreement during the game, Igor and I ended up in a fight.

He was stronger than me, and I enjoyed the challenge of trying to beat him. I also liked being close to him, tumbling and rolling around on the ground to see who could come out the winner. I caught his neck in the crook of my arm and began to squeeze, pushing his head against a tree. I knew I won today, and I reveled in my victory, waiting for a request for mercy. Instead, Igor unexpectedly hit me in the face. I stumbled back in complete bewilderment, wiping blood from my nose.

He won, and I could see he thought this proved he was right, but he wasn't. I was ready to burst into tears. I was not too fond of the smug look on his face and today was the day for me to win.

I didn't want anyone to see my pain, especially Igor, so I ran from the field. I didn't want to kick and chase the ball in a game where your opponents gave you 'friendly' incentives by kicking your shins.

I didn't know where I could go. I felt almost called by those little daisies in the field. So I ran toward the forest, with its branches rising as though they might be arms reaching for the runaway clouds.

As I entered the canopy, the fragrance stirred my senses, as though it might be a cure for every sorrow and sweep away my worry, pain, and fear. The sun consumed my anguish. I was soothed again by the pleasant warmth, the wind, and waving branches. The day was intoxicating, giving me the desire to create and become a part of the view I was lucky to have.

I didn't like fighting with Igor, and now, I wasn't sure if I wanted to be left alone or would have been pleased to have him here with me. I guessed it was both, dancing together to create little storm clouds in my mind.

They didn't last. I started looking at the trees around me, collecting every sound I could. I listened to the birds singing and tried to understand them. I wished I could capture the freedom surging across the grasses and scratching at my nostrils, making me happy to inhale the thriving life around me.

As I continued to meander, I couldn't help but think of how it would feel if I was born in a small cottage isolated by the woods. What would my life have been with no orphanage but with a mother to love me instead, freeing me of lonely nights and tear-soaked pillows? I wished I could live in the quiet of the woods, away from a dorm filled with hundreds of little lungs breathing the same stagnant air. I loved nature. I knew life must be perfect for the people who lived here.

I walked for a while, thinking. Until the soothing symphony of running water interrupted my longings and grabbed me, making my imagination bloom instead, retrieving all the parts I lost to endless sorrow and reasonless regret. The sound was incredible. So, I started running, trying to catch the noise. With each step, I got bolder and let my adventurous spirit rise. And then, finally, I found it. The turbulent river Prut ran in front of me, daring me to run with it. It was one of the most peaceful yet lively places I've ever visited.

We spent hours playing in the river during our stay at camp, swimming, or jumping from an old collapsed bridge into the blurry stream of water. The ruins of that bridge remain there to this day to remind us of our courage. As a child, I always planned my jumps near the banks, hiding that I didn't know how to swim. Years later, after I learned, I returned to what remained of our bridge, and using all kinds of exhibitions, I demonstrated my power over Prut's mighty flows.

But on that day, I didn't dare enter the water. I stood looking between the path back to camp and the river. I wanted to return to my friends, but I also wanted to rush into the waiting river. I looked at the road and then at the river again, with its stone bridge bathed in an eternity of flowing water. It stood crooked but firm, with its roots buried deep into the ground beneath the river. It called to me, but I was afraid to jump. I thought I would be the river and let the water wash away everything that existed. I turned back, following the echo of a trumpet bouncing off the beech trees that told me lunch was nearly ready.

As I stepped beyond the field of wildflowers, Slavik approached me soaked in sweat. They were playing soccer for probably more than an hour. His plump cheeks were rouged bright red, and he was breathing heavily. Finally, leaning over, he grasped his knees and tried to take a deep breath. Then, he sat down on the grass. "Where were you?" he asked, trying to gather the words to create a complete question between sighs and gasps.

"Too much football, huh, Botsya?" I started laughing. I loved calling Slavik by his nickname Botsya. He looked so cute, puffy, and was very funny. I could grab his cheeks and play with them the entire day without getting tired.

He frowned at me, trying to catch enough air to be able to laugh. "What were you up to?" he asked, squinting against the sun, now shining directly into his eyes.

"I wanted to take a walk and look around. Nothing special." I answered. Thankfully, the teacher's voice calling us to lunch rescued me from needing to say more.

As we returned to the building, I could hear my friends' playful screams and joyful chanting as they left their jumping ropes and overused soccer balls scattered amongst the sunbathed fields and high grasses. No one but Slavik seemed to notice I was gone, but I didn't care. I felt transformed after my journey through the forest, but it was like the rest of my friends stood frozen in time, unable to recognize the opportunities in front of them, or maybe they were just stubbornly insisting things stay the same.

8

Queen of Spades

Baba Yaga from my favorite USSR fairy tale.

I LOVED CAMP, BUT OUR MEALS weren't much different from what we ate at the orphanage. We all sat together in a large room, eating the same food almost every day. I knew I had to eat everything, not leaving a single piece, or they would ground me, and I didn't want to take the risk, not in this place. I had big plans for my night. So, when it was time to eat, I eagerly cleared my plate.

Looking around, I could see some of my friends had almost finished their dinner, but I still had several bits of almost raw pork covered with mashed potatoes on my plate. Worst were the chunks of fat staring back at me. Breaking away some of the pork, I put it in my mouth. It was easier for me to chew small bits of meat than to swallow the fat. So, while I ate, I scanned the room, looking for ways to dispose of the remaining scraps. That's when I spotted a dog just a couple of meters outside of the window. A new idea was born!

I looked around to see where our educators were and found them busy talking to each other at the other end of the dining room. They seemed unusually relaxed and happier here.

Eyeing them cautiously, I scraped fat pieces from my plate and put them into the napkin lying beside it. I then wrapped it like a gift and put it into my pocket. The minute they excused me from the table, I ran to the field. Unrolling the fat chunks, I fed them to the grateful dog, who wagged his tail in appreciation.

The dog left more than half of what I gave him. I don't know if he already had his food, or maybe he felt the same way I did about eating so much fat. I wasn't sure, but it didn't matter in the end. I just kicked a little dirt over the place where the last few pieces lay on the ground and covered my crime. Finally! I would have a vacation from the orphanage and from eating fat.

"Vitaly!" I froze for a moment, thinking someone caught me, but then recognized the voice calling me.

Slavik approached, waving his hand in my direction, so I started walking towards him, with the curious dog in tow.

"Oh, I see you already made a friend!" Slavik laughed and began petting the dog. "Igor wants to call upon the Queen of Spades tonight. He said that anyone who doesn't want to participate is a wimp."

I had heard older boys talk about the tradition of telling scary stories or even playing creepy games at night after the educators went to bed. Their favorite was a story called 'A Red Spot, a Black Black Room, and a White Sheet,' and I thought they might tell it, but they wanted to play 'Queen of Spades' instead. I was nervous. I heard it was supposed to be the scariest of all the games.

"We are not wimps, are we?" I frowned, excited and afraid.

Slavik stared at me for a moment, then fired, "No, we are not."

As the last of the day faded from the sky, we decided to gather in Igor's room to make plans. As word spread, the room filled with curious faces. By the look of most, they weren't believers. They just stood in the doorway with mocking expressions on their faces.

I was a believer. I knew the Queen of Spades was a game to evoke a witch named Baba Yaga. Baba Yaga was the worst of the monsters from my childhood. She was known to help honorable wanders she met in the forest, but she was also known to eat children, especially those who didn't do as they were told. I thought of the fat I gave the dog and wondered if this was the best place for me to be tonight. I was scared she might come for me, but I knew I also did good things. I tried to do my best, so I decided to keep my thoughts to miracles and wonders, trying not to give way to dark, ominous things.

Igor was the last to come into the room. He checked to see if anyone was outside before approaching the group. As he did, he spoke with a low whisper, "Some of the teachers are sitting near this room, so if we don't want to be grounded or interrupted, we better go to another place."

It would be time for bed soon, and our educators would be getting to know the camp staff better, making plans for our summer here. So, we knew a session of summoning the vicious Queen of Spades wouldn't be interrupted tonight if we could get where they couldn't hear us.

Igor looked around, waiting for someone to volunteer their room by raising a hand or making a sound, but no one did. I knew it would be impressive to Igor to see me be brave, so I looked at Slavik and raised my hand.

He lifted his as well. "We're at the other end of the hall. We can do it in our room," Slavik said, speaking with a conviction that sounded like maybe he was deciding to convince himself.

Everyone agreed, and we quickly made a plan. We moved two by two, occasionally pausing along the way, so we wouldn't appear suspicious. By the time everyone was there, our room was packed. Kids crowded to find a place to stand. I could tell some of them were excited, but some were anxious too. The anxious ones hung by the door, with the kids drowning in skepticism, seeing it was the safest place to be.

Igor dug into his pocket, pulling out a tube of lipstick.

"You are planning on becoming a girl now?" someone asked, teasing.

Igor sent him a resentful glance, ignoring friends who could barely contain their laughter. "Did you bring the candle?" he asked one of the boys sitting in a circle.

The boy passed a half-burnt candle to Igor wordlessly, trying to hide the fear I saw reflected in his eyes.

"Now, who knows how to draw a door with the staircase?" Igor asked, looking around the room, searching through a dozen or so faces. No one was eager to step forward, but there was no need, "Vitaly? I saw your drawings from art classes. Will you do it?" He looked at me with the assurance that I would do a great job.

Knowing I wouldn't refuse, Igor handed me a hand mirror he found by a garbage pile at the movie theater. I took it and the lipstick and started to draw. Before I could finish a single line, I was stopped by Igor's voice, "Wait. We first need to turn off the lights and light the candle." He dug through his pockets again, searching. "I don't have matches….Damn!"

"Well, does anyone have matches?" a voice from the crowd asked.

Everyone shook their heads in negation.

Igor looked ready to give up, but Slavik finally spoke, "I'll bring matches!"

"You are just trying to run away," Igor said, probably jealous of thinking he should have had the idea first.

"I think you didn't bring those matches purposely because you are too afraid of the Queen of Spades," Slavik said as he walked through the door, standing as tall as he could, with his chest puffed in might.

An expression of uneasiness and shame spread fast across Igor's face. He leaned against the wall, trying to look casual, but I could tell he was bothered by Slavik's comment. We were all friends, but everything between us was a competition. The girls at the orphanage were always there to help each other, but the boys spent their days trying to prove who was best. Slavik had stolen a moment of Igor's glory tonight. I could see it.

A few minutes later, Botsya appeared at the door, and looking straight into Igor's eyes, pulled the entire box of matches out of his pocket. Some of the boys started patting Slavik's back in approval and acceptance, and he strutted, celebrating his victory. He loved rubbing his bravado into Igor's disappointed face.

"So, shall we?" asked Igor, deciding to ignore Slavik's boasting and regain his position as leader. He then nodded, and someone switched off the light, leaving us in the shadows of the trembling flame.

Now, it was my turn. Holding the lipstick tight, I started drawing the doors first, leaving straight lines of red sticky marks on the mirror glass. I felt good to do my part, and I loved drawing. It only took a few seconds to finish the door. Then, I stood back, admiring the accuracy of my work.

"Perfect!" someone from the crowd remarked.

Igor looked in the mirror dramatically, his face floating yellow behind the red lines of my drawing. Then, he began to whisper, chanting the exact five words over and over until we all joined in a dull symphony:

The Queen of Spades, come!
 The Queen of Spades, come!
 The Queen of Spades, come!

We chanted the words with Igor until he raised his hand, silently telling us to stop. The quiet that followed was thick with our fear and with something more as we waited for The Queen of Spades to reveal herself.

Suddenly, the mirror started trembling, and Igor dropped the candle. The impact snuffed it out, taking away the only source of light we had. Gasps cut through the room, sounding magnified against our fear. Everyone in the room was trying to be brave. No one wanted to be the one whose legs shook, even when standing in the face of an unexplainable horror.

Igor's whisper sharpened, "Everybody, back up!"

As our eyes adjusted to the darkness, I could see his reflection still floated eerily, lit by moonlight cast through the small bedroom window. "Nobody move! Who did that?" his voice was trembling, soft like the night I found him lying in my bed. "Who moved the mirror?"

No one answered.

"Is it supposed to do that?" I asked.

Igor shrugged, "I don't know what it's supposed to do."

Footsteps echoed all around us, like a predator stalking us, but we couldn't see who was taking them. Everyone was looking around to see if anybody was moving, but we were all frozen, paralyzed by unwelcomed fear.

Some boys began to panic, but my body was flooded with adrenaline, making my heart beat faster. I felt excited and alive and as if I was standing on the edge of something magical until one of the boys turned on a light.

The shift assaulted my senses. I squinted against it, but the feeling of someone being in the room with us didn't disappear with the shadows. I could still feel it as it lingered, floating from boy to boy like a prophecy of impending doom.

Although no one would admit their fear, boys started leaving the room, creating excuses to avoid spending a second more in this torment. Others sat on the ground, gawking and trying to sort the millions of questions swarming in their naive minds. I was afraid, but I didn't go. I wanted to see if what I was feeling was real, or maybe just my mind playing tricks on me.

However, I didn't have much time to explore the question before the sound of our teachers' footsteps moving through the halls told me we would soon be in the dark again. We would be stuck with the crazy witch still floating over our sleeping bodies.

I didn't want to spend my night being chased by Baba Yaga, but I had an idea. "Does anyone have a deck of cards?" I asked.

"Actually, I brought one along," Slavik said, beaming again at his readiness and desire to show everyone that he was not afraid.

"Ready to lose it?" I asked with anticipation, hoping that my plan would work.

Slavik started going through his unpacked suitcase, looking for a deck of cards. I wasn't surprised he brought them. We liked to play card games when it was raining out. So, it turned out to be perfect. While Slavik collected the cards, I sent someone else to find some electrical tape, rubber bands, or something similar that could help us put the cards together.

We used the tape and a rubber band I found and wrapped the deck of cards tight. I wasn't worried about the other cards in the deck but feared the Queen of Spades might find her way free to ambush us in our sleep.

After making sure the deck was packed nice and tight, we put the cards away in the wardrobe and moved the bed closest to it a little further into the room. We didn't know what The Queen would do if she caught us, but no one wanted to be too close to a Baba Yaga. So, we decided to play it safe.

Besides Slavik and me, two other boys also slept in our room. One was visibly frightened, probably because his bed was closest to the cabinet. "Hey, guys?" he asked, gaining our attention. "Do you maybe want to go to the next room? Maybe one of the older kids knows what we could do...".

I still didn't feel sure about my plan. So, it sounded like a brilliant idea to me. We all agreed and followed him to the room next to ours, knocking on the door. A tall boy with messy blond hair named Andrej opened it. "Hey, friends! What are you up to?"

We told Andrej and his roommates about what happened. As we finished the story, one of them headed out the door, saying, "I think I know what to do. Follow me."

Trembles of anxiety, insecurity, and fear twitched in my muscles like a million tiny ants as I watched him head straight to our room. We followed him eagerly, hoping to alleviate our worries before bedtime. I wanted my fear to go away and struggled to convince myself that the footsteps and mirror were only an illusion we created, or maybe a trick someone had played. My reasoning suggested I was right, but my experience told me another story. I preferred thinking it was just an illusion created from a mysterious atmosphere. Still, my mind wouldn't surrender its worry. All I could think was I wanted that Queen of Spades out of our bedroom.

"The deck is in the cabinet, right?" the boy asked as he entered the room.

We nodded in unison, waiting to see what the boy would do.

He opened the wardrobe door cautiously, seized the deck of cards, and closed the door again. Then, turning back to us, he said, "I suppose someone has a box of matches?" He looked around, waiting for a response from our frozen faces, and opened his hand.

Slavik pulled the matches from his pocket, placing the box in the boy's hand. The boy unwrapped the deck, flipping through the cards until he came to the Queen of Spades. When he found her, he tossed the rest of the deck on the bed. Then, lighting one of the matches, he brought it to the corner of the card.

We all watched as the Queen melted, bending and fading to black until it eventually disappeared. Then, when there was nothing left, the boy picked up the deck from the bed, wrapping it up again and placing it back in the cabinet.

"That ought to do it!" he said, confidently rubbing his hands.

Andrej and his roommate left the room chuckling, leaving us puzzled but somewhat satisfied with the outcome. The rest of us moved nervously, trying to go back to the place in our minds where this had never happened. I picked up the mirror, wiping away the door and staircase I had drawn less than an hour ago to make sure she could never return.

No one spoke as we turned off the lights and rolled ourselves up in our sheets. We all lay silently, curled in protective postures, twitching, and hiding behind our pillows. I could still hear the footsteps echoing in the hall like Baba Yaga was finally coming for us. I wondered if the other boys could hear them too because I knew; even if we didn't believe we were terrible little children, maybe she did.

* * *

I entered my dream flying high, cherished by the clouds, and loved by the sky above me, and even though I was there, with nothing to protect me and nowhere to hide, I felt safe and free. Power ran through my limbs as my arms transformed into the wings I always wanted to have.

I could see my friends calling to me from below, with their arms waving and bodies begging me to notice them. Then, a shadow crossed my face, devouring my peace. I flew faster, trying to escape the darkness. Going forward, I did not look back, but my friends were still standing below me, no matter how far I flew.

When I did look back at the shadows that followed me, feelings of uneasiness stabbed at my chest, causing the poison of fear to spread across my body. It coursed through my arms and legs, slowing my progress, draining my strength and will. I wanted to return for my friends, but the thing chasing me threatened me with eyes lit like fire. If I stopped for even a moment, I knew it would catch me and take me down to be one of the frightened screaming faces.

I reached for the last of my strength, trying to free myself of the beast's paralyzing pursuit. Still, it pulled at me, slowing me down. Fear swelled in me, making me nauseous and full of pain. The air became fire, searing my throat and lungs with each breath as the clouds around me darkened, mirroring the creature's color. My friends were still there, with their screams ripping my mind apart. I was afraid to look at them. I was sure that the ground below was trembling, making the sky quake as well. I couldn't save them. I didn't think I could even save myself.

The fear ate at me, threatening to undo me until I saw the house peacefully nestled amid a cluster of trees near the edge of the horizon. As I flew closer, I saw a field of proud daisies surrounding it. They seemed to watch as I approached.

I landed with unexpected ease and an overflowing feeling of safety. The dark threatening mass faded the moment I connected with the ground, and the sound of my friend's tormented screams faded behind the sound of voices coming from inside the house. I stepped forward, peeking through the window to take in a perfect view. Five little heads leaned over their plates, eating, talking, and giggling, while their mother and father looked over them, satisfied with the pleasant surroundings.

I felt like I belonged inside. I wanted to be inside. I looked back to see if the dark blur of fire and coal had followed me to this perfect place, but all I saw were trees growing to protect and hide me.

As I turned to peer again through the window, I saw the woman standing, pointing in my direction. I knew I must be in trouble, watching them and wishing I could be inside. So, I tried to escape. I tried to fly, to be embraced by the sky again, but before I could push my body away from the ground, she was outside with me, gently grabbing my arm and inviting me in. The whole family was there, letting me know that I was safe.

The inside of their home was warm and inviting. Everyone was kind and accepting. I sat with them, frightened and hurt, lost and confused. I was so happy to be safe, away from the dark cloud chasing me, but I left my friends to the dark blur of teeth and fire. As I realized the depth of my betrayal, my tears flowed. How could I be so happy, knowing I had left them with that beast. With each tear, the air around me cooled, and the sky grew dark until finally, the rain came. I listened to the raindrops tapping on the roof, knowing each was for my friends as the sky cried with me.

"What is your name?" a little voice asked me.

I turned to see a small child looking up at me, wrapped up in innocent curiosity. "Vitaly...My name is Vitaly", I said, rubbing tears from my face.

"Vitaly!" he screamed, playing, "Vitaly! Vitaly! Vitaly!"

"Vitaly! Vitaly! Wake up!"

I opened my eyes, assailed by the barrage of words coming from my educator's mouth. When he saw I was awake—thanks to his thoughtful yelling in my face—he continued calling out to the rest of the boys. He unleashed names, contaminating the air with his shouting and breaking the mist of pleasant dreams along the way.

"It's breakfast time, and unless you get up and get ready, we will be late for recreational activities. Come on, boys! The new day has already begun."

We bid farewell to our beds and staggered across the room to search for clothes.

"Hey, guy! Look at this! Unbelievable!" Slavik was in front of the opened wardrobe holding burnt cards like an offering in his hands. As we examined the deck, I noticed charred scars on only the suit of spades, well, most of them anyway. There was one undamaged spade in the deck, the Queen. She lay crisp and clean atop the pile, slyly mocking us with her twisted gaze.

As gasps and awes grew, a crowd gathered, but no one knew what to say or do until Slavik ran from the room, taking the cards with him. They all followed, but I stayed behind, checking the closet for evidence of a trick. I even checked Slavik's bag to see if he had an extra deck of cards, but I couldn't find anything, not a match or even the rubber band that bound the cards the night before.

I was in the room searching for some time. However, I eventually decided to surrender. If Slavik and Igor were playing a trick on us, I knew one of them would tell me. I didn't know if Baba Yaga was now sharing a room with us, but I was hungry.

As I entered the cafeteria, I saw Slavik calmly eating bread, jam, and butter with tea on the side. To look at him, you would have assumed nothing remarkable had happened.

I sat next to him, asking, "Where are the cards?"

9

Zarnitsa

As kids, we played sports, games, and developed talents

AFTER FINISHING OUR BREAKFAST, our educators sent us outside to embrace every opportunity this beautiful day gave us. Distant fields, blanketed with inviting lilies, emitted the delightful scent of early summer.

We split up into the different games we created from having nothing and played until we heard the voice of Ludwig Viktorovych cutting through the laughs and screams of our joyous creations. "Okay, boys and girls, round up!" Ludwig said, inviting us to join him.

The air was intoxicatingly fresh, and I wanted to dip my toes in the river, catch the sun with the daisies and find the perfect place to build a bonfire, but our educator had something different in mind. "We are playing Zarnitsa today!" he said with exuberance, passing his joy to the children standing around him. "For those who don't know what Zarnitsa is, I will explain the rules, and then we can start playing!"

We were all ears, intrigued by the potential of a new challenge.

"Zarnitsa is an exercise that has different thematic military games. We will be playing targeting today." Octobrist Camp was always a fun adventure, but it had a purpose too. Many of our games were also military drills, training us to be ready if ever called to battle. They challenged us, but in a playful way, making us want to learn.

Ludwig turned, gesturing towards the forest. "We will be playing in the woods," he said, "but don't worry. It's completely safe." He wanted to comfort us, but we weren't afraid—well, the boys weren't anyway. The girls asked to stay on the field and make up another game, but my friends were ready to have an adventure, and so was I. My heart leaped with excitement. I would finally have a chance to wander through the forest after all.

The instructor told the girls they could stay. Then, he guided us to our next task. "I have divided you into two groups, and each group will have its color. That is what these are for." He raised his hand to show us blue and red strips of cloth. "I will divide you equally myself."

As he started calling our names, he distributed colors. Slavik and I ended up in different groups. I was wearing a blue banner while he wore blood-red. Some boys were left confused when the ribbons ran out, and they had no color and no team.

"You will wear your colors somewhere visible, so your teammates and opponents can see which group you are. It's a good idea to wrap them around your arms or heads. Slavik will be the team leader of red, and..." he looked over at my team, "Vitaly, will be leading the blue team," Although I enjoyed being in charge, I started sweating. I knew I would get credit if we won, but being a leader meant everyone would blame me if we failed.

"You will need to come up with a strategy for your team," he continued as we each found a place to tie our bands. "If your flag gets ripped off or taken, that, unfortunately, means you are out and must come back to the field. If it is only half torn, you can compete but are forbidden to run. The boys without sashes will be our judges to prevent anyone from being tempted to cheat. I will also be watching." He paused to give us a significant look of warning before continuing, "No fighting, no beating, no kicking, no biting. We are playing a friendly military game. It is about strategy, not aggression. So any violence will disqualify you.

"I've set flags at your base camps, one red and one blue. The goal is to find and take your opponent's flag. To win, you must either capture all the opposing team's bands or seize the flag and bring it to the field. I already set the bases, so follow me."

We followed Ludwig into the forest. After a few minutes of walking, he stopped and said, "Red team, you will go left and continue in a straight line until you find your base. I marked it with the red flag, which you must protect. The blue team will go right, following the path to their base. You will recognize it by the blue flag, which you will need to protect. While you find your bases and work on your strategies, I will set the watchers. Remember, we are playing fair, with no violence. Now go!"

Slavik and I waved at each other. Then, we disappeared in opposite directions. Everyone was running, driven by the divine rush of adrenaline in our systems. The energy made me wonder whether

I was excited or frightened. I felt both.

My team progressed through the woods, looking for our base. After about ten minutes of running, one of my teammates shouted, "Hey! Look!" He pointed at a rising hill where a large blue banner stood surrounded by a dozen or so lesser flags of the same color. I gazed at our base camp, inspired to protect the majestic prize at our hill's peak.

There were seven players on each team, all of us equally matched. As I was the one leading us to victory, everyone on my team stood looking at me the minute we reached our flag. "So what do we do?" one of them asked.

I forgot the game and tried to think of a way to make my tongue move. "What do we do?" I thought. "How will I beat Slavik and his team?"

I imagined running, trying to grab the other teams' sashes. Then, a plan started to form in my mind. I forgot my fears, and the words came, "Well…I was thinking that two of us should hide here while the rest split into two groups, each heading to either side of the red base."

"That sounds great!" Andriy shouted. He was first to approve, and soon after, the rest of our team agreed. I was glad he was in my group since he always liked to be competitive but fair in sports.

I continued, flattered by the pleasant validation I received from my teammates: "Does anyone want to stay here and guard our flag?"

Two of my teammates quickly volunteered, looking at each other and me, laughing.

I nodded. "So, here is the plan. They probably won't suspect that we have anyone lurking around here, so stay hidden. Then, you can surround him and take off his streamer if anyone comes toward the flag. If you only tear it, you can still catch him since he won't be able to run. Okay?"

They nodded simultaneously. So, I proceeded, rushed by the ticking clock and bursts of self-esteem, "If two or more come, stay low. Wait until you find a good chance to rip off their bands. Just remember to keep them away from taking the flag or your sashes.

"The rest of us will go in search of their base. Two of us will travel through the trees, intercepting any who try to head toward our base, and the group of three will carefully go towards their main flag. Okay?"

"Yes! Let's do it!" they all said excitedly, almost in a single voice.

Andriy and I worked together. We searched the trees while the rest of our group headed towards the red camp. Moving from tree to tree, we tried to remain invisible while watching for anyone approaching our base. Our friends sped up, split one by one, appearing and disappearing between the bark and low branches as they carefully drew on the red camp.

"Should we wait?" asked Andriy.

"I think yes...we better wait for a while."

We waited silently, listening for any noise in the woods around us. Then, after several minutes of nothing, Andriy came to sit where I was, crawling through the high grass to stay hidden on his way.

"No one is around," he said, leaning against both me and the giant tree I was using as a backrest. He was fit and athletic, and I could feel his weight against my body. Heat rose in me, reminding me of what it felt like to have a high fever. Suddenly, my clothes felt too warm and my head too light. I wanted to escape the heat, but I wanted to stay there and surrender to it too.

I wanted to explore the feeling, but it distracted me from the game. My friends needed me if we were to win, and more than any other feeling, I wanted to win. So, I pulled away, pretending to look through the grass, and said, "Maybe we should spread out and look around... Our team is probably covering us ahead."

"Or they lost their banners," he joked with a sparkling smile.

I looked at him, pausing for seconds that seemed like an eternity. I wondered for a moment if it was his heart I felt pounding in my chest and not mine. "Well, let's hope that's not the case," I said, smiling back at him.

"Any sign of the Queen?" Andriy asked with a serious expression on his face.

"So, you believed the story? You believe in the Queen of Spades?" I was surprised.

"Well, you said she was there...plus, you were all scared."

I flushed, embarrassed. "I was not scared!" I said shakily. I wanted to defend my honor, but it ended up sounding like I was trying to convince myself as much as him.

He put his hand on my shoulder, "Vitaly. It's okay...even if you were scared... but you weren't, as you say," he finished, looking away. His comforting voice had the hint of a friendly tease to it. But then, it faded as he looked at me with a more stoic expression. "It's all right. Everyone gets frightened sometimes."

I knew he meant it, but I was too embarrassed to look at his eyes or say anything. So, I just pretended I was looking through the trees, watching for anyone approaching.

The silence hung for a moment when we were suddenly startled by the sound of twigs breaking nearby. I looked up to see one of the red bands standing out from the spectrum of forest green. I grabbed Andriy, dragging him closer to the tree. Then, putting one hand over his mouth, I pointed the other in the direction of the red intruder.

Andriy took a glance, then laid back onto the tree, leaning his body even closer to mine. I knew our time alone in the woods would soon be over. So, I buried myself in the feeling for just a moment. Then, I let it go, and so did he.

"I will get out and distract him, and you jump out a few seconds later and grab his flag. Okay?" His voice was barely audible, kept low as Igor approached us, completely unaware of what awaited him only a step or two away.

A second after I nodded in confirmation, Andriy jumped out of our hiding spot.

"Look what we have here!" he laughed, teasing Igor.

"Oh, Andriy. It's great to see you. Let me borrow your band for a while!"

They started circling each other, but just before I was about to leap from my hiding place, I spotted another boy approaching. They were trying to ambush Andriy. So, I waited for the other red team member to move towards them, so I could jump on him and take off his flag.

Igor kept Andriy distracted as the second boy crept past me. The moment his back was to me, I ran towards them, determined to win and regain the honor I lost with the dreaded Queen of Spades. Everything happened in slow motion. I could feel my teeth vibrating as my feet slammed against packed soil. My heart responded, traveling from my chest to my throat, pounding. Igor spotted me, but it was too late. The blue flag was already in my hands before he could even open his mouth to give a warning.

I looked around to see if more of them approached and saw one of the watchers clapping and pointing his thumb in approval. I felt my pride restored, but I couldn't stay to celebrate. Andriy needed my help.

As I looked at him, he was already stripping Igor's flag. He had taken advantage of the distraction I created and leaped to add another victory for our team.

Igor suddenly started to yell and scream.

The watcher turned to look at them as he approached. His focus had been on me, but he needed to respond to Igor's screams. Assuming Igor's cries were from pain, the watcher held up a hand, "No kicking, no beating, no violence. That's what Ludwig said. You probably hit him, Andriy, so you are disqualified."

Igor and his teammate didn't say anything. They just leaned against a tree, one of them laughing and the other shooting knowing glances at Andriy.

"I didn't kick him or hit him!" Andriy said furiously. "But now I will!"

He lept at Igor, knocking him to the ground.

The watcher and I jumped in to break them apart. The watcher turned to Andriy, "You need to return his flag to him. He has another chance."

"Come on! You saw him! He is laughing! I didn't do anything!" Andriy was trying to defend himself. "He is only trying to get me disqualified because we captured their flags."

"I don't think Andriy would have done that," I said. "I saw what happened."

"And I don't think Igor would have faked someone attacking him," said the other boy.

We all looked at Igor. I could see he was hiding his guilt, but he didn't budge.

Andriy was mad, and I felt like I could scream. Still, we knew there was nothing we could do.

"Here you go!" Andriy said, throwing the red sash at Igor, who immediately tied it around his arm. He occasionally glanced at Andriy with a look of satisfaction on his face.

"And here is another," said Andriy, throwing his blue band to the watcher.

As Andriy headed towards the field, I thought about how unfair it was that Igor could get away with cheating, but I had an idea. I looked at the watcher and asked, "The game is on?"

He nodded. So, I waited for Igor to stand, and when he did, I grabbed his arm and took his band, putting it in my pocket with the other sash I had won.

"Huh? Wait! You can't do that! He can't do that," Igor yelled, looking at the watcher.

The watcher laughed. I think he knew what Igor did wasn't fair, and he liked how I found a way to win. "Yes, he can!" he said. "The game is on. Get off the field, boys. You're out."

I took one last look at three of them as they left. I was disappointed that Andriy was out of the game. I wanted to join him and continue our time on the sunny field of daisies and lilies, but I felt it was my duty to stick with my team. I wanted to win.

He looked back at me, waved, and smiled in approval of what I had done. I was glad he didn't see me as weak.

Turning back to the game, I decided to take a different path and move forward to where I thought their camp might be—heading in the direction of where I first saw Igor. I snuck through the forest, using trees as my cover, and it wasn't long before I saw a boy just a few meters away, hiding behind a tree. I glanced at his arm and saw that his band was blue. It was one of the boys from my group.

"Hey, Volodymyr!" I said in a hushed voice, "Over here!"

He was looking around, trying to determine where I might be. I peeked from behind the thorn bush, where I was hiding, holding my hand high in the air. He looked around to make sure no one was approaching. Then, he came to hide beside me.

"Where are the others?" I asked.

"They are down. A couple of them tried to ambush us, but we managed to take one of their flags," he answered, pulling a red banner from his pocket.

"Good job. They disqualified Andriyj. Igor claimed that he hit him. Liar!" I was angry. "But, I have their bands, so we are square."

"Wow! So, with two of our guys back at base camp, that leaves four against four over here. Do we go for their flag?"

"We go for their flag," I replied. "But we will hide behind the trees and intercept whoever passes through. That way, we can increase our chances. Okay?"

Volodymyr nodded in approval. "Deal!"

We moved quickly. I was proud of my new strategy and wanted to get to their base before they got to ours.

We notice someone coming through the woods in no time, moving toward our camp. I locked on his flag, so I told Volodymyr, "We will let him progress further just a few more seconds. Then, we are onto him. We will attack from behind, but we need to make sure none of the reds are behind us before we move. Okay?"

"Okay," Volodymyr replied.

We could see no one was following him, so we began creeping up from behind him, waiting for the right moment to attack. I noticed one of the watchers could see us from the side, but the boy from the red team didn't even know we were there. Since I was sure he wouldn't be able to fake being hurt, I jumped in front of him, quickly removing his band. Everything happened so fast that the watcher didn't even notice that another boy had just been sent back to the field. So, I held up the band and yelled, "Out! One down!"

The watcher smiled and asked the disappointed boy to follow him to the field.

We had the red team outnumbered. So, we decided to lay low and wait to see if more reds would come. Once we saw that no one was around, we decided to go forward and try to take the flag.

As we approached their camp, we could see there were only three of them left, and that is when I saw Slavik nearing our hiding place, but judging by his look, I knew that he hadn't spotted us yet. Competing against Slavik wasn't pleasant at all, but I still wanted the blue team to win, so I put my finger to my mouth, prompting Volodymyr to be quiet until Slavik was out of sight.

Once I was sure that Slavik had moved away, we jumped out from the trees, yelling as if we were savages. The two boys were surprised by our attack and didn't know what to do. Their mistake was that one of them had climbed up the hill to guard the place where the red flag sat buried deep into the ground.

The other boy tried to take my band, but I knew how to make a secure knot. So, he wasn't able to take it off that easily. I managed to quickly remove his sash as he was trying to take mine, and Volodymyr took the cue. He didn't even think of the boy protecting the hill. Instead, he ran toward the flag, pulling it from the ground while the other boy tried to take his blue mark.

With another red trophy in my hands, I started running towards Volodymyr to help him. The other boy saw me coming and hurried his efforts, finally succeeding at the exact moment as Volodymyr claimed their flag.

A split second later, I claimed my fourth red band, the flag from Volodymyr's assailant. I knew Slavik was well on his way to our base camp, but there was no time to return and fight for his base. Taking the base flag into my hand, I knew that victory was ours!

That night at dinner, Slavik and I were talking about the game. "You won because I had hopeless cases," he whispered, looking around to search for the faces he was accusing.

"Oh, yes, we won because of that!" I laughed at Slavik's hurt pride and made him laugh as well.

"On the bright side, Slavik, you were the last man standing, so that is something right there," I said, trying to lift his spirits.

He pondered the ceiling like he was considering a menu of responses written there. "Well, that's true..," he replied, puffing his chest, soaked in the pride he got back after just one sentence.

"Did you know that there is a Talent show tomorrow?" he asked, taking the win and moving on to the next competition.

"Really?" I asked attentively. I loved singing and dancing, so I was always looking for a chance to show it.

"What were you thinking of preparing for the show?" I asked Slavik.

"Well, maybe I could act or something....I didn't think about it. I'll figure something out. What will you do?"

"I don't know...," I replied, considering my options with pleasant anticipation.

10

Talent Show

I am performing a Yoga move during a talent show

I WAS TIRED FROM THE DAY'S ACTIVITIES, but the exhaustion wasn't nearly as powerful as the lightning strikes of absolute satisfaction I had when I won Zarnitsa. My pride pooled with blissful thoughts of what it would be like to win the talent show, as well. So, I went to bed satisfied and happy, not thinking of all that was missing in my life.

I lay for a while thinking of what I wanted to do for the talent show and how everyone would love it. Still, it wasn't long before the exhaustion weighed heavy on my eyelashes and crawled into my nostrils, slowing my breath.

Soon, I was dreaming again. The woman was back. She was beautiful as she watched the two boys playing in the field of lilies and wallflowers. Every inch of the vibrant green grass was bathed in bright sunlight, drawing out her artificial smile. No one could see me watching. I was present, but my body wasn't there. I was a sentinel, analyzing every move. I could pause when I wanted, speed up or slow down the time, and stop or rewind it slowly.

The fair-skinned boy glanced at the woman, and I could see what he was thinking. He was not as small as he was before. He saw through her twisted grin and how she always tried to make everything perfect, forgetting that humans aren't and never will be. The woman would sometimes go out, still holding onto her smile, but the boy knew that she would put that same smile away every time she turned her back. Her heart was shrouded in secrecy, dark as the starless night. She was a genuine Baba Yaga, the Queen of Spades, hiding beneath her youth and beauty.

I could see how the older boy stood by, ready to protect the young one no matter what, but he didn't have the heart to reveal the truth to the golden child, who still looked upon his mother with unwavering admiration and love.

I woke from the dream feeling like a bus had run over me. Besides the hard work of yesterday's victory, I was tired of vivid dreams and trying to understand the people in them.

I lay in my bed for some time, unable to get up until I remembered there was a talent show scheduled for that night. The moment I realized, I jumped from my bed, dreams forgotten, and began my daily preparations.

The day sped by, and I ran with it, feeling like there would never be enough time to finish my chores and prepare for the show. I rushed as fast as I could, thinking the whole time of what I needed. Still, the sun was already low in the sky as I finished the last of my responsibilities and went immediately to Valentyna Vasylivna, asking her to lend me a dress and some makeup. She was stunned by my question but amused as well. Her eyes filled with anticipation, pondering what I would do as my talent.

I ran back to my room with the dress held close to my chest. My eyes darted the halls, checking the nearly empty corridors to be sure no one could see what I was doing. I knew I had finished my work ahead of most of my friends, so I rushed again to hide the dress under my bed. Then, I ran back to the dining room for dinner.

"Where were you?" Slavik asked, stuffing his mouth with mashed potatoes as he spoke.

"Upstairs, preparing my act for tonight," I said slyly, digging into my plate as well. I didn't want to say anything else. So, I just looked at him, knowing more questions would come, questions I wouldn't answer.

"Oh!" Slavik was excited, "you know what you will do? Tell me, tell me, tell me, tell me!"

Slavik loved to do that. He knew I never liked to say "no" to him, but this time was different. I was determined. So, I smiled, saying, "Let's make it a surprise."

Slavik wasn't satisfied with my answer. "Vitaly, pleeeeeease tell me! Please??" He was jumping on his chair, holding his fingers crossed with hope.

"You will see in a few moments when I start preparing," I said, laughing. "Okay?"

"Oh, it will be funny, won't it?" he continued, hoping to catch me another way, but I just smiled back at his question.

Slavik interpreted my smile as affirmation and peacefully continued with his dinner, leaving me to mine, as well.

Not long after we cleaned our plates, I went upstairs to get ready, followed by Slavik's untamable curiosity. When we arrived, Slavik just stood in the doorway, waiting to see what was next. "So?" he asked.

I ceremoniously retrieved the dress from under my bed, waiting to see his reaction.

"You are going to dress up as a girl?" Slavik was stunned. "That is hilarious!"

I was glad Slavik liked my idea, but I needed to prepare if I hoped to be ready on time. So, I took out the makeup Valentyna lent me, applying color to my face. Since I was already good at drawing, applying makeup came naturally. In very little time, I created a true masterpiece on my face.

"Wow, Vitaly, anyone could mistake you for a girl," Slavik said.

I don't think I have ever been happier than I was at that moment. Slavik said I looked like a girl, and I liked how that made me feel. My high-pitched voice brought me trouble with older kids many times, but I felt more like myself in the dress I was wearing than with any of the clothes the orphanage provided, and now I planned to use it to win the competition.

I chose the funny theme song from "Blue Scarf" that I liked a lot. It was about a cockroach, and I planned to perform it as a female opera singer, using my feminine voice and appearance to convince the crowd and the judges that I deserved to win.

I had always enjoyed singing, dancing, and being praised for expressing myself artistically. So, I knew this would be easy for me. Still, my heart pounded as I left the room and headed towards the gym, where the talent show was about to begin. Everyone was gathering in the hall, anxiously glancing at each other, silently judging their competition.

I didn't worry about the other competitors. I was caught in the moment, thinking about my performance and trying not to forget the words. So, I barely heard or saw anything. I gave the last of my attention to listening for my name.

"Vitaly Mahidov! Please, come to the stage!" The voice cut through the gym, echoing across the high ceiling to land in front of me. I froze for a moment, unsure if it was me they were calling.

"Vitaly?"

"I'm coming!" I yelled, hurrying to my moment, but frankly, I wasn't as fast as I wanted to be. Running in a dress was not as easy as I thought. Still, being comfortable in my disguise helped me relax and tame my wildly beating heart.

I came to the stage dressed to easily fool anyone who didn't hear my name bursting the bubble of noise in the auditorium, and I owned the part. Everyone was clapping in anticipation, waiting for me to feed their curiosity.

It was fun wearing makeup and a dress, feeling and looking like a girl. So, I inhaled, holding my breath until the melody carried me to my moment. Then, words burst forth from my heart,

In the old, rotten trunk
　Fleas are dancing the quadrille.
　In small gray pajamas
　A small bug approached a bald flea.
　'Tell me, flea, do you love Vaska-bug?
　If you do not love him, then you will break his heart,
　And he will run away forever!'
　'No,' said the flea.
　'I do not like Vaska-bug.
　I like the cockroach from under the sofa!'

TALENT SHOW

'Okay, my friend, bye-bye!'

People clapped and began standing, screaming my name even before I closed my mouth. Their acceptance was intoxicating. I bowed to the audience, and their clapping intensified, filling the entire room with the sound of my success. The night was mine.

Filled with pride, I watched as the last of the children finished their performances, but none were as passionate as mine. When the evening approached its end, I heard my name called again. Carried by claps and cheers, I cut through the crowd towards the stage. They awarded me one certificate of honor for my victory and a second for active participation in the social life of the Ivushka Summer Camp.

As I exited the stage a second time, my head felt lighter than a cloud, shined on by the pleasant smiles of my friends and teachers. I did it. I had achieved my goal, and this time, I did it just by being myself.

11

Botsya's Mother

This is Botsya, my dear friend and foster brother Slavik. He was so cute and chubby that we called him Botsya, which meant, little fatty. He loved to be called Botsya.

BORSCHT WAS A STAPLE OF MY childhood and is one of my favorite things to eat. To this day, I eat it more times a week than I eat anything else, and I prepare it with the same careful attention most Ukrainian families use. My mouth is watering as I think of it; chunks of meat with onions, potatoes, beans, and carrots left to simmer for hours in a beet and tomato broth. I serve it with garlic, sour cream, and crispy bread. It's something I've eaten my entire life.

Between meals of fatty pork bits with mashed potatoes and boiled spicy beans with beef, we ate a lot of borscht at the orphanage. Unfortunately, the borscht they served was nothing like the borscht I love today. All I had to do was glance at my plate, and my gut would twist, clamoring to get away from the table and what it knew was coming. It was something no child should endure. Still, I knew I must leave my plate clean and my teachers satisfied if I wanted to go with the other orphans to a movie.

I've always been a person who believed I could have it both ways. So, I often used cunning tricks to make my teachers happy while saving my stomach from sure sickness. After eating all the potatoes, beans, and carrots floating in the broth, I would drink the juice. That was the easy part. I loved vegetables, well, most of the time anyway. When it came to the clumsily chopped pieces of boiled onions floating at the bottom of my bowl, I couldn't eat it. They looked too much like the chunks of fat sitting next to them for me to want to taste them. So, they usually went with the fat to whatever creative way I could find to dispose of them. I used as many different ideas as I could create, but not on Sunday. The rules changed on Sunday.

Regardless of my wit and determination, they often discovered my little crimes. A pile of onion leftovers under my seat at the dining table or a balled-up rag next to my bed were enough to give me away. Sometimes I would get away with my tricks, but they caught me enough that I knew I couldn't take that risk on Sunday. I didn't want to be grounded, beaten, or yelled at today, not when Chernivtsi was waiting for me. So, I swallowed every piece of boiled onion on my plate, stealing my will to prevent myself from throwing up.

After swallowing the last onion, I jumped from my seat and ran to the foyer, where I knew they would line us up by twos for the walk from the orphanage to the city's hub. I couldn't wait for the dimmed lights of the comfy theater, knowing there would be no more work to do and with ice cream too. It was perfection in its purest form.

Slavik was as excited to go to the movie as I was. So, he rushed out behind me. We ended up standing together at the front of the line. As we stood waiting for the other children, I couldn't stop thinking of the icy-sweet aroma of frozen delight and how it might wash away the taste of the borscht we had for lunch. I thought of it as we walked side by side down the streets of Chernivtsi and waited together while our educators found seats for us in the local theater's small projection room.

"It would be so much better to have ice cream first," he sighed as the teacher guided us to where we would sit.

I agreed but didn't say anything. My thoughts had already adjusted to the theater's dimming lights. We were about to watch "Sadko," an adventurous movie made long before I was born. The film's hero longed to bring joy and peace to the ones he loved as he searched for the bird of happiness, and he was willing to fight anyone who stood in his way. I felt like I was fighting with him. I wondered where that bird resided and if I would ever find it. Maybe there was one waiting for me outside the orphanage or even outside Chernivtsi. I didn't know, but I would fight for it every day of my life, the way he did,

After almost two hours of the positive tension caused by Sadko's rises and falls, we went for ice cream. I would always eat mine with great attention, anxiously rushing to collect the drips forming on the edge of the cone. It took all my focus to catch each one as we made our way back to the orphanage. I often thought of what it must be like to gaze at this little group of children from some window high above, eating their ice cream as they buzzed around the city lined up two by two. Of course, they didn't always need to be from the apartment windows. It could be from any house, from any building, from any window. It didn't matter to me, as long as there was a place I might one day call my "home."

Since that wasn't up to me, I would often sense the helplessness slowly climbing toward my throat, choking me in despair and sorrow. I would look around and see a couple, mom and dad, walking with their children. Mothers would hold little hands tightly while children's free hands were getting busy with pastries, ice creams, and candy. I imagined they were on their way to the park or home. Of course, I didn't know where they were heading, but wherever they went, I knew they were never alone, hugging their pillows or crying themselves to sleep. I tried to make the sorrow leave my chest, but I suppose it was too comfortable, as it usually decided to stay.

Today's walk wasn't as bad as most. I had impressions from the movie, memories from our camp, and the surprisingly comfortable noise of cars passing along the road to entertain me. We were in front of our building in no time, embraced by the flowers and greenhouse telling us we were near the familiar comforts of a place I felt tempted to call home. I tried to feel welcomed when I arrived and nostalgic when I left, but I just couldn't. Every association of our little haven on Fastivska Street always brought me back to the point where I had to think about why I was there.

The sound of forks, knives, and clinging plates was there to meet our little group, followed by the scent of some kind of meat announcing it was getting close to dinner time. We were barely in the door, and already it was time to get back to our schedule.

Slavik and I prepared quickly, and then, we sat at the window together to watch the people going about their lives. We were excited to see someone new and think about what they were doing, where they were going, and how it felt to live outside the orphanage walls. After almost half an hour of interpreting the movie and going through the scenes we saw, I told Slavik about the thoughts I had during our walks. I wondered if the people outside ever imagined children at the window of the orphanage, watching them, but there was no one around tonight, not even a passerby. It seemed our little community was too far outside the city to have many people walking by it.

We watched for as long as possible, but it was soon dinner time. So Slavik got up and prepared for dinner. I lingered at the window; my thoughts lost in the image of boys and girls hanging from their father's neck as he came home from his work. He was so happy to see them and overwhelmed with joy by the sight of his family. I could see him approaching his wife. She would be smiling, receiving a kiss, gently placed on top of her head, where it would affectionately mingle with the scent of apple pies. They would later sit at the big oak table, sharing baked chicken, crispy sweet potatoes, freshly chopped salad, and cake she had prepared.

I turned to share my dream with Slavik, but looking around, I realized everyone had already left for dinner. The room was empty, filled only with the ache of loneliness I felt reflected by the barren street.

The following morning, as we were finishing the milk and buckwheat porridge we had for breakfast, we heard a female's screams breaking through the hall. Her raised voice bounced off the walls, ping-ponging through the empty corridors until it landed in Slavik's lap. I tried not to look at him as he began to sink under the table. We all knew it was his mother.

Slavik pretended to be searching for something at his feet. He seemed embarrassed, but at the same time, you could see the relief on his face, as he knew his mother had come to pick him up, at least for a day. Regardless of the time or meal schedules, she was coming for him, always yelling and screaming down the hallway, occasionally berating the orphanage staff.

I looked under the table, trying to catch Slavik's eyes. "You'd better go now, Botsya."

He stood up, rushing towards the exit, as she appeared at the doors, wrapped in grotesque darkness and the echo of her reckless screams. Botsya gave me a restrained wave as he nearly dragged his mother through the cafeteria door.

I knew that Slavik would come back with candy, ice cream, and all sorts of sweets that he would selflessly share with all of us, but that didn't matter much. I was glad that he had a chance to spend at least a couple of hours with the woman who gave him life. He could gather pieces of her to store in his memory and recall later in the swirl of endless nights and dreams. Even if everyone said she was loud and unbearable, at least she was there.

While Slavik was still out with his mother, probably enjoying all sorts of delights, we had to take some time to go with one of our educators to the greenhouse. Besides learning how to knit, sew, sing, write, iron, and wash our clothes, we also had to learn how to take care of the vegetables, flowers, and fruits we grew in the backyard. Although many would consider these tasks too challenging for children, I enjoyed planting flowers, clearing weeds, and picking pears and apples. I liked learning how to take care of the fruits and vegetables we later used to make meals. The smell of the freshly dug soil and fertilizers returned me to my simple pleasures, teaching me what it meant to be in touch with the earth that nurtures us.

Ludwig Viktorovych – one of our educators – showed us how to prune the roses. He also taught us how soil should be plowed and dug for the next planting. I was surprised by how empty my mind could be while working with soil. It was like working on a new invention. So, maintaining the garden soon became one of my favorite chores.

I came back to the dorm, all covered in soil and dust, with my face as calm as a monk in silent prayer when I spotted Slavik. He was smiling above a pile of candy he had spread across my bed. He moved aside, making a spot where I could sit, showing me that he meant to share the collection between us. My face lit up with a smile as I came to sit next to him, almost feeling embarrassed to open one of the sweet treats.

"Dig in!" Slavik said with a welcoming smile spread across his face. Then, he jumped from the bed, "I'll be back. I'm going to find Masha. I bet she will faint once she sees this."

He was off rushing to get Masha and left me to observe the pile of candy. I couldn't help but think of what our lives would be like if we had never met each other. We would have never become friends if we weren't alone and parentless. Of course, it didn't make being an orphan better, but I was grateful to have a friend like Slavik in my life.

I picked one chocolate out from the pile and started unwrapping it with odd attentiveness like it might disappear once the wrapping came off. My fear disappeared when Slavik returned with Masha. Her amazingly bright face, framed with chestnut hair, lit up. She looked at the pile, stunned and full of joy.

Sitting next to me, shyly smirking, she asked Slavik, "Where did you get this?"

"My mother bought them for me," the word mother seemed to catch in his throat.

We didn't ask anything else. We sat on my bed enjoying the candy while watching the cars driving on Fastivska Street, "When I grow up, I think I'll drive a Mazda, black with leather seats," Slavik said as we watched one pass.

"I don't know. I would be a Honda for sure if I could be a car. Honda is faster, so I think it would beat Mazda without question," I replied.

"But a Mercedes would beat a Honda. So I would be a Mercedes."

"Well, I don't think so.... Maybe it could, but if I was the one driving it, no one would beat me," I said with finality though I knew the argument continued in both our minds.

Whoever came in was invited to join our little sweet-eating quest, their faces blooming with a sugar buzz floating above our heads. We ended our adventure with not a single candy left. Our stomachs were full of happiness, leaving everyone in the mood to play, chat, whisper, and sing. We were drunk with joy that rarely came to our orphanage door.

When they announced supper, only a few of us were still able to open our mouths, let alone swallow the food they gave us. The teachers circled us like vultures, checking the contents on our plates.

We all put forth our best effort, knowing that detention was lurking if we didn't find a way to finish. I was looking at my sandwich with thoughts of having time to build something from the engine I buried. I wanted time to work on it, which I wouldn't have during punishment. So, I decided to avoid trouble. Unfortunately, some of my friends weren't as motivated as I was, so I could hear threats and unpleasant pokes, implying detention and consequences. The worst punishment you could get was being beaten with the wooden ruler across your palms and fingers or beaten with a belt or wooden stick, which was usually the form of detention I was getting.

I couldn't help myself not to scream when they were punishing me. I liked to think it was to annoy my punisher or rebel against that system, but it was more likely because I was frightened and wanted someone to save me. So I screamed, choosing the highest pitch I could get, often being bullied by the older kids or laughed at for "screaming like a girl." The only one who stood up for me was Slavik. Somehow you always find someone to patch you up and stick with you, regardless of the challenging things around you. I guess no one should be alone in this world.

I didn't want to face anything that had to do with punishment, so I remained silent, and I ate. In the end, most of us did, so the living room was filled with dozens of children, fighting to find the best spot to watch the long-awaited television show, "Good Night, Children!" The opening song started, and most of us sang along with words well memorized. We matched every pause before seeing the little puppet bear and bunny talking to each other happily. We loved watching the opening credits, observing the moon and the stars made of colored clay, turning into different shapes, and changing colors in a blink. We watched the bear singing, dancing, and telling fairy tales with lyrics while bunny and other puppet animals were having all sorts of goodnight adventures, summoning dreams in our sleepy little heads. Our brains welcomed the enticing invitation to dream but battled it too, wanting to stay up and watch the show.

As the sun left the sky, we surrendered to the darkening night. Though the sugar buzz was still whirling in my head, the intensely sweet burden of a busy day finally fell on my eyes, making me sleepy and hungry for hugs. I dove into my bed, hugging my pillow, and let the sheets take over my muscles. With my arms wrapped around the most consistent form of comfort I knew, I fell deep in dreams, silently lurking around my bed, waiting for me to live them.

The wind was whipping my face, but it wasn't cold. I was high above the ground, but I wasn't afraid. I was flying, able to touch the warm summer raindrops as they reflected thousands of miniature rainbows across the clouds. Everything; the sky, the wind, the eiderdown clouds, and the rainbows were all mine.

In my dreams, I was free, and I knew one day my life would be free as well. It would be full of the joy I knew I deserved to have.

12

Loved Ones Lost

Cemetery in Chernivtsi where people I loved and cared about during my childhood are now buried.

DURING MY CHILDHOOD, the winters I experienced were harsh and biting cold. Wind from snowstorms rocked our building, and we lived daily without the necessities to keep warm. Even when we were inside, I would sometimes wear a hat, gloves, and a scarf around my mouth. Unfortunately, the scarf wasn't wide enough to cover my nose. So the steam from my mouth transformed moisture from my nose into tiny icicles. Between that and frightening snowstorms, living at the orphanage seemed like a constant fight for survival.

As I think about growing up in Chernivtsi, I remember everything as dull and gray. I spent so much of my childhood surrounded by people fighting for something. The soldiers were trying to end a war and ease the suffering of strangers while their mothers, sisters, and wives were humiliatingly fighting over pickled vegetables and sausages in cans any time some lucky seller had a chance to stock a shelf. The city was saturated with the signs of unfortunate stomachs, trodding through the barren shelves of almost empty markets.

Ladies cherished their plastic shopping bags, taping every hole with care and devotion like they might be expensive crocodile purses. The sparsely stocked shelves offered little variety, filled only with pasta, bread, and a meager supply of Hungarian pickles and preserves. Nervous, disappointed people often passed by the markets, hoping for the day when they might have more options. The lucky buyers who carried rare oranges or sausage links or any other fruit or meat in their mesh bags were accosted in the street with desperate questions, asking, "Where did you get that?"

We found some peace being children, partially protected from the more worldly concerns occurring at the time. We didn't understand war. Beyond the fairy tales and stories starring our favorite heroes, we focused on enlarging our gum wrapper collections. When we had duplicates, we would find a way to trade. We even went so far as stealing wrappers from each other when someone had one we couldn't help wanting. Our desire to have the most extensive collection determined our battlefronts, making everyone who had less envious of our treasure. Maybe the people who started the wars weren't that different from us. Perhaps they too wanted to have the most of something, but we didn't understand what real war was, the depths of what people suffered while we were battling over worthless scraps of paper.

Even years after the battles ended, whispers filled the room every time anyone mentioned the conflicts. As orphans, we heard of the horrible conditions of war only after small companies of our troops began coming home, never to be the same after the things they experienced.

"What is the cause of war?" our teacher asked, writing the title of his topic on the blackboard. "Our subject for today will be 'Hot spots on Earth.' So, why do we talk about wars, even when everything is over?"

The class was quiet, solemnly looking at one another. Some were curious and puzzled, not understanding the subject. The rest of us were waiting impatiently to hear what our teacher had to say about the still delicate subject of war.

He mentioned Bosnia, Kosovo, Tajikistan, Dagestan, South Ossetia, and Chechnya, posting red pins across the world map. He then pressed one into a place named Kabul, the capital of Afghanistan, as the center of our class' focus today. We didn't realize that these places, which represented only red dots to us, were, in fact, communities that suffered horror, pain, distress, and losses no one could retrieve.

"Whenever there is a country where war is raging, our country always jumps in, bringing aid and trying to extinguish the fire of unreason. That is the scenario happening in Afghanistan since 1979.

"Does anyone know what kind of country Afghanistan is?" the teacher asked, looking around the classroom as if he was expecting one of us to answer his question. Though some of us probably knew at least something about Afghanistan, we remained silent, letting him fill the room with his words again.

He continued, giving us essential information, "Afghanistan is a country of amazing and unique beauty, with great strategic value on the Silk Road that traverses Central and Southern Asia. The religion is Islamic, as other religions are almost unacceptable there."

He told us about the unique beauties and acts of hospitality, like the tea you could get as a token of appreciation if you ever visited Afghanistan. Yet, I couldn't help thinking about how many places of natural beauty were spoiled by blood and death—crippling, mentally disturbing, wounding, killing, and scarring them for life.

I sat thinking about all of the horrible things happening in Afghanistan. I wanted to help the people there. I didn't want them to suffer, but I didn't know what to do. I was feeling helpless. I did not even have everything I needed to help myself.

"Vitaly!" The teacher's voice was like a hard jolt, jerking me back to Fastivska Street. "Vitaly. Come out of your daydreams and take these books to the principal for me."

I stood, pulling my mind from the events of Afghanistan back into my little life. I took the stack of books from my instructor and entered the orphanage's nearly silent hallway. I wished I could stay in the halls sometimes while everyone else was in class. There was so much I could investigate there.

Every step I took was as slow as I could make it. I wanted to take advantage of every second of being away from class. My adventure was almost perfect until I reached the office. What I saw there ruined everything.

Two of my favorite friends, Nadija and Rostik—twin brother and sister—were standing with several other children just inside the orphanage doors. There were seven children in all; four from the orphanage and three I didn't recognize.

My friends stood with the small group. Their coats and other belongings rested on the floor next to them. I knew what that meant.

They were leaving the orphanage. They had a family. Unlike most days, we weren't receiving three new members to our little family. Instead, we were losing four, and none of them were me.

Strong emotions stirred in me. I was excited for my friends, and I was jealous too. I'd seen it before, and it always set my heart racing. Families sometimes came in to adopt foster children. I hated it. I didn't like losing my friends. I wanted to hate them for going away, and I resented those who took them for not taking me. I was jealous and angry, but I was happy for them too. Finally, they would be with a family, something every one of us wanted for ourselves, and for each other too. Still, I couldn't get away from my jealousy. What made this family choose them and not me? Why did they get to go?

Rostik looked at me nervously. Everything we dream about, and still, he couldn't trust it. His expression made it worse. Why would he be nervous? He didn't understand what he was getting, but I did. He and his sister had a loving family now, a place to call home. They get to be that kid I saw holding an ice cream in one hand and his mother's loving embrace in the other. They get to sit at the window, watching the little orphans lined up and walking to the movies. They get a family, but all I got was one less chance and someone taking another piece of my family away.

I watched as Vasyl Ivanovych, the principal, helped them with the last of their few belongings. I didn't even care that he saw me just standing alone in the middle of the hall. It was painful to watch them go. I wanted to be excited for them, but I couldn't. I wished I could just run back to my pillow because, more than anything else, I felt alone.

All I could feel now was the empty corridor around me. What if all the children found families? What if everyone was gone, and I was the only one left? Or worse, what if I were to go and Slavik or Igor were the ones left standing alone in this hall, watching me go? I wondered if this was how the people in Afghanistan felt, standing over the remains of their destroyed dreams. How are we supposed to be happy with a world full of so many horrible things? Even the little blessings like Nadija and Rostik getting a new home hurt somebody like me. If I got what I wanted, who would I hurt? I wondered.

The worst of my feelings came when my mind quickly answered the question. I didn't care. I couldn't stop wishing that one day I would be with a family, no matter who it hurt.

13

Chernobyl

On April 26, 1986, one of the worst accidents in the history of nuclear energy occurred,
which greatly contributed to the collapse of the USSR. Scientists say Pripyat will remain
uninhabitable for another 100,000 years.

IT WAS EARLY IN THE DAY, and I was still not awake when one of our instructors came to the door of our room saying, "Pack all the clothes you can't use anymore. If it's too small or too torn, put it in this box."

I remembered Nadija and Rostik standing next to all of their belongings and wondered what might be happening to us, "Why are we packing our stuff?"

My instructor looked at me with a sad expression on her face. "We are gathering clothes to give them away. A disaster has created an unfortunate circumstance not far from us. So, we are gathering what we don't need to help them."

With that, she walked away. We didn't know who would get the clothes or why someone would need them. We didn't know that we were collecting clothes for victims of an earthquake in Armenia until later. We only knew that something terrible had happened and that many people needed all the help they could get. The thing I realized was that it could always get worse. I didn't have much, but it was enough that I could give to someone else. I was grateful. Our little orphanage often protected us from nature's brutal twists and from finding out firsthand how cruel the world around us could be.

I was standing in a room full of other boys, but we had shelter, food, and enough clothes to share. Unfortunately, there was no electricity to shine upon the screams that echoed through the city or aid the search for lost children and missing people in Armenia. Only the ambulance's red and blue lights illuminated the broken concrete and fallen bricks.

The wounded, the screaming, and lost, that was a picture hidden from us, a thing we never had to experience. However, as Pioneers, we were called to unite and help, parentless or not. Still, the best we could do was to collect the clothes we didn't use—there weren't many—and give them away to the children in Armenia. As we had an idea of what was going on in the Soviet Union at the time, I was sad and disappointed that I couldn't do much for those children because I knew that I would have wanted someone to help me if I needed it. Still, I was at peace because I knew other Pioneers had more and gave more.

When we arrived at class that day, our teacher looked distracted from the lessons. She was usually standing and ready to teach us, but today she was sitting on the front edge of her desk, gently guiding us to sit in our chairs. A man sat behind her. He was missing a patch of hair over his left ear and had red splotches across the side of his face.

His scars scared me. I had never seen someone like him before, and I wondered if he was one of the soldiers returning from the war. The image of his face stuck in my mind, often returning in my dreams, making me wonder about how bad things could get.

When our instructor began to speak, it was with a solemn voice, "Tragedy poured itself upon dozens of towns in Armenia today. Thousands of people were injured, and many were dead or lost. But I don't want to speak with you about the devastation. I want to talk to you about hope. Armenia will rise from its ashes and broken bricks one day. We all do. Life goes on without waiting."

I listened to her and thought of how I had suffered, abandoned at an orphanage. Maybe the disasters caused us to meet others who suffered and find a way to unite in our search for happiness. All of us were parentless and alone in some way.

Our educators and teachers were giving their best to protect us from the world's cruelties while simultaneously preparing us to be independent and compassionate. So, I was happy to gather everything I could and give it to Armenia. I didn't think old clothes consoled anyone in those times, but, unfortunately, that was the best we could do for the people suffering there.

Our instructor continued, pulling me from my thoughts of Armenia. "There was another disaster that destroyed many lives in Ukraine just a couple of years ago. It devastated surrounding countries, and it will still affect those cities and their people generations from now.

"Chernobyl was one of the USSR's most advanced and influential industrial centers. Then, on April 26, 1986, one of the most significant radioactive explosions of a nuclear plant ever happened there, changing millions of lives worldwide.

"It took just one day to destroy a nearly twenty-mile radius around the ruined power plant. They evacuated almost a quarter of a million people overall, leaving behind lives the people there had worked decades to build. The people of Chernobyl lost their towns and villages, families, friends, homes, co-workers, businesses, their entire lives. They suffered devastating illnesses from radiation and lost all their possessions. People continue to share their grief and memories today and will for decades to come.

"Today, I have invited an important guest to our classroom. His name is Oleg Ivanovich, and he was working at the power plant the night it exploded. I have invited him here to share his story with us and imprint the memories of that event in your young minds. When we can learn from tragedies like these, we can be careful to make sure they do not happen again."

Oleg began, "My parents moved to Pripyat in 1979. When I became a man, I served in the Pacific Fleet on a submarine. After my service, I moved to Pripyat, got married, and then my two beautiful daughters were born. At the time of the accident, we were building the fourth block of the Chernobyl Nuclear Power Plant. We had just started the construction stage.

"My family loved Pripyat. Even after leaving it, we grieved about the place we lost. The city sat on the bank of the Pripyat River. Even though it was young and modern, it was also woodland with beautiful scenery. Although we lived in a city, we truly enjoyed all the village-like charms of something that looked more like a small town."

I listened to Oleg and thought of our summer camp and imagined

Pripyat must be full of fields of wildflowers too.

"On the day of the accident, I went to work at 4 p.m. I worked two shifts in a row that day, my regular shift and one for a friend, who asked me to substitute for him. My second shift began at midnight. A senior operator named Anatoly Kurgur worked the second shift with me.

"Everything seemed to happen at once. I knew they were running tests on the unit, and the reactor power was failing. So, they asked us to evacuate the area. I didn't think much of it then. We had situations before. Still, we knew the safety protocol. So, we didn't stay in the central hall of the reactor. It was a good thing too. I found out later. If we had been there much longer, we would not have survived.

"In a security room, there was a walk-in closet made of brick. I went inside to pick up something for the evacuation, and a few seconds later, I heard an explosion. Imagine that. This tiny closet had just saved me and kept me alive. Everything around me was shaking, and I could hear the reactor hissing. Then, it all began to crumble. I pinched myself. I didn't know if I was still alive or if it was all just a terrible dream. It seemed so unreal.

"The air was sweltering around us, making it hard to breathe, but there was no fear among the workers or the administration. Everyone was calmly doing what we were trained to do. The fear didn't come until later after the second explosion happened. The whole place rocked.

"I fell to the floor, but breathing was easier on the floor than it was when I was standing, so I stayed there, not knowing what to do next. Then, I heard my co-worker, Anatoly scream in pain. I looked in the direction of the scream and could see him crawling toward me. Every motion looked like agony, 'I think we got hit hard,' he said.

"Anatoly had more experience than me, so I knew we had to get out right away. But I wasn't sure which way to go. It was so dark around us that we couldn't see much beyond each other. We felt our way through familiar rooms, but every path we tried had piles of fallen concrete. We couldn't even access the stairs. So we decided to make our way to the emergency ladder. On the way to the ladder, I found a flashlight in an emergency bin, which helped me see things around me a little better, including my partner. I was horrified. Anatoly had almost no skin left on the back of his hands. I guess he must have been out in the main room when the explosion happened and used them to cover his face.

"When we finally found our way out of the building, he was taken away in an ambulance. Along with the other nuclear plant operators, I returned dirty and wet to the administrative building. I washed with the special powder we kept on sight and changed my clothes the moment I got there.

"Most of the workers in our area had already gathered when I arrived. We also had operators from the third block, and we talked about what happened. We knew we had a job to do. So, we didn't panic, although in our hearts, maybe some of us were scared."

Oleg paused for a moment, gathering his emotions before he continued to tell his story, "We made it out, but we still didn't understand the real danger yet. People were walking around, examining chunks of graphite they found on the streets. We were still in the office planning as a glowing column rose from the mouth of the reactor. I just stared. It was beautiful in a way, like the northern lights.

"You know, this may sound strange, but at that moment, it hit me. Everyone said the reactor was destroyed, but I suddenly understood what that meant and thought about my family. I thought about the entire city. Our children, families, and sixty thousand people slept only three kilometers away. They had no idea of what had just happened.

"We all stood, staring at the scene in front of us, not sure what would happen next. We knew it was necessary to make a quick decision, act, and fulfill our duties as parents and workers, but I don't think we knew what to do. What could we do?

"Things were bad, but even then, no one understood the full scale of the disaster. The deputy chief engineer told us, 'Okay guys, there has been an accident, albeit a serious one, but I don't want you to worry. We've made plans for this. First, they will send us to Moscow for medical treatment. Then we will return.' He didn't know that many were already on their way to Moscow to die.

"They took the people with the worst injuries first, while the rest of us stayed behind to try and stop more disasters. But, as the night progressed, I was getting worse. So they put me in an ambulance to take me in for treatment, as well.

"Later, in the Moscow clinic, it turned out that eighty percent of my body was burned, but Anatoly had received more burns than me. I think I was saved by changing my clothes and washing when I got to the admin building.

"It was over a day and a half before they warned local inhabitants that it was necessary to close the vents, go out less, and carry iodine tablets. Before that, the people passed the news through word of mouth. Some women thought it was better not to let the children go to the sandbox. Still, they didn't know the severity of the situation, so many children continued to play outside. It was a day off for many people, so the city lived like things were every day. People gathered to continue celebrating their life events, even though the military wore respirators as they walked along the streets.

"At the time of the accident, I already had two children; one girl was ten months old, the other girl was two months. When my wife heard about the disaster from our neighbors, she gathered the children and tried to leave for a nearby village, but people were leaving that village, as well. As a result, her father drove her to the Gomel region. They ended up going to my aunt's in Minsk, but before they could see my aunt, everyone had to be examined. When they arrived at the hospital, the staff took their clothes, giving them clean garments. After that, they had thorough exams and blood tests.

"I spent days in the hospital unable to move or eat. None of us had any appetite, and in my case, I ended up with a bone marrow transplant. It was excruciating, but the worst part was that I could not see my wife and children when I was in the hospital. While I was fighting for my life in the hospital, my elder brother took care of my family. Thanks to him, we all survived.

"On the twenty-seventh of April, a radio broadcast finally went out in Pripyat, announcing the evacuation, 'You are leaving for three days, take the minimum number of things,' they said. They evacuated the young first but did not tell the elderly to respond in one way or another. Some of us knew what was going on, but no one explained what would happen next. The people of Chernobyl and its neighboring cities faced an uncertain future, and all they had were bits of unclear information.

"Although she had left earlier, my wife took nothing. Our documents, gold jewelry, children's toys, clothes, and other valuables remained in Pripyat. We thought we would be back. So, they didn't take any food, canned goods, toys, or expensive things. Besides the clothes on their back, my wife's only thought was diapers for the baby.

"After a few days in Minsk, my wife and both of our little daughters went to the sanatorium of Slavinsk in the Donetsk region because they managed to get a ticket from the station's trade union committee. I met them there six months later. I didn't work after that because I was now disabled from my radiation exposure. So, we lived on those benefits."

"The doctors later told me, depending on the regions of Pripyat, people were exposed to as much as fifty to seventy REM of radiation. Five REM is considered the maximum exposure anyone should experience in a year. Still, even with their high exposure, the conditions were survivable with treatment for most people. For others - who were exposed to over a hundred REM or higher - they were diagnosed with acute radiation sickness, rated as first-degree. Many of them would not make it.

"Now, years later, we know it is unlikely that your generation and even your children will be able to live in Pripyat's beautiful city. One bad moment and our lives are changed forever."

I couldn't imagine everything he had gone through. It sounded excruciating, and I could see he was suffering as he finished his story. We probably didn't need to know those details as children. We couldn't understand what happened, but we couldn't avoid it either. I remembered sitting in front of the television with my attention caught by colorfully drawn characters of a cartoon that showed the suffering of a family from Chernobyl. The father grabbed hair falling from his head. His son was watching him. The boy's mother passed away, and they were left to live alone and face an unknown future. The cartoon was graphic, and we were missing the complete picture of chaos, disaster, and lost lives that Oleg had endured. We only knew a small piece of the story. Still, we knew disaster happened not far from our own homes.

As I grew older, I heard similar stories of the terrible impact the Chernobyl disaster made on the lives of many people who went through these sufferings. They mobilized thousands of people, but many had already suffered graver consequences than losing all of their hair. Every time I met with a survivor, their stories awoke my childhood memories of Oleg and his family. Even today, I can't help but think of the disaster and what happened there. The world moves on for most of us, but for some, their tragedies consume them.

I learned a lot from the horrible things that could happen in the world. Still, I knew, like my teacher said, life goes on. So, no matter how many disasters I had in my life, I had to let them go. I could not let the tragedies consume me.

14

Pan Kotsky

Pan Kotsky fairy tale book cover

HORRIBLE THINGS WERE happening in the world around Chernivtsi. Our people suffered almost ten years of pain, war, and loss, trying to make things right somehow. If I had understood what was happening in the world outside our little orphanage, I would have been more grateful for the simple things I had and maybe forgotten the circumstances that brought me there. But it is often difficult to see beyond our suffering, to understand others' pain. We notice what we don't have, and maybe we should. Perhaps our pain isn't so bad if it makes us want something better than what life gave us.

Horrible things were happening in the world around Chernivtsi. Our people suffered almost ten years of pain, war, and loss, trying to make things right somehow. If I had understood what was happening in the world outside our little orphanage, I would have been more grateful for the simple things I had and maybe forgotten the circumstances that brought me there. But it is often difficult to see beyond our suffering, to understand others' pain. We notice what we don't have, and maybe we should. Perhaps our pain isn't so bad if it makes us want something better than what life gave us.

We learned to want more as orphans. Every night, we would read a different story to tickle our imagination and sweeten our dreams. The exciting tales showed us more to the world than just our little lives. Our senses became excited every time we heard the words, "Once upon a time...." We would all listen carefully, longing for the rest of the sentence, "...in a land far away...." I always wondered how far that land was and how you could get there, desperately hoping there might be room for one more person.

My imagination ran wild, flowing into the story, creating magical realities and fantastic worlds where anything was possible and where good always won. I loved hearing the news of what would happen next for little children like me. "...There was a little girl named Little Red Riding Hood. She was very kind, and everyone knew her name because she was easily recognized with her red hood bobbing through the forest."

Even though I already knew what was coming next, I was always held in curious anticipation, waiting for the Big Bad Wolf to come.

Yet, at the same time, I was frightened but peaceful, knowing that no matter what, someone would save the day, and the fairy tale would end with, "and they all lived happily ever after."

Even in real life, I hoped that someone would save the day every time I was in bad situations with potentially harmful endings. Usually, I was the one to protect myself, at least in most of my disasters. Who knows? Maybe everyone is too busy to save each other, or perhaps the world is full of too many people. That's how it was at our orphanage. There were so many children. No one could focus on just one. So, I felt lonely most of the time.

Still, I believed in miracles and wonders, hoping for the best. I wondered how it would feel if I were one of the lead fairy tale characters, blindly traveling towards my happy ending. The stories gave me brief moments to hope for the best during the day, occupying my brain until bedtime arrived. Then, I would inevitably come back to my pillow, twitching and clawing, trying to find my consolation. Sometimes I found it in my dreams, but I also returned to the fairy tales for peace when I was restless.

One of my favorite tales was Pan Kotsky. It was a story about a very persuasive and rather fat cat. "Once upon a time," the teacher began, "there was a humble old man who had his best friend cat who proudly wore the name Pan Kotsky. They were the best of companions until their happiness came to an end. The cat was getting fatter and fatter, and his owner didn't have enough food to feed him. Pan became so lazy he wouldn't catch mice, so the house was swarming with those annoying little critters. Finally, with nothing else to do, the old man put Pan Kotsky in a bag and carried him to the forest, leaving him far enough away he couldn't come back. The old man was sad and lost all of his joy, but the cat was so useless and lazy, and with the lack of food on top of everything, he just had to leave him."

At that point, I was always confused about whether I should feel sorry for the old man or sympathize with the cat. Still, even though the cat was in an unenviable situation, luck was on his side. Others accepted the image he created of himself, and he experienced a string of fortunate opportunities. Pan Kotsky even married a fox, who was on his side, claiming he was the fiercest animal in all Ukraine.

The thought that everyone should have one fox beside them struck me. I always thought about how lucky Pan Kotsky was. Though he was a little too proud and pompous, he was an adventurous cat. I knew that I could rest with peace in my heart, knowing that Pan Kotsky would find his fortune, even facing unfortunate conditions.

Little Fox saw him alone in the forest, saying, "Well, you are beautiful! Your tale is so magnificent! What kind of animal are you?"

Pan Kotsky replied, puffed up in glory and self-esteem, "Don't tell me, Little Fox, that you have never heard of Pan Kotsky! I am the fiercest and most famous animal in the entire forest!"

The fox was impressed, instantly falling in love with the vain cat. "Oh, please, Pan Kotsky, would you come to my house and protect me? I am so small and helpless. I would love to have someone like you by my side!"

Pan Kotsky accepted and went to live with the Little Fox. She went out every day searching for food to feed her beloved fat cat. She gathered the food and prepared the meals, so Pan Kotsky didn't even need to raise his tale.

One day, as the fox searched for food to feed her gentleman cat, she ran into Mr. Rabbit. Mr. Rabbit approached, "Little Fox," the rabbit started, "I was thinking about you, wondering if I could come to see you soon."

Little fox said, "Sorry, Mr. Rabbit, but I already have my gentleman, the fiercest and the most famous animal in all the forests!"

Later, she ran into Mr. Boar, and he also asked, "Hello, Little Fox! Can I come to court you later? I was thinking about how beautiful you are."

"No, thank you, Mr. Boar! I already have a gentleman! Pan Kotsky is

the fiercest and the most famous animal in the entire forest!"

Not long after, the fox met Mr. Bear, "Hello, Little Fox! You are so beautiful! Would you care to accept a gentleman like myself?"

The fox replied for the third time, "No, thank you, Mr. Bear. I already have a gentleman! His name is Pan Kotsky, and he is the fiercest and the most famous animal in the entire forest!"

Mr. Rabbit, Mr. Bear, and Mr. Boar gathered later to discuss this Pan Kotsky. "I think we should call Little Fox and her gentlemen to dinner and see if that Pan Kotsky is who Little Fox says he is."

They all agreed, sending Mr. Rabbit out to call on them. "Dear Little Fox, would you come to dinner with your gentleman Pan Kotsky?"

Little fox agreed and began getting ready to go, so proud to have them meet her gentleman.

When the fox and cat arrived at the dinner, there was no one at the table, for Mr. Rabbit was hiding in bushes, Mr. Boar found his place hiding under the table, and Mr. Bear had climbed a tree. Without any manners, Pan Kotsky meowed excitedly and jumped onto the table, devouring everything in sight. As he roared and made sounds, the animals hiding thought he was asking for more.

With each growl from Pan Kotsky, they became more and more frightened. Mr. Boar's tail started trembling, revealing where he was hiding under the table. Pan Kotsky thought it was a mouse to eat with his dinner, so he jumped and bit the tail with his sharp little teeth.

Mr. Boar ran, tipping the table and causing Mr. Bear to fall onto Mr. Rabbit's back, making the rabbit cry, "Help me! Help!!!"

"Pan Kotsky knocked me out of the tree!" said Mr. Bear trembling.

"He hit me in the back!" said Mr. Rabbit, crying.

"He bit off my tail with his enormous teeth!" said Mr. Boar, still frightened.

Little Fox noticed that her fierce and famous Pan Kotsky was also trembling in fear, thinking the other gentlemen wanted to attack him.

Realizing none of them were there to protect her, she said, "I've had enough of gentlemen!!" and she left, locking her door against any caller.

I loved the story of Pan Kotsky. The moral of the story seemed to be, "He who talks big doesn't always act big." I knew this was true, as I could think of many people in my life who were a lot like that greedy cat. They often made big promises they didn't keep.

I didn't know how to think of people like Pan Kotsky. Every time I listened to the story, I found myself wanting him to succeed and fail at the same time. I was not too fond of the cat's behavior, but I did appreciate how things always worked in his favor. I wanted my life to be like Pan Kotsky's. Of course, I didn't want to be fat and lazy, but I knew I could get what I wanted if I had the same confidence as that crafty cat. I just had to figure out how to have one without the other.

15

The Lord's Prayer

Many of the Orthodox Churches in Ukraine, favor a Russian style of architecture.

DURING THE TIME I WAS GROWING UP in the orphanage, Ukraine was a place where religion was considered useless. The only belief system we were allowed to worship was communism. As children, they taught us to be honorable, hard-working adults and that religion would only hold us back. The USSR focused on scientific facts only, racing to advance technology and being first above other countries. They believed there was no proof that God existed, and we should have faith only in what our eyes could see. "Religion is for unintelligent people!" they said. "God does not exist, and there is nothing above the human race, except the clouds and the stars." They thought we should live our lives using intelligence and the pure power of deduction.

The Soviet ideology stated that cultured and enlightened people could not be believers of religious fancy. Our Government persecuted churches. They arrested priests and tore crosses from rooftops, determined to prohibit and limit all spiritual activity. This mandate included removing religion from all government activity, including the public schools. As Soviet citizens, we could sacredly believe only in the victory of communism. It was a way of life for me.

Still, believers silently believed, practicing their faith privately. They didn't talk about their opinions or even go to church, but they believed in their God. I've often felt the teaching of communism wouldn't have been so devastating for Christians if only they were allowed to believe in what they wanted. Someone trusting that Jesus was God would not harm those who didn't. Science and spirituality didn't need to contrast one another, but that was not the opinion of the Communist Party.

Eventually, Communist Russia did leave our fair city, and the consciousness of the Ukrainian Government changed. As I was entering the years where I no longer wanted to think of myself as a little boy, the world around me was also feeling a little more independent. Communism had left its mark and still had its influence, but people began believing again, though they did so with caution. The teachers at my school were not allowed to talk about religion, but some of the teachers were brave enough to try and introduce us to

Jesus. Martha Ivanivna was my favorite teacher at the orphanage and the first to unveil ideas about someone out there who loved me that I could not see or hear.

"Isn't that the point of religion?" Martha once asked us, "to provide us with the strength to face challenges we meet along the way. That's why it's called faith."

Most of our guardians wouldn't say such a thing. I don't know if they had faith in religion, but they always said religion was useless in our classes, and communism was the only "religion" we needed. Some of the teachers taught us that faith in Jesus was misleading and as destructive as Satan to our way of life.

As young minds prone to readily adopting our teachers' knowledge, we gave it our faith, following the example of Vladimir Ilyich Ulyanov, better known by his alias Vladimir Lenin. We didn't know if Jesus was as horrible as the Bible preached Satan to be, but they said we shouldn't trust his teachings. So, we didn't think that the stories about Jesus were authentic, and we could not understand why people followed them. I always supposed that children whose parents were silent believers could still believe, but we all listened to what our instructors said at the orphanage, obliging and following their lead. Well, most of us did, but not everyone.

One night, when it was Martha's turn to watch over us and take care that we were all in our beds on time, she came into the room, carefully checking the hall first to see if there was anyone outside the dorm doors. Then, she sat on one of the beds and smiled at all of us. I was excited for our next bedtime story as she carefully drew a book from underneath her sweater.

Looking toward the door one last time, she asked, "What do you know about Jesus Christ?"

We were confused by her question. We didn't know much, only that he wasn't a favorite of the communist party. I realized later that rules aren't written by the masses, no matter how progressive they are. Individuals who rule the people decide what their lives will be.

"Jesus and Satan are evil, and we shouldn't believe in them," someone said from beneath a blanket.

"Jesus is bad," another voice followed.

"Jesus is not a God," I followed. I wanted to say more. I had many opinions about Jesus, but I didn't want to look stupid, so I didn't say everything I thought.

Martha listened to us, not blinking, not replying. Then, she took a deep breath, her faith unwavering, and peacefully replied, "Let me tell you a story, my dears. One day, thousands of years ago, a woman made a mistake, just as many people still do. It doesn't matter whether you say something bad or do something wrong; we all make mistakes that separate us from God. He could have made sure that we never do anything wrong, but he loved us so much as we are all his children that he gave us free will and the ability to make our own decisions and choices, even if they are mistakes."

We listened in silence, wrapped in curiosity, waiting to find out where Martha's story was going. You could tell by her face that the words she spoke weren't of an ordinary tale to her. She believed them profoundly and with steadfast commitment.

She continued, "We all made mistakes, and there are always people ready to judge us and sentence us, although they are also making their own mistakes. The people were ready to kill the woman for the mistake she had made, throwing stones and rocks at her." She paused, observing our silent faces before continuing, "However, there was one man who thought that violence and judging people were wrong. So, he stood in front of that unfortunate and frightened woman and said, 'You can throw your rocks at her, but whoever is without sin may be the one to throw their rock first.'"

She smiled for a moment and then continued with excitement in her voice, "And do you know what happened? Just as everyone knew that there was no such thing as a sinless human, for we all make mistakes, no one threw their rocks, sparing the woman painful and horrible judgment. The man who stopped them all from killing this woman was named Jesus Christ, or Jesus of Nazareth, as they knew him in the Bible.

"Besides trying to make things right and helping people understand that there is always a way to be better people, he also healed people from devastating and fatal illnesses. He didn't do this to demonstrate his power but to help people, for he loved all people more than he could ever love himself. He died to save us from our sins, nailed to the cross, only to be resurrected and brought to heaven to watch over us. Although he no longer walks the Earth, he can still hear our prayers and help us with doubt or pain. He is there when we are sad or when we are going through hard times."

As she finished her sentence, she opened the book she had been holding in her lap the entire time. Then, without saying anything further, she began to read.

"Our Father who art in heaven,
hallowed be thy name.
Thy kingdom come,
thy will be done,
on Earth, as it is in heaven.
Give us this day our daily bread,
and forgive us our trespasses,
as we forgive those who trespass against us;
and lead us not into temptation,
but deliver us from evil."

Martha finished reading, casting a sincere smile upon each of us. "This is a prayer each of us should know to protect us in our lives and help us be purer." Then, she stood up, concealing the book underneath her sweater.

I knew she had not hidden it as a surprise to us but that she was hiding it from the other teachers' curious eyes.

"Good night," she whispered as she left the room.

Caught up in the impressions born of Martha's stories and her promise that someone was out there watching out for me, always there when I needed them, I got up from my bed, almost running after her. She was already halfway across the hall, but I managed to catch her.

"Vitaly, what are you doing in the hall? It's bedtime, my dear. It would be better if you returned to the room and had some good sleep."

"I know. I will. I am sorry," I said, "but I wondered if you could maybe write that prayer you were reading out of the book. I would like to have it," I looked at her nervously, nearly jumping from one foot to another, partly because I was impatient and partly because the floor was too cold.

Martha smiled at me. "Of course. I will write it out and give it to you tomorrow at breakfast, but for the sake of both of us, don't hand it out to anyone or tell anyone that you have it, alright?"

I nodded.

She smiled and pinched my cheek, "Now, go to bed. Goodnight." With that, she turned her back, walking down the hallway as I returned to the bedroom.

The following day, after breakfast, Martha stood in the middle of the hallway, discretely observing children as they were walking by her. "Good morning, Vitaly," she said, handing me a piece of paper that she had carefully folded into a small square.

"Good morning, Martha," I replied, taking the paper. Then, I smiled at her as I walked away.

When I was alone, I unwrapped the piece of paper and saw she had written "The Lord's Prayer" above the words she had recited. I liked reading those words. They made me feel safe and less alone.

For weeks, I recited the prayer, studying it line by line until I knew it by heart. Then, I would walk the halls and repeat it in my head, over and over, making sure that I could recall it any time I needed it. As I recited the words, I felt protected by them. Like the woman in Martha's story, I knew I was no longer alone. I knew Jesus would love me, no matter how many mistakes I made.

Like Martha, I believed the prayer had power, and I wanted it to protect me. I was always a target for older kids to harass me and beat me up for nothing. So I was grateful to now have this new power to protect myself.

One night, right before we went to sleep, one of our educators, who was supposed to make sure that we were all in our beds, wandered away to do something down the hall. She was an older woman who would often be the one to take care of us at bedtime. We hated when we heard her coming because she would make us scratch her feet, only because she couldn't do it herself. We never wanted to be the one she picked, but we were also glad she was there because she protected us from the older boys. Whenever she decided to leave, that meant the older boys from the room across the hall had their chance to come into our room and torment us. I was the one they liked to target the most, and I always knew when they were coming. I could hear their laughter bouncing off the empty hallway from a mile away.

As the laughter rose, drowning out the click of the woman's shoes, I pulled my covers over my head. Then, remembering Martha's words, I began repeating the prayer I memorized. I was sure I must be saying it aloud as I fervently recited the sentences, thinking of them as protection, as some kind of shield or immunity.

Two of the older boys came in, and instead of picking on me, they immediately started messing with Slavik. Although I was glad I wasn't their victim, I felt sorry for not being able to help Slavik. I was safe and sound, hidden under the words I was reciting, but he was still vulnerable, not believing in the things Martha taught us.

I prayed harder, thinking of Slavik and how I wanted him to be safe as well. Before I even finished the prayer, it. At the exact moment I said, "but deliver us from evil," someone in the hall yelled that the supervisor was coming.

The older boys immediately left the room, and I finished the prayer, "Amen." I felt so much joy. I believed my prayer worked and always had faith it would protect me, not just from the older boys at school, but from more threatening monsters as well, like from witches that like to hide in little boys' closets or some of the teachers that weren't as nice to me as Martha.

I always believed in Martha and her kindness, and I was interested to learn about Jesus. So, I often asked her to tell me more. In return, she brought her new testament and shared a couple of stories from it with us. It was always easier to sleep following one of her stories about Jesus than from the scary stories the other teachers like to tell us.

Faith is an exceptional power of the human mind and was an incredible source of strength for me. Whether it was the high values of communism or following in the footsteps of Jesus, I knew what Marth was teaching me would help me through my life to do good deeds for others. Still, having faith in Jesus would also bring me help when I needed it. So, I fostered the belief that he was my helper and silently prayed to him when I wanted to be loved or appreciated, especially when I needed a family.

16

Too Bloody Curious

I remember pulling down bench seats like these in our cafeteria growing up.
It is where I spent much of my time talking with friends and avoiding chunks of fat.

THOUGH MARTHA'S STORIES BROUGHT ME MORE PEACE and joy than anything I had known in my short life; I was quick to learn that there were times Jesus could not protect me, especially when I needed some protection from myself.

As the snow came that year, covering my misfortunes and my treasures under the white gown of winter, the joyful screams of children cut through the orphanage. Everyone ran for the doors the moment the opportunity presented itself, as we escaped our redundant days. We made makeshift sleds to take advantage of even the smallest of hills, and when the snow was deep enough, we split into two groups. Then, we would set out in opposite directions to make our bunkers. The first to finish their masterpiece would call themselves winners and gain an immediate advantage in the game, sending a flurry of snowballs announcing to the other team who had won the first contest.

The cold cut through the gloves we wore, freezing our fingers while the fresh but biting wind slapped our faces. Mother nature was a constant reminder to honor our instructor's commands to pull our woolen scarves over our mouths. It tried to remind us to avoid catching a cold, but our dedication never lasted. Our fingers became numb, and our scarves fell away, as did any thoughts of our suffering. Nothing felt as good as burying the other team under an onslaught of tiny white cannonballs and forcing them to retreat. So, we would have spent hours trying to conquer and ruin our opponents' bunker.

Still, there was an inevitable end to every battle. The prize? Pride, an opportunity to claim a small victory in a world where we often felt like we might be losing at life. For others, the game ended with sneezing, coughing, and feeling nailed to a bed for a couple of days. Being sick for me meant being condemned to listen to the occasional snowball hitting a window or the cheerful screams of other winners.

The cure used for banishing any cold was one cup of hot tea combined with one spoon of strawberry jam and one of honey, served to us still steaming. When I was the unfortunate soul stuck in bed, I knew I could still enjoy the sweet and tasty treat. With sweat dripping from my forehead, I savored the medicine, knowing just a few cups would make everything right again so I could return to the game. As good as the elixir was, nothing was quite as good as a snowball fight.

Between the snow and the holidays, we all looked forward to the joys winter brought. Winter was like every fairy tale I ever read coming true. Dreams became a reality, intoxicating my senses with warmth and celebration. We spent the last week of December preparing for my favorite day of the year, December thirty-first. We escorted it in with great pomp and serious commitment. Santa Clause—the one we called Did Moroz or 'frozen old man'— was a merry grandpa with a silver beard who would visit us on the last day of the year to celebrate a new beginning.

We followed the New Year's Eve celebration with an entire month of holiday cheer. We all trusted January first to bring more joy and prosperity through the coming year. So everyone shared their gifts with friends all around, visiting neighbors with candy and other treats. Of course, the best part of January for me was that children were off school during the entire month. So I rejoiced in not visiting classrooms. It meant less time trying to keep my fingers warm while writing assignments the teachers were giving us and more time for snowball fights or eating the treats brought to us by generous donors.

On January sixth and seventh, we celebrated Christmas Eve and then Christmas. Though our celebrations were modest compared to most, we celebrated the glory and monumentality of the New Year's spirit. We accepted humble festivities, improving the atmosphere with modestly made costumes and each taking our turn to perform holiday songs or recited verses to receive a gift from Santa. I liked to memorize poems before the event to get my present from Did Moroz. They were easy to remember and always impressed the jolly old man.

Bearers of goodwill from Germany and other nearby countries donated the gifts we received, along with candy and delicious food to savor. I was so enamored with the generosity of the donors, I often convinced myself that somebody would remember us on other days, as well, but somehow, those gifts weren't finding their way to our orphanage.

Fortunately for us, the candy we received at Christmas came in large portions, with various shapes, colors, and tastes, many of which I tasted for the first time. I preferred gummy bears when I got candy, always eating the red and yellow ones first. Then, continuing to green and orange. Sometimes I saved the gummies and ate the exceptionally made Ukrainian dark chocolate first, even though it inevitably made me hungry for more. Lucky for me, I didn't need to share my treats with anyone during that time because I knew they were also getting sweets. So, I had the fun game of exchanging the ones I didn't like in search of the candy bags I enjoyed the most. These little rituals allowed us to feel the carefree spirit of the celebrations and festiveness, even if it only landed on our doorstep but one day a year.

I loved thinking about the candy and the presents we received, but they were never enough to capture my full attention. I always wanted something more to do. I remember one holiday when I was bored from all of those empty hours without classes. I couldn't stop thinking of the mechanism that made our Christmas tree rotate. The tree sat in the center of the room, where we held our New Year celebration. It sparkled, the lights twinkling as it turned, begging me to come and see what it had to offer. Since the tree was a significant amount taller than I was, the entire phenomenon likely appeared more interesting than it was.

I was fascinated by machinery, so I decided to take my chances and discover how it worked. I snuck to the tree when I noticed no one else was near it. Checking over my shoulder one last time, I decided to explore. I knew there was no way I would see what was happening at the top of the tree, but the space that separated the tree bark from the ground was wide enough for me to fit underneath.

After one last look, I slid under the branches. The tree's trunk slowly spun, its base sticking out of an engine planted to the floor. I could see how the engine rotated, causing the tree to turn and catch the light from the ceiling. I poked at the mechanism, searching for the magic that kept it alive and running.

Unaware of the power of rotating force, I drove my finger into one of the holes at the base of the mechanism. That is when I discovered that dozens of differently sized gears and pinions interlaced to instigate the machinery rolling and spinning. My finger joined the tangle of equipment, firing sharp pain from the tip through my entire arm. My head reeled, and my stomach turned at the sight of fresh blood gushing from the hole, causing a pool of red to spread across the floor. Forgetting where I was and even the thing that caused it all, a scream escaped my lungs, causing everyone to drop what they were doing to rush towards me.

Tamara Vasylivna arrived first, grabbing me to guide me to the isolator, "Vitaly, what did you do? Why did you put your fingers where you are not supposed to? Who told you to go under the Christmas Tree?"

New pain burst from where the teacher's fingers cut into the muscle of my arm. I was running to keep up with her brisk stride as she dragged me down the hall, speaking words that carried a whole new kind of pain, "You know you won't get to spend time now with other kids at the movies this week. You must stay in the medical room until your wound heals!"

I looked at her with tears in my eyes, wishing I could say I made a mistake, but I felt that it wouldn't matter to her as it seldom did. She wasn't kind like Martha, often looking for ways to cause us trouble. I trembled inside for the fear they would ground me and that I might miss our weekend adventure.

Scream or no scream, anyone in the school could have easily found me in the clinic room by following the bloodstained trail I left lingering in the hall. Still, after a few more stings of alcohol mixing with red liquid and torn skin and tissue, the teacher left, and I was left to wait for the pain to go with her.

I didn't care about the discomfort. This incident wasn't the first or even the last time I did something where I ended up screaming in pain and grounded. I was often left with a tightly-wrapped bandage, hiding the excruciating pain of what a few gears could do. But, even though it often brought me pain, I couldn't resist experimenting with the mechanisms I found. They fascinated me. I loved revealing their core, their function. So, it was no wonder you could often hear my screams bouncing off the walls of the orphanage, but it wasn't always like that.

Moments of excitement existed in sharp contrast to the other side of my nature. I also enjoyed knitting and sewing, carefully adopting everything my teachers taught me. Still, beyond the mayhem, maybe the two sides weren't so different after all. I liked to know how things worked, and I wanted to create new things from the scraps I found. It seemed to be the way I approached my life. Every time I felt overwhelmed, overcome by the inner stirrings of my mind, it was hard to resist. I would do something I wasn't supposed to do, intentionally forgetting everything about being beaten and grounded.

Still, luck was with me that day. The spirit of celebration saved me from being punished. I played games and ate candy until both the day and the games were exhausted. Then, because I was too listless to play football or chase around with Masha and Slavik, I sat at the window watching the sky transform, spilling a spectrum of colors onto the peaceful clouds that danced over the children playing outside.

Then it happened again, I was bored watching others have fun, so I decided to look around the orphanage to find something to entertain me until dinner. I could feel the restless vibration boiling in my stomach again. I could only hope it would not end in pain or punishment this time.

I wandered the hallway, burying my hands deep into my pockets, and that's when my discovery happened. My fingers touched on a pair of wires I had found in the backyard just lying around with no potential of ever being used. I took the wires out of my pocket, holding both pieces in front of me as I walked. Then, I headed to the playroom, carefully observing those tiny strings, wondering how I could use them.

Dozens of buzzing voices began filling up hallways as the children came in to prepare for dinner. I entered the dorm, still alone, still observing the wires with great attention when I spotted a power plug next to the TV. My interest peaked for the first time since getting hurt. A new experiment was underfoot.

I linked one end of the wires and kneeled in front of the outlet with only one question in mind, "What will happen?" I wondered.

I put one end of the wire in each hole, creating a power string. After a single pop of electrical contact, I heard a couple of screams that slowly transformed into giggles. I had managed to shut off the power in most of the building, leaving only one part of the orphanage lit and visible to anyone passing on Fastivska Street. I didn't want to admit my misadventure, knowing that I could potentially be punished or even beaten by a teacher. Instead, I ran out of our playroom and into the hall, trying to calm my beating heart.

It wasn't long before they restored the lights, and Tamara Vasylivna was back to dragging me past the confused faces of my friends. Some of them were still giggling, linking the image of someone hauling my body through the hall to the sudden power outage. Even though I knew I was on my way towards my next punishment, all I could think was, "That was amazing!!!"

While everyone else was having dinner, my dramatic screams broke through the building again.

17

My Dear Mommy

My mother when she was 29, almost ten years before I was born. She was beautiful and very smart. But chose to live a different and difficult life.

O NE DAY, AFTER THE FESTIVE BUZZ OF THE HOLIDAY, HAD WORN OFF, our instructor wanted us to practice our writing skills. The teacher had arranged the classroom with a few dozen chairs and some outdated desks donated to the orphanage by those who no longer wanted them.

The sun danced off Vasylyna Tanasivna's golden curls as she approached her desk, saying, "Hello, everyone!" Her smile glistened almost as much as her hair. She was one of the few instructors who made sure she provided everything we needed to live outside of the orphanage one day. I enjoyed what she taught most of the time.

"I thought we could maybe practice our letters and check how good you have become at writing." She looked at us, silent for a moment before continuing, "You are going to write a letter to someone you care for...."

"A letter to a friend?" someone from the back asked.

"No," she grinned. "You are all going to write a letter to your mom."

Everyone was quiet. I felt frozen and hot all at the same time. My palms began to sweat as I imagined most of my peers were probably feeling the same way. I didn't know what I would say.

Winters were always fun at first, but as the season progressed, it was often too cold to go snowballing, which narrowed our amusement options to watching television, storytelling, and making up games. When I didn't have adventures to distract me, I often thought about my mother. I wondered if she was okay or where she spent the holidays. My time was full of too many hours for questions, but I had no answers.

Vasylyna probably knew it was difficult for us to think of the parents who abandoned us, but she continued with the lesson. "Now, please, take your pens and papers." She drifted across the floor, slowly pacing the front of the room. She kept her hands locked in front of her the entire time, her fingers tangled in a mild grasp.

"When writing a letter to someone you care for," she said, "you will always start with 'Dear' or 'Beloved.' At the end of the letter, you will put 'Sincerely' or 'With love' followed by your name. All right, children?"

We all nodded.

Trembling, I stared at my piece of paper, not knowing how to start. I sat, wondering how I should address my mother. What name should I give her, or was I even allowed to call her "Mom?" Finally, after minutes of torture that felt like hours, I let the pen touch the paper. I felt far away from the classroom, like a puppet master slowly moving the hand of his puppet, causing it to form letters that turned into words and, eventually, sentences.

Dear Mommy,

Today, I played my favorite game with my friends. It's called hide-and-seek, and it was really fun! I found Igor hiding in a wardrobe in one of our dressing rooms, where I hid once too. There were a lot of birds flying over the rooftops when we played, and one of the birds pooped on my best friend's head. It was so funny we both laughed! My best friend's name is Slavik, and he is great.

Slavik's mom came to visit him, and she brought him some sweets that he later shared with me. I thought you might want to know that I drew a picture of you and the sun. I think you are very pretty.

My teacher Martha started teaching me German letters because I like listening to the language and want to understand what the soldiers are saying when I watch our people fight fascists in the movies. It is very nice here. I have lots of friends and good teachers. We learn everything about everything, and it's fun, but I would really like you to come and visit me sometime. My teacher also told me that I have a brother, so you could maybe bring him along. I would also like to meet my brother.

I found out today that a family in Italy adopted my friend Sasha Bykov. We used to build electric toys together out of parts we found in the backyard of our orphanage, so I was sad he left but also envious because he has got a new family to care for him.

When will you come to visit me, mommy? I will be waiting for you. Tell my brother that he can come to see me too if he likes.

Love,

Vitaly

I didn't sleep that night as all I could do was think about the letter. So I sat under my blanket with a hand-made battery light instead. I spent most of the time cross-stitching, so I could be sure that my cross-stitch table cloth was ready for the upcoming talent exhibition at our school. Working on it was calming. I liked preparing for competitions. The little victories always made me feel better, and the cross-stitching helped me relax and express my creativity.

Because I spent many hours needing to relax, I was proficient at crafts, carefully concentrating on the details the instructors liked to see. My table cloth would later win first place at the event. I would be proud of myself, but sad too. Because even after hours of work, my winning entry would not return to me. I would not see my tablecloth again, but I didn't know it that night. All I knew was that I was grateful to have the cross-stitch instead of thinking about my letter.

When I finally laid down to sleep, I was so disheartened, diving into a dreamless night, not even imagining that tomorrow wouldn't be the same as every other day at the orphanage.

I did what I could to find distraction and soon realized I probably had the best one right in front of me. I enjoyed learning, and I listened to our teachers with rapt attention. It was my only way to escape, so I pushed myself to be better. I ensured that I sat in the first row in each class, right in front of the teacher. So, when I raised my hand, she would call on me to share with the class what I knew. My schoolwork was the only place where I could stand out and get everyone's attention, not with cuts and bruises and my teacher's punishments, but with my knowledge and good grades instead. To the teachers at the school, we were a sea of never-ending faces, the abandoned children they needed to help live in the world. I loved it when one of them noticed me. I wanted to be the center of attention, standing and having everyone see me.

A few of the children living in the orphanage were getting frequent visits from their parents. They were confused by the circumstances, but at least they got to see them, to talk to them. We were all clawing for bits of affection and savoring even just a couple of hours of undivided attention like it was gold. Anything was better than nothing.

I could tell because I was one of the unfortunate children who didn't get a single visit from my mother. The letter I wrote for her seemed more like some fairytale our teachers told, with no chances of coming true. If reviving that fairy tale required only my will and desire, it would have come to life a long time ago, but my hope wasn't enough. It required my mother's will and desire too, and she didn't seem to have any. So, I let it go.

I woke every day to the repetitive habits of another routine. I don't know how many days we followed the same pattern. One day flowed into another, each just like the last until I began to move with no memory of yesterday or hope for change tomorrow. We got out of our beds, went to the bathroom, and dressed for the day. After a short break, we all went to breakfast and attended our classes. We learned basic subjects like writing, reading, math, history, and art.

After finishing our lessons, before we were to do our homework, we headed to freshen up and prepare for lunch. Again, the smell of borscht joined the children exiting classrooms, filling the hallway with the echoes of yesterday, where we all knew the sounds of spoons and forks clinging would soon follow.

My days were long and exhausting, so I was always ready to dig into my plate. Most days, I did, but there was one day I will never forget, a day Martha interrupted me. I watched her slowly moving towards my table, and I remember thinking that she would show her teeth at me because of the fat chunks still floating on my plate, but the mild expression on her face didn't fit the story in my mind.

I froze, unsure of what to do, stung by the unexpected concern in her eyes,

After taking a deep breath, she said, "Vitaly, dear. Can you please come outside for a moment?" She never called me "dear," so, at that moment, I knew that this day was not going to be like any other day. Something had happened or was about to happen, something I hadn't experienced before.

While I was still trying to understand what was going on, Martha led me out of the dining hall. My friends were staring at us, glancing over their shoulders, trying to see what might happen next. Then, abandoning their plates, they whispered and exchanged their guesses about what I had done or what Martha was about to do.

I followed Martha, finally escaping their curious whispers. As we walked through the hallway, I wanted to ask my teacher why she called me to leave the dining room, but the worried look on her face confused me, leaving my tongue paralyzed and my mind empty.

"Vitaly..." she said as she stopped and dropped to her knee. Then, grasping my shoulders, she looked at me with a level of compassion I've still not seen equaled to this day, "I'm bringing you to the office because your mother has come. She is here, Vitaly. Your mom is here to see you."

Everything seemed distant but clear at the same time as years of hope and pain stuck in my throat. A flurry of feelings flooded my body, making my chest tighten and my stomach churn, but my face remained cold and expressionless. As I tried to untangle the knot in my gut, I remember thinking, 'Why does Martha seem so sad?'

"Vitaly, are you all right?" Martha asked, unnecessarily consoling me with that fearful look in her eyes.

"My mother is here?" was the only thing I could say. Blinded by disbelief and surprise, I still couldn't understand how this day turned out to be so different from any other day I spent on Fastivska Street. Without a single warning, everything in my life had just changed.

"Yes. She is right at the end of the hallway. So you do wish to see her, right?"

I looked into Martha's eyes. I didn't nod or use any words. I didn't need to say anything for her to see what I wanted. So, she took another deep breath, and what I think might have been a sigh. Then, she rose, and we continued walking, side by side, down the hall.

I remember the sound of our steps falling synchronously on the polished hallway floor, and then I saw her. My mother stood with her back to us near the school's front doors. The only way I knew about my mother was her golden hair. It was one of the first things they told me about her.

She looked ready to leave, and I wondered if she might have been gone had we taken an extra minute or two in the hall. Everything in me tightened at the thought. As we approached where she stood, I couldn't think or breathe. I wanted to be perfect. I wanted her to like me. I wanted her to hug me and love me.

She didn't turn as we approached, but I noticed she held a small bag of something I hoped was for me. I thought maybe she brought something tasty or sweet, as the other parents who came to visit their children did. I stood silent for a second, only a few inches away from her, collecting my breath to speak up. My mouth felt so dry. I had spent my whole life thinking of what she would do when she saw me for the first time. That's when I would know. That's when she would finally see the boy she left here to grow up in an orphanage.

"Mom?" I asked as if I couldn't believe that she was standing right in front of me. I experienced her presence through a fog of disbelief.

Having her was too perfect to be true. In my memory, she stood perfectly framed in the soft lighting they sometimes use for taking portraits. I saw her as if she was a vision, the one that tricks you into believing in miracles.

I think I still see her as some angel descended from heaven. I'll probably never see her for who she truly was that day. She lived on the pedestal I made for her. I lived hungry for affection, wanting to feel at least for a second how it was to be unconditionally loved.

We didn't spend much time together. I don't remember our words or if I ever did receive any of the things I wanted from her. Of course, as circumstances were at that time, what little she gave me was going to be enough, even if it wasn't. Even if the only thing I did get from her was a few seconds of affection in a timeless eternity of waiting for something more, that was the world to me.

Still, more than anything my mother did that day, what I remembered most was Martha and how she reminded my mother of what mothers should do. They were only a few feet away from me as I stood waiting for Martha to take me back to food I didn't want to eat. I don't know if they knew I was listening, but Martha's raised whisper was more than loud enough for me to hear. "I think it is disgraceful how you waited for your little boy to send you a letter before you came to visit him. It's been eight years! Eight years! He is an exceptional young man, and he deserves to be visited at least once a week."

Martha left my mother speechless. She didn't have anything to say in response. So she walked away, leaving me with a kiss on the cheek. My heart broke, wishing it could be more.

My mother never returned to the orphanage. I know now that Martha was right for doing what she did, but I was angry for a long time. My face burned at the thought of what she said to my mother. I was afraid my mother wouldn't return after the terrible things Martha said. What if she took away my chance to show my mother how good of a son I could be? If my mother could see how special I was, I knew she would want me.

Because of Martha, I was afraid I would never have that chance.

18

Surprise Visit

This is the same trolleybus we took from the orphanage to the movies after Subotnik.

A FEW MONTHS AFTER SEEING MY MOTHER, Martha interrupted one of my meals again. However, this time she had a more satisfied expression on her face, and I hoped that meant she hadn't ruined things between my mother and me after all. She seemed far more cheerful this time as she said, "Vitaly, there is someone outside who wants to meet you."

Her words burst the bubble of expectation floating above my head. I thought my mom came back, the way Slavik's mother always came back to visit him with ice cream and sweets. However, when she used the words "meet you," I knew it couldn't be my mother. My hope tried to argue, but eventually, logic won the battle. Someone I hadn't met before was here to visit me.

Though it seemed my mother might never return to the orphanage again, at least someone else thought I was worth visiting. I was disappointed, but I was also excited to see who it might be.

A young man stood facing us as we exited the front doors of the orphanage to a warm and sunny afternoon. He stood alone in the yard, tall and robust, like the kind of man I wanted to be one day. As he smiled a broad smile, I could only stare, walking as slow as possible. He seemed familiar to me, like someone I should know, but I didn't. He sure acted as if he knew me, but I didn't know how.

He was too young to be my father, and even if I had one, no one knew him. Our educators told us as much as they knew about our families. My mother was the only parent on record. So, I never really expected to see the man who created me, but he wasn't the only man who might be in my life. My heart swelled at the thought. I knew I had a brother named Roustam. I could only hope this man might be him.

The closer I got to him, the more he smiled until he finally decided he couldn't wait. He approached us to intercept me, obviously excited to see me. "Hey, big guy!" he said as he kneeled, tangling my hair. "Look at you! I didn't know that you had grown to be such a strong young man."

I could hear the thrill in his voice, and it made me smile. I felt safe and protected by him. Unlike my mother, his presence felt permanent.

It was a place where I could finally stop worrying, hoping, and praying someone might eventually come. It was as if every tone he uttered was the call of my blood.

I observed him for some time before I found the courage to say anything, "Hello!" I finally responded. "My name is Vitaly. Are you my big brother?" I held my breath waiting for his answer.

"Yes, little guy," he smiled. "I am your big bro, and I know your name. But, I got to tell you..." he leaned as though we were about to share a secret, "...I like your name very much. It's awesome, just like you!" He ruffled my hair again, making me giggle. "In case you didn't know, little brother, my name is Roustam."

My brother stood up, and at that point, I realized that he was there to show me who I could be when I became a man, even though I didn't know anything about him. Before I met him, I just knew him as someone who existed. That was all I could say about my big brother. But now, seeing him so confident and happy to see me, it was every dream I had come true. Finally, I had a family, someone to love me.

"Madam," he looked at Martha, "thank you for allowing me to spend some time with my brother. I really appreciate it. I want to ask you if Vitaly and I could maybe go for a walk and to the movies after."

I could barely contain my excitement when I heard his question, praying silently that my teacher would give her approval. I loved the movies more than anything and now, to go with my brother by my side was everything. It would be my turn to be like the people I always watched, not marching in rows of abandoned souls, but walking with my brother, someone I could have that was just mine.

Martha smiled, looking at my brother, then back at me, nodding her head. Her nod was the key to my brief freedom, an entrance to a divine new world, a world where I had a family.

As we began our walk down Fastivska Street, I couldn't help myself from jumping. Each leap set free a pleasant tickling in my chest. I guess it was the feeling of being accepted, of belonging somewhere. Anywhere. I almost exploded from it.

"So, what do you do for fun, little brother?"

"Well, I like making things, and I also enjoy going to the movies each Sunday. Today will be the first time I am going to the theater, and it is not Sunday."

He chuckled at my excitement. "Well, I think we ought to change that! Any day is a good day for a movie."

"Do you know I make my own toys, big brother?" Calling him brother scared me a little like he might turn to dust and float away because I said the word out loud. Still, I had to take the chance. I saw my brother was invested in my every word, and I wanted him to know about all the cool things I did so that he would like me.

"Really?" he asked, honestly surprised. "Well, to tell the truth, Vitaly, I knew you were a smart boy the moment I saw you. You will turn out fine once you grow up to be like me. I know that."

I was so happy I ran out of words. He said I could be like him. All of my dreams were coming true.

We stood at the trolleybus station for a few minutes, waiting for one to arrive. I was impatient, eager to ride the trolley with my brother for the first time. It was like a rite of passage for me, a way for us to begin our life together as brothers.

Finally, just as I felt I couldn't wait one more minute, a trolleybus stopped in front of us, squeaking as it was slowing down.

As we entered the trolleybus, we saw it was half empty, so we sat down. "Always make sure that you give your seat to an elder or a mother with a child if you have a seat and there isn't one available for them, little brother."

I nodded eagerly and then sat looking through the window, observing buildings and people as they blurred together, appearing and disappearing in time with the rhythmic pattern of the trolley's wheels.

When I found my words again, I turned to Roustam, trying to catch his eyes, "Do you go to school?" I asked, "What do you want to do when you finish school? What do you do for fun?" I couldn't stop the questions once I began. I was anxious to learn everything I could about him, still worried that this might be the only chance I would get to see my brother.

Roustam started laughing. "Easy little bro...One question at the time. We will get to know each other." I smiled, relaxing a little as he continued, "I'm going to school to be an architect, but I think I'll join the army. I want to be a soldier after I finish school.

"What do you want to be when you grow up, Vitaly?"

"I want to become a soldier, too," I replied, not because I thought he would expect that answer, but because I wanted to be like him. Everything he wanted to do, I would do too.

After we finished a movie I was too excited to remember, I continued my onslaught of essential facts I wanted him to know about me. First, I tried to explain life at the orphanage, but it wasn't easy. All I ever wanted was to live with my family. I didn't know the words to tell him what it was like to live without one.

Roustam looked at me seriously before responding. "Little brother, you are lucky to be living there, trust me."

I could tell there was more he wasn't saying, but I didn't ask what it was. I didn't understand his words, and I don't think I wanted to. Of course, looking back now, I know what he meant.

He could see I wasn't ready to hear what he had to say. So, he dropped the thought, mussing my hair again. "You will grow to be a great guy," he said, smiling at me.

I smiled back. All I wanted to do was be happy with my brother for as long as possible. He took me to show me the tiny two-bedroom apartment he shared with our mom. He said he lived somewhere else most of the time, but he came to stay there on the weekends. He showed me his boxing gloves and a few of the moves he used to beat his opponents. I felt empowered because I had someone to rely on when other boys asked for trouble.

The day I spent with him was the best day of my life, but it couldn't last forever. After a few hours together, being real brothers, we returned to the orphanage, and I had to watch him leave again, not knowing for sure if he would return. But he could see my worry, and I think he wanted our day to end happily. So, before he left, he took me aside and filled my hands with chocolates and candies.

I looked at him, joy bursting from me in a massive grin.

He laughed again. "Knock yourself out, little brother! I will be back soon," and with a final tussle of my hair, he was gone, leaving me with the memory of his smile and a warm brotherly hug.

I couldn't wait to tell Slavik all about my brother. I ran through the hallway, trying to find him so I could share my sweets, as he always did after his mother's visit. I don't know if I've ever had a happier moment in my life. I felt I could be up every day and night just waiting for Roustam to return.

Somewhere inside, I knew my mother wouldn't be back. A small part of me was hopeful, but it didn't have much strength behind it. On the other hand, I felt different inside about Roustam. I believed in him, but I had to be careful. From a very young age, I had learned to lower my expectations of others. So, I wouldn't end up hurt and disappointed if things didn't go as I hoped. I couldn't let it ruin me if he didn't come back.

Luckily, that wasn't the case. I believed Roustam would return, and he did. For one of the first times in my life, my hopes and expectations didn't go unrealized. Only two weeks after his first visit, Martha came to me with a smile, and I knew that Roustam had returned. I was playing outside when he arrived, searching for more parts to go with the secret I had buried. I thought of making an electric car once I found all the parts I needed to build it, but I discarded the thought the moment I knew he was there.

We walked around the orphanage for a while, having a good chat. I showed him all of my favorite places to go, and then, once we were alone, far from the other children, he stopped and pulled a large piece of the watermelon out of a grocery sack he was carrying. I couldn't remember the last time I had watermelon, but I never forgot its sweet and refreshing taste.

While he left to wash it, I couldn't help myself from taking a peek at the other treasures that might be hiding the sack he left behind. I found a jar of jam, toothpaste, and a few apples, so I knew he was planning to stay with me for more than just an hour. He wanted to spend time with me. My heart raced at the thought, but I also felt tremendous peace settling in my belly, leading me to a blissful place. For the first time in my life, I realized that I was not alone in this world. I had a big brother.

Roustam returned wearing an honest smile that made me smile as well. At that moment, I knew what it meant to be truly happy. Dropping his jacket to be used as a picnic blanket, Roustam sat with me on the worn grass near the tree where Igor and I once buried ourselves. Then, in one of the most memorable moments of my life, he pulled an army knife out of his pocket and pierced the sweet meat of our watermelon.

I dove into the massive piece Roustam handed me, which was about twice the size of the piece he kept. I savored the familiar sensation of pure bliss sliding down my throat. It almost made me forget about every horrible thing I tasted until that moment, even the haunting pieces of pork fat I choked down every day at dinner.

"You have a really cool knife... " I mumbled between squishy bites.

"You like it?"

I nodded.

"You can have one too in a couple of years."

I smiled in response. I was so happy. I couldn't think of a thing to say.

"Is anyone bothering you at school or the orphanage...?" Roustam asked, mildly surprised by my interest in the knife.

"Well....." I was deciding whether I should tell or just skip the question. I didn't want him to think I was weak, but I decided to take advantage of having an older brother to protect me. So I told him, "there are some older boys who are picking on me and my best friend, Slavik."

"Well, you tell them that your brother will come to talk to them if they don't let you alone. And I surely will. I will always have your back, little brother."

I smiled. I always dreamed of what it would be like to have a brother like Roustam, and now it was even better than I could have imagined.

Roustam visited me often, always finding a way to bring me something sweet and make my day. I appreciated it. I knew he didn't have much money. He told me about the struggles he had living with our mother. Although he only saw her during the weekends, sometimes it was too unbearable. So, he would skip his visit and stay at the boarding school where he lived instead. He was trying to teach me what kind of person our mother was without killing my childish innocence, but I guessed he was probably hiding the worst of it.

I sometimes wanted to hold the image of my mother I had built in my mind, but it was becoming increasingly difficult. I learned from Roustam that living with the woman who gave us life was no fairy tale at all. While I was still hoping she would return, Roustam showed me she probably never would. Our mother left me here to be alone, to face the loneliness of sunsets and the silence of sleepless nights.

In the end, I heeded my brother's advice and tried to make the best of living at the orphanage. At least I had a brother to come and tangle my hair, someone I knew I could always trust to have my back.

19

A New Family

This is our first summer camp. I am in the front with my two sisters, Masha, Nadya, and the rest of the girls. My brothers Serhij and Slavik are at the back.

A S I GREW OLDER, ROUSTAM'S VISITS LESSENED. He still came by every couple of months, giving me glimpses of how it felt to have a family of my own. Still, it didn't fill me. My desire to have a real family sat like the pain of hunger in my belly. It was always present behind the laughter and tears of childhood. I wanted a mother's lap when I felt like crying and a father to give me sage advice.

On Thursday, May 9, 1991, it happened. The day was set aside as a national holiday to commemorate the heroes who gave their lives fighting for peace during the Second World War. Every year, there was a massive celebration with thousands of people flooding the streets of Chernivtsi. The town gave tribute to lost grandfathers, fathers, brothers, and lovers. Our class celebrated with the rest, but we did so within the walls of our orphanage.

We arrived at our classroom that day to see an honored Veteran standing against the front wall. His posture was proud and strong, but I thought I could see remembrance and maybe some regret shining beneath his short eyelashes. As he began to give tribute to his lost comrades, he straightened up his body and tapped on the classroom floor with his shiny black boots. He was a statement of unshakeable pride. It was as if his division commander was right there beside him. I could see all the years of pain and suffering on his face, but he lasted. He survived. He was there, regardless of what he had to do, of what he saw, of what he knew.

"No matter how many years have passed, we will always celebrate our victory over enemy forces, even as we forget our differences, but remember those who have fallen fighting for peace and life." He sighed but still held his head high as he reached for the memories he would share with us that day.

"Millions of Soviet people, tens of thousands of residents of the Chernivtsi region, laid down their lives on the battlefields. We worked in victory's name to live peacefully, so all can work and raise children and grandchildren today. We spared no effort, and now we live without fear that our life might end the next day. This festival is how we honor the heroism of those who fought on the front lines, forging this victory for our country. It is how we express gratitude to those whose courage and heroism will always serve as an example of loyalty and devotion to their grateful homeland. All Veterans, war Veterans, and home front workers are our heroes. They bore brutal wars and won the most difficult but majestic of victories. This holiday will remain forever in the history of our country, celebrated so we will never forget them."

He finished his speech, and I felt like each little head in the classroom understood what true patriotism meant. We listened to the Veteran speak, and then the teachers gathered us to stand in front of a large audience and sing "Den' Pobedy"—a Victory Day song—to commemorate the celebration. The anthem was well known in the USSR and has always been part of the festival.

I loved to sing. So my teachers allowed me to sing a solo while the other kids stood with me as background singers. I showed my talent at a very young age. Unfortunately, besides singing carols to make money during the Christmas season, I never had an opportunity to develop my singing talent, so it fell by the wayside with many of my other childhood dreams.

I will never forget this Victory Day Celebration, not only because of Commemoration Day but because, like our little town of Chernivtsi once did, I also had a whole new opportunity in front of me.

After the celebrations were complete, a teacher pulled me to the side, saying, "Vitaly, today you will be meeting some potential foster parents. I want you to prepare a few items before going to bed tonight. You'll be going with them right after breakfast to spend the weekend, and please, Vitaly, while you are visiting, try to be on your best behavior."

I couldn't believe it. It wasn't even bedtime yet, but I rushed to my room, making sure I set myself to make the best impression possible. I had watched so many children visit foster homes and later be adopted permanently. This visit was my chance to have a real family.

The family we were meeting had already taken three of my friends from the orphanage: Masha, Serhij, and Nadya, and although I didn't know them that well, I learned Slavik was also coming to our new home. I was so grateful. Slavik was one of my best friends, and he knew Masha, Serhij, and Nadya very well.

"Do you think we would be better at the foster home, or would it be better if we decided to stay here?" I asked Slavik.

He looked around our dorm room, secretly examining everyone to see if they were listening. Then, he turned back to me, "Well, I think it wouldn't hurt to try, would it?"

He was more casual than I was, even though I tried my best to stay calm. I wanted to believe what Slavik believed, but I thought things might be more comfortable for him since he knew the other children very well. Slavik was my botsya. He was my best friend, but I wasn't sure what it would be like sharing my new opportunity with people I didn't know very well.

"What is Serhij like?" I asked as we left to gather our meager belongings. "I mean, I know him a little, but not as good as you do." Even with my stomach full of porridge, it felt empty, like I hadn't eaten in weeks.

"Well, he is cool," Slavik responded casually, "He is a good friend. So you don't need to worry, Vitaly."

"And Masha and Nadya?" I was still nervous.

"Well, you know Masha a little, and I don't know what you think of her, but I will tell you that she is also a great friend, as well as Nadya. Believe me, Nadya's like one of the guys. She loves to hang out with boys and do boy things. So we couldn't end up with better even if we asked!"

Slavik was in a good mood, so I tried to pick up some of his positivity and get ready for the adventure. Still, no matter how hard I tried not to be nervous, anxiety took its toll. When the teacher told us about our foster parents, she said they had already taken two other children from our orphanage, but they didn't keep them as those kids were still young and peeing on the sheets.

They gave them back, and we're coming to find other children they could take home. I didn't like that Slavik and I won our fortune on someone else's misfortune. It was like we were merchandise with a return policy, and I worried about Slavik. Slavik sometimes wet the bed in his sleep, and I didn't want our foster parents to decide they didn't want to keep him.

The teacher warned us to be careful, but I couldn't stop thinking about the kids who came back to the orphanage only because they were soiling themselves. Still, I couldn't say, "No." I was finally getting my chance to have a family. I wanted to see what it felt like to have a home with parents and even siblings. I wanted to experience a dining room that was warm with family, not overcrowded and noisy. I wanted to see if another mother was waiting for me out there. I didn't want to ruin it.

I climbed into bed that night, reliving some of my past adventures and the trouble they might cause. I remembered breaking my wrist, getting my fingers caught in the Christmas Tree gears, and the time I made a bonfire with fallen leaves, dry twigs, and some matches I found in the shed. As the fire grew, I decided to experiment with watching things burn. My favorite was an old hula hoop I found in a storage room at the orphanage. I held the hula-hoop over the flames, and as it started melting, I leaned it over to watch the once hard plastic turn to liquid. Unfortunately, I became so mesmerized by the spectrum of colorful drips I lost track of the flame, and one of the melted drops of plastic fell on my pinky. The pain was as sharp as the smell, and once again, my screams broke through the orphanage.

Laying there in the dark, I could still feel the scar. I had a lot of scars.

The instructors were always scolding me for one thing or another. I lay for hours that night thinking about it, examining the reasons for my experiments, hoping I might be able to leave them and their punishments at the orphanage. I played imaginary scenarios in my head, planning my behavior, and hoping that I wouldn't get myself into trouble.

Masha, Nadya, and Serhij were with our foster family for several months before we joined them. The fact they didn't come back gave me hope that everything would go well. I knew that most families in Chernivtsi had less than six members. So even though my new foster home would have more than seven with Slavik and me, I wasn't worried.

I remembered meeting a family that had accepted many children from the orphanage and had more than twelve souls in the house, of which eleven were children. I heard their life was modest but peaceful, and you could tell that this family had a lot of love to share and give. Even though only some children were their own, they raised the parentless kids as equals. I hoped my new home would be the same. I wanted to be loved and for a parent to care about teaching me to be a good adult.

I went back and forth between my dream of having a family and the comfort and security I felt at the orphanage. I was torn, trying to imagine two possible futures. Even though I always felt sure I wanted a new family, I suddenly didn't know what was best for me. Even with my misadventures, I thought of how the staff cared for us, working to raise healthy and intelligent children. I wondered if it would be the same with a foster family. I hoped they would treat me like their son, but I wasn't sure they wouldn't just reject me like my mother.

It was like every dream I ever had was coming true, and I couldn't trust it. So, I finally returned to the one thing I could count on, Slavik. I couldn't imagine living anywhere without Slavik. He was the only constant in my life besides Martha. So, even though I was a bit nervous, I decided; if Slavik was there, I wanted to be there, and even if they chose to send Slavik back, I could decide to come with him.

Consequently, I decided to dive into the new opportunity and try my luck.

Our new foster mother spoke with the principal as we posed like dolls at the marketplace. She would occasionally glance at us and make another comment to the people around her. I felt exposed like we were being graded and evaluated. I guess we were, but I wasn't sure if we were measuring up just standing there and not having a chance to show her our talents.

Eventually, she headed toward us with a warm smile, reminding me of the woman from my dreams. She seemed kind, and her smile visibly honest but somehow forced.

"You don't need to worry," the principal said as she came to stand before us, "because you have a pair of smart and hard-working boys there. We have raised them as polite and compassionate young men. So, they will listen to you, do their chores, and avoid getting into trouble." I felt his eyes on me with the last sentence. I imagined him hoping that my curiosity was tamed and set to be silent.

He didn't mention anything about Slavik's occasional bed-wetting, so I was at peace, knowing that I wouldn't have to say "Goodbye," to my best friend.

The principal introduced us, guiding us to call our new foster mom "Tyotya Valya" which translated to "aunt Valya," and her husband was "Dyadya or Uncle Grisha." Children in Ukraine called any close family friends their aunt or uncle. I didn't know if they were close to us, but Tyotya Valya and Dyadya Grisha were the first aunt and uncle I ever knew.

As Tyotya Valya approached us, she offered her hand. "Hello, boys! You must be Vitaly," she said, looking at me, the curl of her mouth never wavering until she turned slightly to continue, "and you are Slavik!"

"Good afternoon," we said in unison, looking like a pair of ducklings ready to follow their mother across a busy road.

"You boys are adorable, and I am very pleased to meet you," she said as our teacher approached.

"Well, that's it," our instructor exclaimed. "Boys, you can go with this new family now. You are in safe hands."

I knew we had just the weekends to spend with our foster family, as she tried us out to see if living with us would work, and I was determined to show her it would. I committed to being on my best behavior, so she would want to keep us in her home forever, and I could finally have the family I always wanted in my dreams.

II

Foster Care

Happy families are all alike; every unhappy family is unhappy in its own way.

—Tolstoy "Anna Karenina"

20

Bazaar Food

These are the traditional Ukrainian dishes that we made for celebrations. I wish Tyotya Valya made delicious meals more often.

AFTER SPENDING SEVERAL WEEKENDS with Tyotya Valya and Dyadya Grisha, they decided to foster us full-time. So, Slavik and I gathered our meager belongings and left the orphanage for good. I had prayed to leave that place every day. Still, I didn't feel the excitement I expected to feel. Instead, the pain struck me, making my stomach linger and twitch.

I missed a lot growing up in an orphanage, though I found ways to get the most of every moment. I was curious and inventive, and the orphanage gave me enough freedom to explore my creativity. I could only hope that my new home would allow me the same opportunities to create new things, but I wasn't sure. I was facing an uncertain future.

Our new foster mother said she didn't want us to bring junk to her house, so I left the toys I created behind. Of course, I didn't think the things I made were something to be cast aside. Maybe it was because I knew how that felt or perhaps because I could always find a use for things others didn't want. I believed that everything was valuable to someone. I hoped my toys were something the other children could enjoy.

As we approached Fastivska Street, I turned one last time to look at the only place I had ever called home. The tree where Igor and I built our den looked back at me, reminding me of the time we nestled under it, praying for a day like today. I thought about the melody of rain drumming fallen leaves and the comfort of another body next to mine. I remembered all the dug-up plastic and metal scraps I used to make toys. I eventually made an electric car from the motor I found in the shed. It even had a miniature light bulb attached to it to show the way in the dark. I was so proud of that car. I worked on it for months, but I had to leave it, like everything else I had there.

I imagine I would have given anything to be away from hordes of children and live with a family of my own. Having a family is often taken for granted. Being raised in an orphanage, I learned to appreciate little things. I did my best to show I cared and was grateful for every effort someone made to do something nice for me. Right now, it was foster parents. Even if my new home didn't live up to the dream I had of it, I knew I would do my best to stay with Tyotya Valya and Dyadya Grisha. So, I left with only a couple of worn-out pieces of clothes and a lifetime of memories.

"Vitaly!" I heard Slavik's harsh whisper and turned to see Tyotya Valya crossing the street. She didn't check to see that we were behind her but expected us to follow her wherever she needed to go. I ran to catch up, and we walked together to the trolleybus stop.

"So, boys, the first place we need to visit is the bazaar. We have some things we need to bring back home, so follow my lead and stay close." Valya spoke as though she had known us our entire lives. The words "bazaar" and "home" woke something in me that warmed my heart, but that last sentence is what caught me off guard. Her words reminded me of my brother's visits to the orphanage. I hadn't seen my brother for a while. It seemed that Roustam had forgotten me, but I held a tiny flame of hope burning, waiting for my brother to return. I couldn't stop believing he would.

As our trolleybus arrived, I couldn't help remembering the day I rode with Roustam. I waited for Tyotya Valya to sit first, as I always remembered what he taught me. Luckily, there were enough seats for everyone, so I had a chance to sit with my nose stuck to the window and watch as the bus made its way through the jungle of cars and other buses.

I tried to remember every meter of our trip. I wanted to memorize the many parts of Chernivtsi I hadn't seen, so I noticed every building. I noticed the theater as we passed, another memory that screamed Roustam's name. Everything about this trip reminded me of my brother. My stomach ached every time I thought about him. Here I was, setting off on this new adventure while also facing the reasons why I needed this family to foster me in the first place. Joy and sadness tangled with each other in my heart, and I didn't know if they could live together without destroying one another, but I had to try. I had a new family now, and I hoped maybe they could help me fill the void my brother and my mother had left in me.

Eventually, we arrived at our destination, and it gave me a break from thinking about my brother. I think I recognized my passion for cooking the moment we exited the bus. The stop was only a block from the bazaar, so the pulsing mist of warm spices engulfed me almost instantly.

We joined the crowd while hundreds of tempting scents overwhelmed my senses. It was nearly impossible for me to know which way to look. There were honey buns, spices, green, red, and yellow vegetables, apricots, peaches, oranges, bananas, apples, and watermelons. Every juicy delight imaginable lay neatly arranged and guarded by the sellers, who were all trying to draw attention, tempting us to pick their products.

The bazaar was critical to the people of Chernivtsi, who were surviving on a low budget. It's where all the middle-class families with many children would buy food, dishes, and even clothes and shoes. Everywhere you turned, you could see hundreds of colors, different materials, and endless lines of faces; some of them selling, some of them buying. Most people were cheerful and in the mood for little chats, and I enjoyed listening to the bits and pieces I could catch.

As we traveled the market, observing the goods around us, Tyotya Valya asked us to help her with the many bags we had to carry. Of course, we were happy to help as we filled the bags with fresh meat, fruits, and colorful vegetables. I think we were both looking forward to an authentic meal at a real table and no fat chunks to eat to avoid punishments.

"And now, we need to find one fine piece of watermelon," Tyotya Valya said, walking in front of us, assuming we would follow. We passed by a couple of butcher's shops and tenders with cabbages, potatoes, fresh cucumbers, and tomatoes before stumbling upon a beautifully arranged stand filled with strawberries, cherries, blueberries, and watermelons. The watermelons were brilliant green, but all I could see when I looked at them was the perfectly pink fruit awaiting us inside. I was looking forward to sinking my teeth into it. Tyotya Valya picked one from the bottom of all the stashed watermelons. It was so big she was barely able to carry it.

After we finished gathering food, we each got a new pair of jeans and some shirts, so the worn-out clothes clumsily packed in our bags soon became useless. "You two will be so handsome once you jump into your new clothes!" Tyotya Valya said, trying her best to make us feel comfortable, not knowing that she had already won us over with all the delicious food we would be eating.

My positivity spiraled into anxiety as we neared Tyotya Valya's home. Though I knew Masha, Nadya, and Serhij had already found their home in the lap of dear Tyotya Valya, I feared I might not be accepted or even able to fit in. Tyotya Valya seemed to sense my fear and paused to smile at us. Her smile encouraged me, telling me we were welcome in her family. So, we gladly followed as she turned and entered the building, still carrying the most substantial watermelon I have ever seen.

Tyotya Valya, Dyadya Grisha, and their children lived in one of the old communal apartment buildings. These remnants of the communist party's declaration that all houses were the state's property were more the rule than the exception in Chernivtsi. Some things had changed since the collapse of the Soviet Union, but much remained the same. People just found ways to adapt. We walked gray cement halls banked on either side with doors leading to small apartments. Every door had lists of names carefully written on the wall next to it. Next to each name, there was also a doorbell.

I enjoyed looking at the names. Many of the apartments housed ten or more people. I saw one apartment door with a long list of names written to the side of the door. I later found out it was a single four-bedroom apartment where over twenty people lived. It seems funny now when I look back, but it made sense then. I was used to full bedrooms and busy dinner tables. It seemed life outside the orphanage wasn't that different after all.

We walked through several long halls and climbed what felt like a hundred stairs before Tyotya Valya finally reached for one of the doorknobs and entered our apartment. The entrance was another hallway that seemed like a narrow, never-ending tunnel. As we passed through the hallway, I heard a baby crying in one of the rooms. So, I knew other families were living with Tyotya Valya's family, still sharing the spirit of communism. I glanced at the mother trying to put her baby to sleep as we passed, curiously absorbing every impression I could. I noted every scuff on the floor and counted the olive-green doors that banked the dimly lit hall. We would later paint the doors a beautiful marine blue, but I will never forget that green. It was the first time in my life that I had a real home with a real family.

We continued down the long-dimmed hallway until we came to a room where Tyotya Valya's husband, Dyadya Grisha, was leaning out the window, having a cigarette. Serhij, Masha, and Nadya sat on the floor beside him, watching television. Tyotya Valya stood for a moment, waiting for someone to notice her. When they didn't, she cleared her throat, and they all turned to look at us.

"Oh, hello, boys!" I could tell Dyadya Grisha was happy to have us there, moving from the entrance so we could squeeze in. The room was a lot smaller than the orphanage's living room, but it felt warmer, more personal.

"Shall we all go to the kitchen to dig into that watermelon we brought?" Tyotya Valya asked with cheer in her voice.

"Oh, you brought the watermelon?" Masha was barely able to contain her joy.

"Oh yes," Tyotya Valya responded, "and Vitaly and Slavik had to help me carry it. It's huge. You will see."

Dyadya Grisha was the first to stand up. "If it is that huge, we would probably have some trouble cutting it open," he said, moving toward the kitchen.

"Let's go, kids!" Tyotya Valya invited us to join as she followed him.

As we walked through the hallway, Masha, Nadya, and Serhij were bumping into each other, giggling. They were so happy to see us. I thought they might be missing the orphanage, but that was almost impossible since they had everything they ever needed in this apartment. Tyotya Valya would make sure of it. I could tell she always tried to make everything perfect, exactly as it was supposed to be.

"We knew they were going to keep you two!" Masha whispered to Slavik, making him smile at the compliment. "You'll see it's very nice here."

As we carried the bags of groceries and gigantic watermelon to the kitchen, I was confident it would be.

Even before we made it to the kitchen, I heard a drawer squeak, followed by cutlery rattling as Tyotya Valya looked to find a knife big enough to cut the watermelon.

Everything about that day made me feel like I was finally that child I always wished I could be. Now I had the close relationships I once watched in others randomly passing by. Finally, I was one of those children who could hang on a parent's elbow or grasp at their hands, feeling linked to them for life.

My mind relaxed. Every muscle in my body softened, and I could feel myself getting warmer at the thought. Finally, we were together. I'm sure the moment might appear trivial to some, but for me, it was everything. It was the kind of moment children who grow up in orphanages seldom get to experience.

21

Seconds

*My new family together, eating dinner in the small kitchen of our new apartment.
From the front left: Tyotya Valya, Slavik, Me, Nadya, Serhij, Nastya (Yura's wife), Masha,
Yura with his girl Valya and Sasha, Tyotya Valya's son.*

THERE WERE FOUR BEDROOMS and three kitchens in the apartment. One of the kitchens was enormous, with a high ceiling. The walls were a tapestry of peeling paint and traces of evaporated grease, layers of fat risen from the numberless meals cooked there. Dozens of wires clumsily hung from the walls, draped in a tangled mass that led to the phone in the hallway. Despite my natural urge to experiment with electricity and fire, I didn't want to get sent away. So, I didn't think to stay and investigate what the wires did or what new invention I might create with them.

A few steps from the phone lines, a schedule for cleaning day hung on the wall. It was similar to one we had back at the orphanage. As perfect as my new home seemed, I could see that Subotnik was not behind us. We would all have our obligations to keep the house sparkling clean, but I didn't mind. It was a small price to pay for what we were gaining.

We all followed Tyotya Valya to the kitchen, carrying the giant watermelon. Even though Tyotya Valya's kitchen was the biggest of the three kitchens, it still felt crowded. A massive wooden dining table with more than ten chairs around it occupied most of the space, leaving little room to navigate. Still, we didn't care. All we could see was the familiar green and white striped ball that now consumed the middle of the dining table, just waiting to be cracked and tasted.

Dyadya Grisha sharpened their largest knife while searching for the best place to begin cutting. He dug the blade deep into the giant melon when he found his spot, carefully cutting the slices. We all sat in silence like those gathered for church services, observing and waiting for our turn to taste the sweet treat. Finally, Nadya stood up from the table, helping Tyotya Valya with plates and little blunt knives we used to help us get rid of the tiny black seeds disturbing an otherwise perfectly pink pallet. By the time we passed the plates, Dyadya Grisha had finished cutting, and we all dug into the sweetest fruit I had ever tasted. I savored every bite, thinking of Roustam again, whom I missed immensely, but this time I ate with the hope, I would see him soon and be able to tell him about my new family.

"It's good, right guys?" Tyotya Valya looked around the table, observing our happy faces. She smiled, honestly relaxed.

"May I get another slice, please?" I asked, and I got one, escorted with Dyadya Grisha's smile. Everything was so perfect as our little family enjoyed such a pleasure together.

As soon as everyone saw I got another piece, they quickly asked for the same. "I want one, too," Serhij said with his eyes wide open. Then, Nadya and Masha followed his lead. Only Slavik held back, cautious not to take too much.

Dyadya Grisha smiled at them. He was happy to see everyone excited until his eyes met Tyotya Valya's. He froze when he saw her face, standing back and waiting to hear what kind of reaction was suitable.

I felt an uncomfortable cramp returning to my stomach for the first time that day. Then, with regret and a bit of shame summoned by the sweet taste of watermelon in my mouth, I froze as well. Maybe I shouldn't have asked, but I did, and it was too late to take it back, as my plate bore little more than castaway seeds and a watermelon rind.

Tyotya Valya's posture was as tight as her tone as she responded to Dyadya Grisha's pleading look, "I didn't think it was a good idea when Vitaly asked, as I think you should always spread the joy and save a piece for tomorrow as well." You could tell that Tyotya Valya was unhappy with how things turned out. I wondered if my birth mother would have reacted as she was reacting. I wanted to believe she wouldn't.

Serhij, Masha, and Nadya frowned, fixedly exchanging glances.

I think Dyadya Grisha felt the burden falling on his back, as he was the one that gave me the second slice. He paused for a moment, and then, he smiled, saying, "Let the kids eat."

That is when I realized that he would never let any of us feel neglected or torn apart, but I could see the uneasiness stuck between his teeth, making his jaw twitch when he hastened a glance in Tyotya Valya's direction. She just moved from the table in silence, taking her scorn back to the kitchen island, where she began chopping the vegetables and meat she needed for dinner. She was morbidly silent, so I stopped eating my watermelon, feeling too guilty to enjoy it.

Dyadya Grisha continued cutting, sharing equal pieces to everyone around the table, "Eat, don't let it wait," he smiled at me, determined to set things right. That's who he was; a man made to be a father, a man to make you smile and laugh. He was always joking with us, which made me accept him as my parent and trust him to be my family.

All the impressions from that long day buzzed in my head as Tyotya Valya remained in the kitchen preparing dinner while the rest of the family sat watching television. I could only imagine how hard it was to make a meal for more than five people. I remembered seeing the wrinkles on her face announcing that she was growing tired from the endless obligations she had. Cleaning and taking care of children seemed to be an infinite cycle of dull repetition, especially when you had more than a couple of them. You could clean after someone, wash their clothes, scrub, rub, and dust, but after only a few days, you needed to repeat the process. Thinking of Tyotya Valya's work reminded me of Sisyphus rolling his rock up the hill every day, over and over again, waiting for redemption. Of course, Sisyphus was immortal, but Tyotya Valya wasn't, and she was doing it out of motherly love, the way only mothers can do it, but you could tell that she was tired.

I wished I could do something to make her work more manageable, but I was afraid she was nursing anger about the 'watermelon incident.' So, I decided to stick with the others and play a game while Dyadya Grisha watched the news.

It wasn't long before Tyotya Valya's voice broke through the hallway. "Dinner time!"

Dyadya Grisha stood up, gesturing for us to join him.

I was hungry and looking forward to dinner as I inhaled the spicy smell coming from the kitchen. Tyotya Valya served her special pork cutlets and mashed potatoes. They were a delicious surprise, and even though I didn't see the salad I wished for, I didn't think of asking. The dish she served us was extraordinary. The meal from Tyotya Valya's kitchen tasted so much better than the food we had at the orphanage. Maybe it was the quality ingredients or because she prepared the meal for her family. I didn't know for sure, but I did wonder if the orphanage cook's children—if they had any—had better meals at home or if they had to swallow fat chunks to avoid being grounded or punished.

The cutlets Tyotya Valya prepared for us had no fat chunks or anything else that would make me leave a single morsel on my plate. I was ravenous, and the food was delicious. So, I savored every bite, but I didn't ask for seconds. I remembered the painful expression on Tyotya Valya's face as she walked away from watermelon treats, and I didn't want to upset her.

After finishing our cutlets with potatoes, Tyotya Valya served us cherry compote. The compote we had in Ukraine was more juice than cherries, but I loved it, and even though it was something I had at the orphanage my whole life, Tyotya Valya made it taste even better. I finished dessert quickly but still enjoyed every sip.

That first meal at Tyotya Valya and Dyadya Grisha's home was a feast, but it wasn't what we ate every day. Tyotya Valya made delicious food, but meat was rarely on the menu. It was expensive, so we only had it about once a week if we were lucky. Tyotya Valya also had many rules to follow while we ate our food. She reminded us to keep our elbows below the table while eating. We were not allowed to talk to others at the table, chew loud, or with our mouths open. If we needed something, we asked politely, unless it was for seconds.

As we finished eating, I thanked her for the delicious meal she had prepared, but she did not respond. Instead, she simply turned her head and began clearing the table, giving her gratitude to the other family compliments. That was when I first saw the temper that boiled in Tyotya Valya's heart.

I thought many mothers might be bitter and tired of everything they had to do around the house, but I didn't understand why Tyotya Valya was so angry. She wasn't the only one rolling that rock up the hill in this house. It was evident from the start that we would all be pushing it as well. Nadya had helped to prepare dinner, and just minutes after leaving the dining table to play in the television room, I heard Tyotya Valya's voice again, calling the next worker. "Masha? Masha!"

Masha winced, moaning as she stood up. "Oh, yes, I'll be right back," she said, but she wasn't back for a long time. It took until almost bedtime to help clean up after dinner. Later, I learned we would all have our turn. We each had a day when we would help in the kitchen, cleaning up after every meal. Monday was Masha's day. On Tuesday, Nadya helped. Wednesday was Serhij's. Thursday, Slavik's and I helped with cleaning on Friday. I hated doing my chores, but I always listened to Tyotya Valya, convincing myself that some things just needed to be done. There are many things in life we don't like doing, yet we must do them. So, I made peace with my obligation and decided that it made playing for a few minutes after I finished even sweeter.

Later that night, making beds started with Dyadya Grisha trying to transform the couch into one seemingly cozy bed, but that wasn't in the cards for Slavik and me. Nothing he did seemed to work.

Tyotya Valya stood with one hand resting on her hip, looking at Dyadya Grisha. "When were you planning to repair this couch?"

"Well, I guess I'll look at it tomorrow. Unfortunately, there is not much I can do now," he said, looking at us sheepishly, "Sorry, boys. It looks like you will spend your night on the floor."

Tyotya Valya's agitation grew as she placed clean sheets on the functional couch, arranging the bed for Masha and Nadya, while Dyadya Grisha was setting up a camping-cot for Serhij, leaving a place on the floor for Slavik and me. Tyotya Valya placed a few blankets over the space, one on top of another, making something that looked like a bed. I wouldn't say I liked the idea of sleeping on the floor, but I already felt like I was on the wrong side of her, and she was taking her anger out on Dyadya Grisha. I didn't want to cause any more problems than I already had.

After making the beds, everyone settled for the night and waited for our favorite show, "Goodnight Children." None of us would have missed that show for anything in this world. It was the one constant in our lives, and it was thirty minutes of the sweetest goodnight you could get, and now, we finally had a family. It was the one thing worth the sacrifice of sleeping on the floor.

There was a second room where Dyadya Grisha and Tyotya Valya slept. As the show ended, Tyotya Valya left to get ready for bed while Dyadya Grisha stayed to smoke one last cigarette. It was one more in the endless haze of smoke that lingered in our house, saturating the walls. You could always tell when Dyadya Grisha was home. Even the hallway smelled of his cigarettes.

"Goodnight, boys! Sleep tight!" Dyadya Grisha smiled as he left the room.

Tyotya Valya turned off the lights with a brief and slightly harsh, "Goodnight." It felt nothing like I hoped my mother's goodnight wish would sound, but I was still happy. Finally, I was with my best friend, and we had a home. Having a mother who was angry at me was better than having no mother at all.

There were many ways Tyotya Valya was scary. However, I could still tell there was a motherly figure underneath her strictness and the disciplinary measures she was implementing in our lives. I estimated that she wasn't off track as a parent and tutor, but I suppose that no child likes chores and the yelling that always followed our wrong decisions and reckless, childish actions. I knew she was doing her best, but I wished she was more patient. After all, we were only kids learning to see the world as it was.

As they left, closing the door to their room behind them. I could still hear their muffled voices in the distance, reaching out to me through the long, dimmed hallway. It was the only sound left in the apartment until a barely audible whisper broke my attempts to hear what they might be saying.

"Hey, guys?" It happened again, but I didn't know who it was. I could barely see anything beyond Slavik's head turned in the direction of the sound.

The voice was persistent, continuing to call to us, "Hey, who wants to play 'I spy with my little eye?'"

It took just a moment longer to realize that fatigue had already laid on Nadya's and Masha's eyes since there was no sound coming from their bed. There was the only other boy in the room, so I quickly realized Serhij had something different in mind than sleeping,

The changes and excitement of the day took away the last bit of energy I had. Still, even though I was tired, the excitement of the day wouldn't let me rest, not yet, so I answered Serhij's question, "How can we play 'I spy with my little eye,' when we can't see anything in this darkness?"

Slavik started chuckling, giving his best not to burst into laughter.

"Well," Serhij was trying to persuade us into curing his boredom. "We can choose any object, as long as we know there is one in this house."

"Not a bad idea," Slavik replied. "Who will start first?"

"I can." Serhij's voice echoed through the darkness again.

"Ok...," I said, trying to be quiet. "Let's start then!"

"I spy with my little eye...." Serhij started the game, and even if I could not tell in which direction he was looking, I knew that he was searching the room for the perfect object, "...something with the letter...F!" he continued, almost yelling.

We were silent for a moment, waiting to see if anyone heard us, and then, Slavik's voice broke the silence, "A fart!"

We started giggling and chuckling, trying to choke our laughter in pillows, but it didn't work. We soon heard Tyotya Valya's voice echoing from the hallway, and we knew it was over. "Quit it! I can hear you! NIGHT IS FOR SLEEPING! Not fooling around!"

The sound of Tyotya Valya's voice—trembling in anger—ended our fun. As quickly as the game had started, our room turned as silent as a graveyard. At that point, I knew that living with Tyotya Valya wouldn't be as easy as it felt the first time I saw her.

22

Bra Dag, Sweden!

I am sitting in the center of the picture with five other orphan girls and singing a Ukrainian song for Danish and Swedish people.

THE KITCHEN SOON BECAME my favorite room in the apartment. The whole family would gather at the table for each meal, sitting in the same order and leaning over the rich choice of different dishes Tyotya Valya was preparing for us. It was amazing to have a family and not too many children screaming to get just a bit of attention. Still, as much as I loved having a family, the thing I liked best about the kitchen was that no fat chunks were floating on my plate. So finishing my meals was a pleasure.

As time passed, I would gladly join Tyotya Valya in the kitchen. I wanted her to love me, and I also loved helping her cook, as culinary skills became one of my passions. Of course, food is something we need to consume to stay alive and healthy, but it becomes so much more in the circle of family and friends. It becomes a bond, an excuse to give a compliment, a reason to smile, and an occasion to share.

Not long after moving in with my family, thinking I couldn't be more blessed than I already was, another great opportunity appeared. As part of our government's initiative to help parentless children and children from large families, they created a summer program offering the opportunity for children over twelve to go to Sweden for the summer. If accepted, we would spend our time there with an assigned family. Tyotya Valya favored Masha and wanted her to participate. Still, I was the one closest to twelve, so Tyotya Valya asked the social workers to include both of us on the list.

Although I was grateful for everything I had, I was also looking forward to expanding my horizons, meeting new people, and seeing new things. I wanted to see if there was more to the world beyond the orphanage walls and our communal apartment.

My desires paid off. I was one of the children in our area selected to go to Sweden. When I heard the news, it was as though my feet had turned to gelatin. I was so happy. However, since I was the only one in my family near the age of twelve, I was the only one who could go. I felt terrible for Masha. Between the feelings of joy I had for myself and the empathy for my friends who didn't get the same opportunity as I had, I felt ripped apart inside.

From the moment I found out until the day we took off, I couldn't stop thinking about all the new and unknown things waiting for me on my next adventure. I was anxious about leaving Ukraine for the first time, but my heart overflowed with positive expectations, and eventually, my fears and anxiety disappeared. For the first time in a long time, I was able to say that I was delighted with my life, although my thoughts often return to the many orphaned children I knew. Unfortunately, we don't all get the same opportunities, which sometimes made me feel guilty. Life didn't work the way I dreamed it could as a child, but I was growing up now. The rose-colored glasses I wore as a young boy fell off, making me see what I couldn't see before. We all need to take advantage of the things that come our way, even if they aren't there for everyone.

The day I was supposed to get packed and ready for my two months away was as beautiful as it could be. They told us we would get new clothes once we arrived in Sweden, making my packing pretty easy. So I floated through the day as the enchanting smell of summer flowers embraced our city. Even our kitchen smelled less of grease and fried food as the windows were open almost the entire morning.

The concrete outside was lazy and lonely as I finished my lunch and ran to wait outside the door of our apartment building. The people in our neighborhood usually went out in the morning and late afternoon. So, the streets were pretty quiet as I got into the bus that would take me to the airport. Today, the twenty-plus children on the bus and I had one of the few with a good reason to face the heat of mid-day.

The trip to Sweden also meant that I would set foot on an airplane for the first time in my life, which made my legs shake, but I knew that wasn't fear. I was excited. Everything about this trip was exciting. We stopped on the way to the airport to pick up one of my friends from the orphanage, a girl named Nadya—not the Nadya who lived with us.

This Nadya lived with a large foster family in Chernivtsi. I thought she was probably grateful she could take some time apart from the nine people she was living with at the time.

I was never sure why some families accepted so many children from the orphanage, but I suppose some were in it for the money. Our foster families received an allowance from the state for each orphan they fostered. Looking back, I doubt we were getting half the benefit of that money in the form of new clothes, shoes, and good food. Of course, we didn't care. Orphans didn't have a lot of options. We either lived at the orphanage or with foster parents. I knew any child would quickly choose a family over a cold orphanage. Even Tyotya Valya wasn't what I expected, but we all have our light and dark times. So, I didn't think much about the worst of it. When I was a boy, I judged by the moment, often forgetting things that happened in the past. I guess all children see the world in the same manner, making each moment an entire universe in their hearts.

After a long buzzing drive to the airport—where I learned more about Nadya and her jolly nature—we boarded the plane. Nadya later told me that she was feeling sick the entire time we were in the air, although that didn't stop her from looking forward to visiting Sweden. Unfortunately, I don't remember anything from that first flight as I was asleep within minutes of leaving the ground. So, I didn't get to see the clouds by my side or get a chance to fear the height like Nadya did.

When we landed in Stockholm, we didn't do a lot of sightseeing. It was probably best for Nayda as she was still recovering from the flight. But for me, I immediately noticed the physical differences between people from Chernivtsi and those in Sweden. I had never met anyone from Sweden before, but I couldn't resist the feeling of being utterly comfortable, thinking that I could stay forever and be happy. The people were so kind and generous.

The first person we met after landing was a pleasant-faced man who took good care of us on our way to the place we would live while in Sweden. Calle, our guide, was tall and corpulent, waiting for us with a wave and a big grin that made his face seem familiar. I couldn't help but smile in return. He was an almost perfect incarnation of Santa Clause, which made me feel more than comfortable in his presence. The only thing missing from him was the well-known white beard, but he still reminded me of Santa without it, especially when he hugged us. His hugs made me giggle as he had the same round belly I saw in the holiday stories we watched about Did Moroz.

We followed him to the minibus that would take us to the camp. As we walked towards the car, Calle was giving out his warm welcome, and even though we couldn't understand a word he was saying, anyone could tell that he was a delightful and friendly person. The man sitting in the driver's seat, Calle's friend, waved to greet us and show us we were welcome, as well. "Bra Dag!" he said, and I knew what he meant without needing a translation. That was the only saying I memorized. Bra Dag, Sweden! It meant 'Great Day, Sweden!' It was a great day, one of the best I ever had.

I climbed aboard the minibus, excited again for another step of my adventure. I had never ridden in a shared taxi before. During communism, Chernivtsi had established a trolleybus system similar to one created in Germany. It was a form of public transportation that people could afford. After introducing the trolley system, Soviet Russia also introduced Marshrutkas or routed taxi cabs. They were primarily minibusses that you had to pay a little more to use, but you could go anywhere you wanted to go and get there faster.

The road we traveled was sleek, with almost no bumps, and the van Calle's friend was driving was far faster than the long crowded buses in Chernivtsi. One of the windows was open, inviting the playful summer breeze to tickle my nostrils, presenting the scent of a new country, of different soil. The seats were so comfortable I dove in and relaxed.

Our destination was a little town called Höör, and as the drive was long, I was asleep almost the entire trip. I tried to outlast my sleepiness by looking through the window. However, as soon as we left the city to traverse a road with village landscapes and slideshows of numberless trees, fields, and bushes, the view quickly turned into green and yellow blurs that became a sedative to my senses. I was asleep without even knowing.

When I woke, it was to several different voices, speaking unfamiliar words and strange tones. The conversation was a random blending of foreign sounds mixed with the familiarity of Nadya's words spoken in a language I could understand. She was trying to answer all the questions our new friends were asking. Still, as we didn't know how to speak English or Swedish, everyone spoke their language slowly, trying to read each other's facial expressions for a gist of what was said.

I slowly opened my eyes to watch the interchange and noticed that most of what they were saying, they said in a language we all understood. Every face I saw was full of smiles.

We traveled for miles even after I woke up, and I was trying to remember as many images of the passing landscape as I could. I wished I had a camera, but I knew a camera could not capture the relaxing atmosphere, enchanting scents of summer, or friendly faces mixed with unfamiliar words and odd gestures. The pictures alone weren't enough. The experience was a feeling that mingled with the memory of strange, majestic birds that had snow-like feathers and a thin black stripe on each wing. The birds took me back to my dreams as I watched them fly in circles above a seaside that was occasionally visible as we hurried toward our destination.

More people poured "Bra Dags!" on our heads when we arrived. Everyone was so happy to see us, but they weren't what surprised me the most. I was amazed by the natural tidiness of the place. Neatly trimmed bushes surrounded the building, and though the windows looked a little old, the glass was spotless. The hotel was impeccable, with perfectly placed pavers, neatly manicured grass, and as we were in Höör—near the southernmost point of Sweden—we were not far from salty water and the hypnotizing sound of waves crashing against rocks on the shore.

I thought of how I could learn the language and settle in nicely here. I was ready to stay with these happy faces and clean streets. Still, as the sun began to set, the sorrow of homesickness returned, and I realized that I was already missing Slavik and even Masha, Nadya, and Serhij. I imagined Nadya probably felt the same way about her foster brothers and sisters. I guess we all learn to appreciate what we have once we are away from them.

Circumstances in Sweden turned out to be great. This beautiful little town where we stayed made sure that two months felt like barely two weeks had passed. The morning after we arrived, when I woke up, the only thought in my head was, "I wish I could dip my feet in the ocean." So I set a goal to walk on the beach with my feet bare and put them in the water before they asked anything else of me. I didn't realize how far we would travel to get to the water. Still, I was lucky. As it was summertime, our educators told us right away they were already planning days at the beach, not the list of chores I would have expected at home. The only thing I had left to worry about was that I didn't have a bathing suit, and I knew the same was true for Nadya. It seemed we might need to figure something out if we wanted to get more than just our feet wet.

Before visiting the beach, we had a breakfast of peach jam, butter, toast, and fresh-squeezed orange juice. After breakfast, one of our educators came into our room carrying a couple of bags, and as we opened the bags, a wave of relief passed over my entire being. The bags were full of the new clothes we were promised, along with the bathing suits we needed.

I didn't sleep this time as the van began rolling its way toward the ocean. It took nearly an hour to get from Höör to the beach in Malmö, but it felt like minutes to me. This trip was my first time visiting a beach or even seeing the ocean. So, I couldn't wait to jump into the water, but I would hold myself until I knew it was okay with our instructors.

We piled out of the van, carrying everything we would need to enjoy a day by the ocean. Walking on the shore with bare feet was even better than walking on the grass. My feet sank into the soft sand, and although it was hot enough to burn, I savored every step.

"Children, please do not swim further than two meters in length, and those who are not particularly good swimmers should stick to the shore," one of the educators warned us.

I ran towards the water, not even waiting for him to finish his sentence. I was still slightly frightened by the vastness of the sea, but the moment I saw other children entering the ocean, I knew I was ready. As I learned how to swim a couple of years before, back when I was at the summer camp with the other children from the orphanage, I went as far out as my educators would let me.

The water was colder than the sand, but it was still warm enough for me to enjoy on a summer day. I could only stay in for a few minutes at a time before I began shivering, but it felt so good to come out of the water and lay on the sand to warm myself up again.

As I rested on the beach with my skin soaking in salty water and my feet dug deep into the sand, I didn't think about anything. I felt as clear as the water, without a single worry. It was like I was in another dimension, a place where it didn't matter whether I had problems or who I was. The feeling that I could be anyone and do anything gave me a freedom I had never considered before, and I hoped it would never go away. Every day I spent soaking in the sun was a piece of heaven for me. So, I finally understood why all the people who could afford it were going on vacations.

I swam, and I stood sometimes amazed to silence in the face of the pristine beauty of the sea. I was thinking about everything that this sea could be hiding underneath, remembering myths and fairy tales about mermaids that were enchanting sailors. I wondered if any pirate had ever dropped the anchor of his ship on this shore.

I felt like I had set sail on one of their adventures. I was so grateful that my days at Tyotya Valya's had somehow magically transformed into days in Sweden with far fewer obligations. It wasn't that I didn't love living with my family. I just enjoyed a break from the greasy kitchen and overcrowded apartment. Still, I couldn't escape them. While others jumped, danced, and splashed in the salty water, I thought of how Slavik would love it here. It was so wonderful. I considered not telling him about the adventure because I didn't want him to feel bad. He didn't get to see what I saw.

Every time we went to the beach, I escaped time missing my family. But, as we came back, they always returned. Lucky for me, it would be just in time for lunch. So, I found something to enjoy again. I was always starving, exhausted from the water and hot air, immediately diving into my plate and leaving it completely clean.

Within just the first couple of days, the things I experienced would have been enough for me, but our educators tried to make Sweden as enjoyable as possible. So they were taking us everywhere, although everywhere was not as extensive as it sounds. Höör was a small town, so there weren't many places to go. Still, staying in this little peaceful piece of heaven was relaxing. Everything was quiet and clean, with barely any traffic, crowds, or noise.

I was assigned to stay with a small family: mother Elm, father Ulric, and their sons Phillip and Fran. It was strange to call any adult by just their first name, but I supposed this is the way things were in Sweden.

The family took us to the nature park one day, and it was so exciting. I had never been to the zoo, so naturally, I couldn't stop smiling and feeling amazed that days like this were happening in the world. Nicely carved wooden benches where you could enjoy the scenery or rest in the shadow of tall trees lined the zoo's walkways. I didn't know where to look first. I gazed at cages that divided us from zebras, lions, bears, penguins, and a seemingly infinite variety of tropical birds that were constantly tweeting and singing. The birds were louder than the rest of the town, but it was peaceful at the same time. I savored each chirp and burble, trying to guess from which animal it came.

We went to new places every day. One day, we visited Stockholm, but we spent most of our time nearer the family home, visiting castles with lakes. We also saw windmills and shopped for different cheeses to take on a picnic. As we traveled throughout the town, I enjoyed noticing the differences between Chernivtsi's people and those in Sweden. We were unique in so many ways, each with different attitudes, foreign words, and ways of life. Even the air here was distinctive, which I guessed was due to the salty breath of the sea. It floated, lifted by the breeze, and no matter where you were, even if you weren't near the beach, you could feel it in the clouds or lightly salting your lips. It worked well on my appetite for sure. I couldn't remember ever being as hungry as I was in Sweden. Every meal was tasty and nicely prepared. Of course, Tyotya Valya's food was delicious, but it seemed food made with cheer was more delightful to eat.

One night, after hours of observing and enjoying every moment, we returned to the family's home to finish the day by having a feast with other orphan children and their families. The sun was slowly setting, and as there were no clouds anywhere, we all admired the last moments of warmth the sun offered. Then, we sat down on the soft woolen blankets one of our educators brought to eat our dinners. I enjoyed a ham sandwich that Phillip made for me. To make it, he placed the ham between two slices of bread covered with butter and cheese and heated it for forty seconds in the microwave oven. I had never eaten anything prepared in a microwave before. It was such a delight. I savored every bite, occasionally sipping orange juice and reaching out to touch the pointy green grass. I wanted to memorize every second and keep it forever; every taste, every sound, the temperature, and the feeling of bare skin merging with soft but stubborn spikes of grass.

I was deep in my thoughts of how wonderful Sweden could be when things became even better. I finished the last of my sandwich, and Phillip turned to me, asking, "Would you like more, Vitaly?"

"I can have seconds?" I asked, not knowing any other way to answer.

"Of course, you can," he said, laughing. "You can have as much as you like. Here. I'll show you how to make one for yourself."

I ate until I couldn't take another bite, and then we relaxed until it was time to go to bed. I never knew what to think of how they treated me in Sweden. When I was hungry, they let me eat as much as I liked, and even when I broke the glass door on a bookcase because I was throwing a ball in the room, no one was upset or punishing me. Instead, everyone understood it was an accident. Life in Sweden was happy and loving the way I always thought a family should be.

I was exhausted as I went to bed that night. Of course, it was the pleasant kind of exhaustion I liked having after a long day of fun. I sometimes tried to end my night flipping through the pages of a Pink Panther comic book I found by my bed. I wanted to grasp all the memories I had collected that day, but it never lasted long. In no time at all, I was flying again, up high, but now there were no clouds and no one to chase me. There was only the endless blue of the sky blending with the mirror of a peaceful sea.

23

Our New Home

Almost the entire second floor belonged to our family. There are seven windows visible in this picture. Two windows to the left are boys' bedroom windows.

AFTER TWO MONTHS IN SWEDEN, I returned to Chernivtsi and nostalgically remembered how much I loved my home. I was happy knowing that I had someone waiting for me.

Unlike the many times I had returned to the orphanage from summer camps, only to hug my pillow, be grounded, or even beaten if I did something wrong, I now had a family and the joys of seeing them again.

"Look, here comes our Swedish fellow!" Dyadya Grisha joked as he waved at me. He and Tyotya Valya came to the bus stop to pick me up, and I was happy to see them and tell them all about my journey. I couldn't stop talking about it. I shared story after story, talking the entire way home, thrilled to have someone listening to all I had to say. I avoided mentioning how great the food was since I didn't want Tyotya Valya to think I liked any food better than hers.

Tyotya Valya was one of the best cooks ever, and I'm sure she knew it. Still, a woman who put all her energy into making a home might be offended if I said someone else's food tasted so delicious. So, I decided to keep my stories to adventures and the great presents I received.

I wasn't a little boy anymore, but a stuffed bear was the best gift I received while in Sweden. I had always wanted a bear to cuddle with at night, and one of the educators there heard me talking about it. So the next day they met me with a surprise. As I told Tyotya Valya the story, she reminded me of how grateful I should be that the people of Sweden were so generous to me, and I was. But, of course, she believed I should later express that gratitude and share my treasures with the family. She began the sharing by taking my bear and giving it to her son Sasha the minute we got home. I think I could have forgiven her for taking any other gift I received. I would have gladly given them, but I finally had a bear to hug at night and not just my pillow. It seemed Valya believed my memories were enough to cuddle with instead.

Despite a few disappointments, I was so glad to be back. Of course, everyone in my foster family was also happy to see me, but the person most thrilled by my return was Slavik. Seeing him, I remembered how much I missed his humor and the unconditional friendship he gave me.

As we settled back into our daily routines, I discovered I wasn't the only one who had stories to tell. Tyotya Valya had some novelties as well. She was always looking for ways other people could help her get what she wanted. Just as with the program that made my trip to Sweden possible, Tyotya Valya loved to keep track of every advantage she could gain in the foster care programs. While I was on my adventure, she found out that the state gave apartments to parentless children living with their foster families. Tyotya Valya was the first on the list to get us a better apartment.

Even though she took care of us, Tyotya Valya always thought about herself and her family first. Maybe it was natural, but I often felt I embraced Tyotya Valya because I had no choice. Of course, I could always do something reckless and earn my way back to the orphanage, but I felt more comfortable in my new home with my friends than in a room with dozens of lonely children. So, I did my best to behave and be obedient, but I knew I would never think of her as my mother.

I knew who my mother was, and I still believed she would come back one day. The most enduring tie possible linked us. Blood bonded us for all time, and I could never forget that. I didn't even want to. So, I tried not to think about how Tyotya Valya treated me or my mother's lack of interest. I decided to think about my brother and how it would be if we all lived together instead.

Besides, things weren't too bad in our new home. I had Slavik, and Dyadya Grisha made my life so much better, as well. Of course, he wasn't the one dictating the mood in our home, as Tyotya Valya pulled all the strings, but he was kind when he could be. In the end, it was an improvement from my life at the orphanage, so I was happy.

I think she was happy too, as she managed to get her hands on that apartment, thanks to our existence. She also had more help around the house. Even though she received money to care for us, Tyotya Valya's favorite thing to tell us was that we also had to "earn our keep." I realized very young that I needed to work for everything I got and the things other people got as well, sometimes.

Not having much, I also learned to be grateful. We didn't have the same great adventures with Tyotya Valya as I had in Sweden, but we did have what we needed, making life better for everyone. We ate meat once a week and had a nice place to live. The new apartment was massive and very pleasant. It was on the second floor of the building, near the city center, on Vavilova Street, right across from Chernivtsi National University. So, the neighborhood was better, and everything we needed was near our home, including access to our school. To get to the secondary school we attended, we could walk across the street and catch the trolleybus that would take us the hour drive to our classes.

The apartment itself was everything that one family could want. It was nothing like the place that was my first home outside of the orphanage. They built the rooms that made the apartment seem like a labyrinth. There were so many doors, all of them leading to different rooms, so I was never sure which way I was going. But I think that was also the first reason I liked it. It had high ceilings, five large bedrooms, two kitchens, one bathroom with a beautiful tub installed, a separate toilet, and two long hallways.

I was excited to see that we would finally have enough room for everyone, but I still didn't understand Tyotya Valya then. Everything we gained from her was to gain something for herself. I'm sure she would have thrown us out of the apartment if she could have. Lucky for us, social service workers were there to make sure she didn't do that. She needed us to have the apartment in the first place. It now made sense why she adopted more children she didn't want.

Everything the government gave her was for us more than it could ever be for her. Still, we were children, and we didn't understand such things. Tyotya Valya knew how to take advantage of the system and keep everything in her hands, pulling strings in her favor. Even though there were five bedrooms in the new apartment, she put the five of us, Slavik, Serhij, Nadya, Masha, and me, in two rooms that were joined to one another but separate from the rest of the family. A pair of doors divided the space between the boys and the girls, but you still had to walk through the girls' bedroom to get to the boys' bedroom and our bathroom.

The girls' bedroom didn't have windows, so it was dark. The boys' bedroom, where I slept, had two windows. I thought she would have put the boys in the darker room with no windows, but it was tiny, even for one person, so luck was on my side this time. Three growing boys wouldn't fit and ended up with the bigger room with three beds. I guess the girls were small enough that Tyotya Valya thought they would sleep in the smaller just fine, and in the end, they did. Tyotya Valya had Dyadya Grisha set up the couch they used in the old apartment for them to share. It wasn't what we deserved, but it wasn't the living room anymore or an orphanage. So, we were thankful, feeling like life was getting better for everyone.

We spent most of our time playing in the larger bedroom. It was away from Tyotya Valya's angry hushes, and everyone had fun playing together with light streaming through to remind us of happy times. I remember how much I loved that room until I broke one of the windows trying to do a handstand so our neighbor could see my feet through the glass. Tyotya Valya was angry, especially since it happened during the winter. So, she didn't fix the window right away. I guess she decided to punish us by making us sleep in the cold. I did what I could to fix it with tape, but it felt like being back in the freezing orphanage most nights. Lucky for us, there was a point where Tyotya Valya stopped being angry, or maybe she was tired of the cold. Either way, she finally decided it was time to make Dyadya Grisha fix the glass.

Tyotya Valya kept the rest of the apartment for herself and her family. Tyotya Valya, Dyadya Grisha, and their son Sasha lived in two bedrooms connected as our bedrooms were. She gave the fifth room to her daughter-in-law, Nastya, to have with her husband, Dyadya Grisha's and Tyotya Valya's older son, Yura. He was in the army at that time. So, they took care of Nastya, giving her one of the rooms to have for herself.

Even if I wanted to, I couldn't say that I wasn't happy living with Tyotya Valya and her family. My life was better, and to me, that made it a good life. Still, I was often the target of Tyotya Valya's brandish demonstrations. She loved giving me pointed stares and shouting orders, along with continually reminding me of how grateful I should be for all the sacrifices she made.

I didn't see her sacrifice much, but she didn't need to. We didn't care about material goods, as long as we were part of a family, and we were. In addition, we didn't have anyone to stand up for us. Dyadya Grisha kept us going with his cheerfulness and kind words. Still, he usually succumbed to Tyotya Valya's cutting glances, so we accepted what we got, and he accepted his life with her as well. No one wanted to pick a fight with her, so we did what she wanted, telling her how grateful we were for her willingness to foster us and find such a perfect apartment.

I never resented Tyotya Valya for what she took. She was the only mother I had in my life, and it was good to be out of the orphanage and in this beautiful place. I was happy having a family and my friends there living with me. I loved it, and for a long time, I thought it was the way it was supposed to be until the social workers visited.

The social workers would announce their arrival a couple of days in advance, and Tyotya Valya would use those days to do things around the house and train us into saying what she wanted the social workers to hear. I was still young, and I couldn't stand up for myself or my friends, but I knew what she was doing was wrong. I always wondered what would have happened if they appeared at our doors unannounced. Although I knew we would still lie for Tyotya Valya, she knew it too. The life we had outside the orphanage was too precious to be tossed into the wind. Still, I wondered if they might see a little more of the truth.

Seconds after finding out they had scheduled a visit, she would line us up, marching and shouting orders as if we were back in Oktobrist training. "The social workers are coming in a couple of days, and I want you all to behave and do as I say. Is that clear?"

We all nodded, although I didn't feel like agreeing to her deceit. I was disgusted with all the lies she made us tell.

"Now, listen! The social workers will ask you some questions, and if any of them asks which room belongs to whom, I want you to say that the girls are sleeping in the room where we set the television." She worried about that room because they designated it to be our playroom. It was the most beautiful room in the house, as it had many windows, bathing it in the comfort of the shining sun. But, of course, Tyotya Valya took it for herself, and she couldn't let the social workers know. When they asked about the bedrooms, I glanced at Tyotya Valya, who said everything she needed to communicate with her eyes. So, I said what she wanted me to say. None of us wanted to go back to the orphanage or get in a fight with her.

Tyotya Valya was greedy, and I don't think she ever cared about us as much as she cared about what she could have for herself by fostering us. But we didn't understand that then. We were only children. It was unimaginable that someone would want to hurt us or take advantage of us, especially if that person was supposed to nurture us and raise us properly.

We believed in her because we had to. We had no one else, and even if we wanted to tell them the truth, we didn't. The entire time the social workers were in our apartment, Tyotya Valya was pinching us with her striking glances, ensuring that none of us said anything we weren't supposed to say. It wasn't long before we didn't need her stares. We seldom made the wrong move when the social workers came.

"What would you say about the food here?" One of the workers asked us, making notes in our file.

We lied, of course. We said that we had everything we wanted, but we didn't. We didn't have toys or new clothes. Having meat with our meals went from once a week to roughly once a month, and then, only on special occasions when we had visitors. Life wasn't as it was on the first day Slavik and I came to Tyotya Valya's home. We barely had enough to nourish ourselves.

The only thing we weren't lying about was saying that she cooked well. Of course, she did, but we didn't mention that she complained about how much we ate, talking about how she didn't have enough money to feed us, although she was getting money for food and forbid us from asking for seconds, even when we were hungry.

They asked about our clothes and shoes, and we weren't as nervous about those questions as we were when one of them asked us how bedrooms are divided. The social worker passed over the clothing because Tyotya Valya took credit for the new things I received in Sweden. As I was the oldest and growing quickly, my clothes never lasted long, so she passed them on to Serhij and Slavik, whose wardrobe roughly consisted of my old clothes. Tyotya Valya didn't mention any of that, and neither did we. We didn't tell them we wore our sneakers until they got holes and cracks in them, so they didn't know our feet were soaking wet whenever it was raining.

"All right, great..." the worker responded absentmindedly to all of our answers. I wondered through the whole thing if they heard the answers we were giving or if they were only pretending to listen. Looking back now, I realize the social workers probably knew how things worked in our home, but we were just numbers in their book. Getting us out of the orphanage and into a home, any home, meant they had done their job.

It seemed many people were looking the other way. The positive thing was that we still had each other, a feeling to which no room, even the largest, brightest, or prettiest, could compare.

24

Playing Games

During my visit to Sweden, I had my first adventure on a giant slide. This is me splashing into the water.

WE LOVED OUR NEW APARTMENT, making it more like home every day. We didn't get the best room, but we weren't on the living room floor, either. There was also more space, so it was good for us. We loved playing together, both inside and outside, in front of our building. We enjoyed the dull noise of tapping as we bounced a ball against the wall or traveled the neighborhood areas to search for new misadventures.

I always imagined how Tyotya Valya must have felt relieved whenever we weren't around, having all the space she needed, just for her family and herself. So, she let us roam, probably more than she should. Still, I didn't think about that as much as I thought about new ways of having fun with my brothers and sisters and our new friends.

Although I wasn't at the orphanage anymore, I still enjoyed finding scraps near the dumpsters to make toys. We didn't have toys magically come to us during holidays or even birthdays like sometimes happened at the orphanage. Tyotya Valya did not like buying toys for us. Most of our gifts were candy or the clothes we needed from growing so fast. So, we played with anything we could find lying around, always coming up with new ways to use it. I wanted to show my brothers and sisters that there was more to do than watch television. Not to say we didn't enjoy our time in front of the television, watching our favorite shows like "Chip and Dale." The bright and sunny room made us grateful for our new apartment, even if we had to be careful of upsetting Tyotya Valya when we were there.

Most of the games we played were fun, and all of the kids liked to play them together, though not all of the games were games girls wanted to play. Nadya acted like a boy more than a girl and enjoyed all boys' games, such as football. Serhij and Slavik also loved everything related to ball games and spending time on the streets looking for trouble, so Nadya spent a lot of time with them.

Masha was the only one who didn't like the things the boys wanted to do. It was hard for her, as she was often left needing to find other girls to play games with her. I liked girls' games as well, so I stayed with her and the other girls on the street sometimes to play the games they enjoyed, like "Rezinochka," commonly called Chinese Jump Rope in America. It took at least three people to play, two to wrap the elastic around their legs, and the third to jump and do tricks. Masha and I loved watching how fast some girls could do their tricks.

My best times were when I wasn't around the house, watching television, or doing my homework. I wanted to be out in the open, testing all the toys I made. Sometimes I had Slavik's help, and sometimes I was by myself. Either way, those were the moments when nothing else around me existed, the moments where I was alone with my thoughts, inventing, and creating from scraps of outcast material. We even went as far as to use condoms to make water balloons to throw at each other on hot summer days. It doesn't seem reasonable to think of those water balloons now, but we were just children and didn't know any better. It gave us ways to play.

One of my favorite games to make and play was darts. All we needed to make a little fun was four matches, glue, some cardboard for making the dart stationery, thread, and a sewing needle. We all knew how to make darts out of those materials. As boys, we were competitive. So, we would often gather around the building and find a tree or some doors to be our target for shooting. May the best dart maker win.

We would bring the game inside if it was too cold or wet to be outside, using a carpet I hung on the wall as a target. One time, during our competition, it went as far as aiming at each other. One of my friends became angry and threw his dart at me, hitting me in the arm. I shot back at him and hit him in the stomach. We stifled our cries so that no one could hear us. I was afraid and ashamed to admit what happened, so I never told Tyotya Valya.

Almost every game we played involved shooting. As boys in Ukraine, that was our main point of interest. So we played with boomerangs and spitting tubes we called harkalka. One of our favorite activities was collecting calcium carbide we found at construction sites, or what we called magic stones. When we gathered enough, we would toss them in the puddles, put them into the plastic bottles filled with water, throw them, or burn them, and excitedly observe the reactions. I remember the distinctive, nostril-pinching scent coming from our experiments, but what I loved most was the flames. We learned from all the different effects we could create around us, but it was the fun that mattered the most, so we found as many new and creative ways to use our precious stones as we could.

One of the best ways to use carbide was to make handguns, which felt more like bombs as the explosions were massive. The main trick was to take an empty bottle and add carbide. We would then spit in it, shake it well, and light it with matches. That was all we needed to produce brilliant explosions that could keep us busy for hours.

Although many of our games revolved around shooting and explosions, I also enjoyed doing things that felt more peaceful. For example, I used colored wires and old telephone cords for making braided bracelets and figurines. It was relaxing and fulfilling on the days when quiet thoughtfulness settled on my soul, and, as it turned out, I learned to appreciate what I could create when I put some effort and time into it. I also liked reading the Bible and learning something new every day. I was always trying to be better than anyone else in the group. Being smart, paid sometimes.

I also liked to keep myself busy observing the tiny lives around us with a magnifying glass. Of course, the bigger the glass was, the better. I loved watching insects and seeing what was too small for me to see otherwise. I also liked magnifying glasses because I could start fires with only the help of the sun. I could repeat the process as many times as I wanted, and I never grew bored.

One of the games we enjoyed playing together was Gorodki. In Gorodki, we made a square-shaped area called a Gorodok, which means 'the city.' Inside the city, we would set up five cylindrical pins called 'villages.' We would throw sticks, knocking the villages out of the city. The goal was to do it with as few throws as possible.

I enjoyed playing Gorodki, but I also liked being with our neighbors wandering around the city, discovering new things. I loved hanging around girls, but boys understood when I wanted to play rough and laughed with me when one of us farted. Most girls didn't like that.

While growing up in the orphanage, the boys all slept together on the second floor. The girls had their dorms on the third. Since we didn't always like the same games, it meant we never really spent time together. I was with boys most of every day for the first eleven years of my life.

Wrestling with the other boys was one of my favorite games. I like to prove how strong I was in physical challenges, but sometimes matches, where we wrestled, became confusing too. Of course, it didn't happen with everyone, but I would get odd feelings with some boys, like the feelings I had with Igor. My skin became hot when we wrestled, and my face flushed. I had other sensations, too, in my groin, like everything became tight and constricted and wanting to explode at the same time.

We all had ways we comforted each other growing up with so many people crammed into one building. Everyone needs love, and there were a lot of different ways we expressed it. I loved it when people could touch each other. As a young boy, I never felt like the instructors hugged us enough, or ever really. So, nights like the one I spent holding Igor were the most comforting for me. It happened a lot that we would find comfort being close to each other, and we experimented with how far that could go. We were as curious as any other child about our bodies, and we only had each other to answer those questions.

As I got older, my focus shifted to thoughts of physical attraction. My hormones drove my cravings for touch to become something more. I felt this way about Serhij, as he had the same raging hormones as me. So, many of the games we played at night were different. When everyone went to bed, and the lights were off, Serhij, Slavik, and I sometimes continued our fun by pretending to be striptease boys. We would roll up our boxers to look like the thong underwear dancers wore, and we would dance in front of each other, laughing the whole time.

Serhij also liked to go to the girls' bedroom and visit Masha. I think she wanted Serhij's attention, but Nadya didn't. Of course, she didn't tell anyone that until later, even though they both slept on the same bed.

Serhij would return from their bedroom and brag about his time with girls. He would touch himself a lot as some teenage boys do and I would get very aroused by his actions. I spent many of my nights lost in the moment of watching him, not knowing how to act or what to do.

I often climbed into bed with him at night, after everyone was asleep. I liked to feel his warm skin against mine. It gave me the same comfortable, safe feeling I felt that day in the rain with Igor. When I touched him, everything became quiet in my mind and calm. Unlike the flying in my dreams, it felt more like floating on a boat in the middle of ocean waves, gently rocking me.

After the first time I climbed into bed with Serhij, I felt uncomfortable the next day, not knowing if he wanted to talk about it. He never mentioned it, acting no different than he did any other day. He never told me he did or didn't want me to do what I did, but as time passed, I noticed he would do things to get me excited at night. Maybe he didn't want to feel alone either and just wasn't brave enough to say anything. Realizing he wasn't rejecting me relieved me from the burden of feeling like he might get upset.

Communism forbids boys from touching other boys, and it was a sin in the Greek Orthodox Church as well, where most Ukrainians who weren't communists were members. So, I learned from a very young age that it was not okay to do what I was doing. I felt like what I was doing was wrong, but hugging pillows wasn't enough. They weren't as warm and comforting as I hoped they would be. They often smelled of chlorine, and like anybody else, I needed the feeling of being close to someone.

I wanted to think of my whole life as a game. I wanted to have fun and forget about the difficult things, but to be honest, none of it was a game. Under everything I did was that deep desire in my heart to be loved. Most of what I wanted to do got me into trouble, but I was curious, and I loved to explore, discovering new things. I worked to impress the people around me to inspire them to keep me. I also wanted the love of a mother, but I didn't have it. So, I found ways to get it.

Everything in my life was the same desperate search for happiness I think we all have. I found that happiness with Igor and later with Serhij, but having it put everything else at risk. To the world around me, none of my misadventures were as bad as the thoughts I had or the things I did with other boys. So, I made sure I never told anyone, not even Slavik, and especially not Tyotya Valya. I hid it from her, and I focused on "earning my keep."

I cherished the friends I had by my side and the games we played. I did enjoy the priceless innocence of my childhood as much as I could, but I also lived endless nights of restless dreams and the inexplicable loneliness that nested in my chest. I managed to pretend it wasn't there most of the time, but I was sure that it would always be a part of my soul.

Being close to Serhij was the only thing that made it feel better. Now that Igor and I were apart, I thought he was the only one who ever would. I didn't know then that the person who would make that feeling disappear forever was yet to come into my life and show me what it meant to free the bird trapped fluttering inside of me.

25

New Friends

Masha with her friend, Nadya and her two friends, then the three boys in the front are Slavik, me, and Serhij

SEPTEMBER FIRST IS CALLED "KNOWLEDGE DAY" in Ukraine because it is the day children return to school after the summer break. We were all excited for our first day back to school.

So when we awoke early to the pleasant smell of sausages and fried eggs, followed by the sound of Tyotya Valya's voice telling us to hurry, everyone was happy to listen. We jumped from our beds, quickly dressed, and then rushed to the kitchen to eat.

Tyotya Valya was supposed to come with us that morning since it was our first day at a new school, but for some reason, she didn't. I guess it was because Sasha, her youngest son, was still a little boy, just three years old, and somebody had to look after him. Dyadya Grisha couldn't come either because he worked all day at the brewery, making beer. So, we all headed across the street to catch the bus on our own.

As we were leaving, I turned to see Tyotya Valya standing by the window, watching over us to make sure we walked to the trolleybus stop and didn't head off in some other direction. So maybe she did care sometimes.

We were at the stop only a matter of minutes before trolleybus number two arrived. The moment the doors opened, everyone scrambled to get on first. Of course, we all wanted a seat, almost running over each other to grab one. I hated fighting for a good spot, but we all knew the ride was nearly an hour, which was too long to be standing.

Other students and many adults going to work used the same bus we took to get to school, so we didn't always get to sit the entire trip. Sometimes, there were so many people on the trolleybus the doors wouldn't close properly. The bus driver would yell through the bus, "Does anyone need to get off at the next stop?" If anyone needed to exit, the bus driver would pass the regular stop by a few meters and let people out so that no new people could get in. If no one answered, he would skip the stop and go to the next one. People sometimes waited hours for a bus that had room for them.

Even if we all managed to get our seats, there was always someone who thought they deserved it more, even though we were already using it. So, we often listened to intentionally loud complaints as we stared out the window pretending to observe trees, shops, and streets we had already seen hundreds of times, only to avoid giving up our spots. Sometimes, when we left the house soon enough, we could walk back along the route to the University stop to catch a bus with more available seats.

The stop where we exited was right near the Russka Street Orphanage, which was very close to the orphanage building where I lived, so I knew those streets and buildings and houses like the back of my hand.

Because I started school late, I was in the same grade as Slavik, even though he was a year younger. I didn't mind because I was always happy to have him in my classes with me. As we lined up on our first day, we met all of our teachers. Some of the children already knew them by reputation as they taught their brothers, sisters, and older friends, but I always attended an orphanage school. So, I was going to meet everyone for the first time.

The person I most remember meeting on that day was one of the twenty kids who would be in my class. His name was Zhenya, and he stood behind me during the introduction ceremony.

I was too shy to say anything, but Zhenya came to me immediately, saying, "Hi. Are you Vitaly?"

I was nervous, but I answered, "Yes," and asked him, "How do you know me?"

He replied. "The teacher told me that you came from the orphanage. Is that true? Did you live in an orphanage?"

"Yes, but we moved to foster care."

"Oh, cool. I love to go to the orphanage on Fastivska Street to get fruit sometimes."

I smiled. "That's the orphanage where I lived. I guess I might have seen you there if I hadn't gone to foster care." I noticed that Zhenya's clothes were not as clean as mine, and I wondered if he might be an orphan like me, but his comment told me he must have a family. I guessed they didn't take care of him very well. Still, I enjoyed talking to him and was sure we could have fun hanging out.

"Let's hang out after school sometime. Okay?" I said.

"Yeah! Sometimes my friends and I go to gather apples and pears after school. You are welcome to join us if you want."

"That sounds great," I said. He looked like a decent guy, and I found him somewhat attractive, so I hoped we could become good friends. "I go home that way, so maybe we can go home together sometimes." I offered.

"It sounds great!" he replied. "So, what do you think about your new family?"

"I like it! Slavik is my foster brother," I said, glancing over my shoulder to search for Slavik. I quickly found him and called out, "Come, Slavik, meet Zhenya."

"We live with three other kids that are in the fifth grade. We are on Vavilova Street, in a nice big apartment. It looks great and is almost two times bigger than the last place we lived. I share a room with Slavik and our other friend, Serhij." I explained while I waited for Slavik to join us.

"Oh, that sounds like fun! It sounds like things have worked out just fine for you," Zhenya responded.

Slavik approached and was naturally very quiet, but he did not mind making new friends. So, he shook Zhenya's hand. I could tell he wasn't as interested in the conversation but could see in my eyes that I was eager to speak to Zhenya. So, he stayed, and we all visited until the lineup was over. Then, we said our goodbyes and all went to our classes.

Everyone was excited about our first day of school, which grew to pleasant euphoria once we met our teachers. I liked sitting in front of the teacher, leaving one desk between the window and my desk. Slavik usually sat at that desk, although he didn't like sitting so close to the teachers. Eventually, he would discover the pleasant perks of sitting next to me as he enjoyed correcting his answers during the tests by looking at my paper, but that first day, he wasn't happy about it.

Our class master, Vera Mariyivna, took care of our group and taught us English. I loved her class right away, as I enjoyed learning English, which she recognized and rewarded every time I made progress. She was a great teacher, and I appreciated her attention, but I was also distracted during her class. Even while she was teaching a critical lesson, I couldn't help but stare at her teeth. They popped out of her jaw, looking as if they belonged outside of her lips, and I found it uncomfortably fascinating.

As we finished our English class, we joined another class I loved, information technology. I was always fascinated with technology and planned to enter the world of computers one day. At the time, PCs were still in the early stages of development, and as our school worked with a limited budget, we used old and donated computers. Still, no matter how old the computers were, Informatics was one of my favorite subjects. I was amazed by how I could manipulate software and interact with the computer hardware. I admired technology and everything revolving around computers. My teacher saw my dedication right away and was eager to teach me everything he knew. Another passion was born.

My first day of school was long and exciting, but it eventually came to an end. As we rode the bus towards our building, I recalled everything I experienced that day. I couldn't wait to get home and tell Tyotya Valya everything, but she didn't seem interested in hearing about my day. The moment we walked in the door, the only thing she wanted was for us to do our homework and finish our dinner.

I was almost always the first to finish my homework, even at the orphanage. So, I helped Nadya, Masha, Slavik, and Serhij finish theirs as well, as they struggled with math and physics, a subject where I excelled. Helping them helped me because I wanted to do more fun things with them, and I always made sure that my efforts were rewarded, asking for favors back in the form of sweets or even just the confetti wrappers I was collecting. It was a good deal. I helped them ensure their homework was correct, had extra treats, and we all finished with enough time to play outside before dinner.

As we finished our work, I rushed down the stairs ahead of the rest, stumbling upon our new neighbor. His family had recently moved into an apartment above ours, so we shared the building.

"Hello!" he said.

"Hello to you! What's your name?" I replied.

"My name is Vanya. And yours?"

"My name is Vitaly. Do you live in this building?"

"Yes. My family recently moved in. Two weeks ago, we moved here from Kyiv. My dad was a governor and now teaches at the University. Where are you from?"

"We just moved here too. We lived in a different apartment. I guess it explains why we haven't seen you before on the street."

"We are on the fourth floor."

"I live on the second floor."

"Do you have any friends around?" Vanya asked.

"Yes, I know a couple of friends. You should come with us. We can hang out. We are going out to our favorite place where there are lots of garages, and we can play 'hide and seek' there."

"Yes, with pleasure! But I must be at home to do my homework at eight p.m." He frowned mildly.

"That's okay. We have to be home then too." I replied, "We have dinner at eight."

I introduced Vanya to Serhij and Nadya. Slavik stayed at home that night, still finishing some assignments where he didn't need my help.

We all left together for the garages lined up around the blocks of buildings through our neighborhood. We often looked for the unsupervised, empty garages and made up games to play in them until our dinner time would come. As it started raining while we were still on the streets playing hide and seek, we took Vanya to our secret hideout. It was a perfect place to play and find respite from the rain, as well.

After our introductions, I started to hang out with Vanya whenever I could, playing with him until our dinner time would come. Vanya liked hanging out with us, and I enjoyed his company, but not long after meeting him, he stopped showing up, and we had an empty place in our group once again.

I remember him mentioning something about his parents discouraging him from spending time with our group. I always thought it was because they were from a reputable class and didn't want their son following our footsteps or copying our behavior, although I wasn't sure why someone would think that we were poor company.

Whenever I would run into him in the hallway, he would say, "Hi," but only if his parents weren't around. When they were there, he would look at the ground, too embarrassed to look at me, obviously respecting his parents' wishes. I was okay with that as long as he was fine. It wasn't his fault, and I always had my friends to play with after finishing my homework. So, it felt good to let him have his life, knowing I would not be alone.

Besides my friends at home, I also had Zhenya. Every time after school, when Zhenya was heading towards his home, I tried to walk the short distance to his house with him before going to the stop to catch my trolleybus and go home. I did everything I could to spend time with him. He was very handsome, and he liked the same things I liked, but the things I loved most were his pretty eyes and smile. I was utterly infatuated and wanted to spend as much time with him as

I could.

I walked with him and helped him with math. We often returned to the orphanage, collecting juicy pears and apples after classes, catching up with my old friends, or spending time alone in the orchard. My favorite times together were when we would go to the orchard and wrestle. He was strong, and I liked the feeling of his strength pushing up against mine. We would both fight to win, but winning wasn't all I wanted. I liked how it felt to wrap my hand around the muscles on his shoulders or feel his thick thigh pressed against mine. He liked it too, often lingering a moment with his breath hot on my neck before the grappling would begin again.

He was stronger than me, and sometimes he made me cry, not because he beat me, but because I felt like he rejected me when he was too aggressive. It sometimes felt like he hurt me intentionally. I don't know why he was angry, but I think sometimes he took that anger out on me when we were fighting.

One time I was so upset, I went to sit under a tree, and I cried. I cried so hard I curled up on the ground, wishing I still had my pillow to hold.

Zhenya came and laid behind me, wrapping his arms around me, saying, "Don't cry, Vitaly. I didn't mean to hurt you."

I didn't respond at first, but he began rubbing my back, and I felt better. No one had ever rubbed my back before. I was always touching someone or cuddling up to them, trying to get as close as I could, but he was the one rubbing me this time. I felt so loved. I couldn't be angry at him for hurting me anymore. He was so kind now.

As we lay there, I noticed the feeling of something hard against the back of my thigh, and I knew what it was. The familiar feeling of heat rushed through my body, making my breath heavy. He continued to rub my arm and back, gradually moving his hand around my waist to touch the front of my pants. I reached my hands back to touch him, as well.

Something happened to me that day. Something different from my games with Serhij. My heart raced, and I think I surrendered. I was never sure if I was doing something wrong before, but it was different with Zhenya. He never pulled away from me. He also wanted someone to touch him and hold him. I never knew anyone since Igor, who also didn't want to be alone. I had a crush on Serhij for a long time. Even up to secondary school, we wrestled, but it wasn't the same. My time with Zhenya was different. It meant more to me than anything else I had in my life. I knew he would never turn me away, but how was I supposed to live the life I wanted and know society would not accept me. I wanted a home and a family with children someday, but I didn't know how to have that and feel this kind of joy, as well.

Maybe, I needed this more. I wasn't sure. I was confused, but there was no one else to love me. I wanted to spend my time being loved, touched, and held by someone who wanted to hold me just as much as I wanted to hold them, but what if someone found out. I didn't know what would happen to us if they did.

26

The Power of Words

I am performing for one of the talent shows, reciting my poem, and showcasing my handmade baskets.

I ALWAYS ADMIRED MY TEACHERS, thinking that it must take a lot of courage to hold such an important role. As a teacher, you must be patient, friendly, highly educated, and specialized in your subject. You must also possess the ability to pass your knowledge onto your students, knowing you might spark something to make them want to study your subject further and make a profession of it. Moreover, a teacher must deal with thirty or more different personalities and try to get the best out of every child in each class.

Teachers open a passion for learning and the potential of opening doors. They offer relationships and sometimes feed the emptiness created by abandonment. Teachers like Martha were the parents I never had. When I did well in school, they gave me the attention and the admiration I needed to build confidence. Even Tyotya Valya was proud of me when I did well in school, or she was less cruel, at least. Good grades meant no punishments.

Not all my teachers were as great as they should have been, but I know that some of them will forever be on my mind. They wanted me to succeed, and they were willing to help me do that. They showed me the many gifts education brought. The more I saw how school improved my life, the more I hoped to go to university one day. They taught me to succeed and gave me the hope that maybe my mom and Tyotya Valya and all the people in my life could see how much I have to give to the world.

I've heard it said that success is ten percent talent and ninety percent practice. I think it also requires encouragement. As I moved beyond middle school and entered senior education classes, my favorite teachers, Ganna Svitlanivna and Olga Larysivna, were the most adept at motivating their classes. They taught with understanding and always tried to make their subjects intriguing and comprehensive. As I had a natural affinity for physics and math, which later led me to engineering studies at the University of Chernivtsi, Ganna Svitlanivna and Olga Larysivna always encouraged me to do well in those subjects. They helped me develop my talents and go beyond my past capabilities, continually testing my knowledge, intelligence, and skills.

There were also strict teachers I didn't enjoy as much, but I did well in secondary school. My grades were always top of my class, but those instructors didn't inspire me to enjoy their classes much. One of our most rigid teachers, Mariya Vasylivna, was a great teacher, although I always thought she took her subject more seriously than she should, making us take long classes with endless dictates. She was teaching our native language, and I loved the sound of it, only that I thought that her lectures were a little boring. I imagine it wasn't uncomplicated teaching us a language we were speaking, even in our dreams, but I think she could have still brought a little more excitement to her lessons. She might have encouraged me to do more.

Occasionally, she took a break from saying so much, allowing us an opportunity to do the one thing I did enjoy in her class—poetry. I loved memorizing the long poems of brilliant Ukrainian poets, and we had a lot of those to remember during my school years. For example, I remember studying "Kamenyari," a poem written by one of the most brilliant Ukrainian poets ever to live, Ivan Franko. Kamenyari, translated to English, means "The Stone Breakers." It was one of my favorite poems, and as it had almost fifty long lines, it was a real treat to recite it from memory.

Ivan Franko disapproved of the Soviet system, and he wrote the poem as a metaphor for the tyranny under which we were living. The stone in the poem was representative of slavery, and the stone breaker or "Kamenyar" was Ivan himself, breaking the shackles of oppression and dreaming about freedom. He lived his life speaking out against the totalitarianism he experienced while we were under Soviet rule. For all he accomplished while he was alive, they made a statue depicting him as a Kamenyar, which he was.

I remember reading that he lived as a poor man, barely having enough to eat, neglected for his talents, and left by everyone. He lived his life alone and eventually died alone, as well. Through reading his poem, I was able to feel his desperation and pain, but the will to fight as well. His words reflected, to me, some moments of my life. I admired him, so none of his poems were difficult to remember.

In addition to Franko's work, we paid respect to other brilliant Ukrainian poets as well, studying "In Eternal Memory of Kotlyarevsky" and "If Only You Know the Rulers" by Taras Shevchenko and one of my favorite poems, "Seamstress" by Pavlo Grabowski. Even though Mariya Vasylivna's class wasn't one of my favorites, the brilliant poems we were studying inspired me. Learning about them taught me more about my urge for artistic expression and the need to transform feelings and emotions into words.

Most of the poems I wrote in her class were about my mother. As I practiced my writing skills, I tried to depict everything I felt. My thoughts had always revolved around her, no matter how often I tried to walk away. I felt stifled, trying to understand why she made the choices she did. I searched for resolution through my poems, trying to explain my life to anyone who would listen.

As if on cue, Mariya gave us an assignment, asking us to write an essay about our mothers. I wrote a poem. I still remember the heavy silence that fell upon the room as I recited it to the class.

Mom, why have you left me early in life?
Why? I am asking you. I'd understand.
Have I caused any pain and scars?
Tell me more to your only friend.

Try to remember, my mom, how I've spoken.
My first sounds to you in your arms;
Then when I grew up a little bit older
I've written poems about you, mom.

Again, I whisper to myself, "My Mother."

Again, I'm sketching these words with such zeal.
Again, these letters appear "My Mother."
Again, I'm searching for a smile in a dream.

Why could not I love you, my mother?
Why could not I say to you, "My Mom?"
My heart was broken; my soul was devoured.
But I believed you were the one.

When will I hear your voice so tender?
Carried through the air to me by the winds?
When will I catch it, will it deliver
Happiness, joy, and fulfill all my dreams?

Will that voice teach me first letters?
Will that voice bring me a smile?
Will it remind me of my childhood years
That vanished away from me for a while?

When can I write to you, my mother,
A few poems about us in a dream?
So, you know your son is now older,
So, I can hear, like a nightingale, you sing.

I think I can. Believe me, my mother,
To love you deeply in my adulthood heart.
And scars and pain will be gone forever.
You are my family, and we are now one.

All eyes were on me as I stood in front of the blackboard, feeling naked and vulnerable and full of pride for the feeling I put into my work. At that moment, I knew that everyone in the class felt compassion for me, as most couldn't imagine what it was like to live without a mother by your side. They all had their mothers cooking for them, taking care of them, singing to them, reading bedtime stories, and what was most important, caring for them and watching them grow.

Oksana, one of the girls in my class I admired, was always polite, kind, and very smart. She could solve even the most complicated math problems, often doing math with me. Today, I saw her hiding her face from the rest of the class as she sobbed quietly. Although I felt sad to see her affected by my poem, I was also amazed by how the words could summon her compassion.

Even the most brutal boy in the class, Oleksiy, who was something like a class leader, approached me after our session ended. "So," he said, hesitating, "you live in an orphanage?"

"Not anymore. I live with my friends and a foster family now."

"What is it like? Are they treating you well?" He was careful not to be too pushy, which I appreciated.

"It's great. We get to live just like anyone else, except I get to live with my friends."

"Cool!" He smiled, and I could feel the somber mood lifting, "That sounds really awesome, you know?"

"Thanks, I guess," I mumbled, surprised by the course of our conversation.

"Hey, Vitaly," he said as he was leaving. "Let me know if there is anything I can do to help you out."

"Thanks, Oleksiy...."

He was indeed one of the strongest boys in school, so his affection meant that I had a protector from potential bullying, and there was a lot of that around the school. Even though children are often considered innocent and pure, it is surprising how cruel they can be at times. Oleksiy's help came in very handy.

As everyone recognized my talent for writing poems, they often invited me to write and present my poetry to various school events and even those initiated by the government. Many of my teachers committed to helping me develop my talent. I loved writing, but as I did it more, I began to understand why Mariya Vasylivna was so demanding. It wasn't always easy.

She did ask a lot from us, but I learned that the key to great poems, aside from expressing your emotions and using metaphors, was using correct grammar, format, and punctuation. She taught me how powerful words could be and how to use them to inspire the soul. However, she also helped me understand how they could devastate it.

27

History Lesson

I loved spending time in the Computer Science room filled with Electron computers made in the USSR. Lines of code on the blackboard are in a BASIC programming language.

EVERY DAY I LOOKED FORWARD TO SCHOOL and learning new things. Then, after school, I would see Zhenya and pick a few apples and pears on my way home. My life felt so amazing.

Although math and physics were my favorite classes at the school, I also enjoyed history. Most of the students yawned at just the mention of the word, but I liked to hear interesting stories about our country's origins and the events that changed them.

Our first day began with a brief account of World War II. Our teacher wanted to remind us of the horrible events occurring during those frightening years. I was stunned and terrified by the stories he shared with us, thinking about how people can do great things, but sometimes those things can turn into real-life nightmares. Each story began with one man wanting to be all-powerful and ended with catastrophic consequences that caused thousands of people to suffer poverty, death, and loss.

I think everyone in the class struggled to understand the reasons for such horrible events. I often closed my eyes, imagining that I lived during those unbearable times. I imagined being scared, lonely, and frightened, unable to find my way home. I wasn't even sure if I had a home. Chaos was everywhere, a thousand lips were screaming, and I didn't know what to do or where to go.

I would soon need to open my eyes, grateful I wasn't alive then, but I remembered that my mother was a baby during that war. I wondered where my grandparents lived at the time and what they were doing to survive. I've never met my grandparents. I didn't even know if they survived the war. Was my grandfather a soldier? Was my grandmother forced to take care of my mother all by herself? What was the story of my family history?

I didn't know anything about who I was and how I ended up in an orphanage. I felt like I had no roots to hold me to the ground. What did my mother go through as a child? Maybe I could understand my story if someone gave me some history about her.

The teacher changed from the subject of battle to talking about relations between the countries. I tried to focus on him and throw away the questions I couldn't answer, but they never disappeared completely.

That night I fell into a world created by the mist of dreams. I was in slippers, shorts, and a t-shirt, running through the darkness. It was cold, and I could hear monsters speaking. They were running around in madness, killing people. I was trying to figure out what was happening as I watched people's lives ending in pain and agony.

The creatures had cloaks, all dressed in black, as they were growling at people, running around through strange masks they wore over their faces. I didn't understand their language. Still, as their voices broke through the night, I knew what they were saying. "Get them! Wipe them off from the face of the Earth! I want them all dead and gone by midnight!"

I could barely see through the thick darkness around me. Chaos was unraveling everywhere, and I didn't know why I was there, running around clueless with my heart in my throat. My slippers were continually falling off my feet as I tried to speed up and run away. Why was I wearing slippers? It didn't make sense. I didn't know what I was doing, nor what I was supposed to do. So, I hid in the bushes.

I watched the creatures as my shorts and shirt suddenly transformed into a towel wrapped around my waist, the knot at my hip the only thing keeping it in place. They concealed their faces beneath black robes, but something was missing from the garment. I wasn't sure what. That's when a flashback hit me. I knew I should place red threads on the black robes to end this madness and finish them all. I searched the ground around me, trying to find a way to stop them when I realized that I was holding the threads in my hand the entire time.

As I carefully approached the creatures, a man ran in front of me. He was a blur, cutting off my path to jump onto one of them.

"We will always be here. We will always be a part of you. You can't control that!" one of the creatures said to the man, lifting him in the air with an invisible force.

They struggled for some time, and although I wanted to help, I couldn't. I stood frozen, not in fear but wrapped instead in the inexplicable strings of my dream. Sometimes, no matter how hard I tried, my dreams just wouldn't let me do what my mind wanted to do. Like when I tried to run faster, everything would move in slow motion, controlling me beyond my comprehension and set above my will.

I could barely breathe, covered in a cold sweat, my forehead burning with fever. Then, something in me shifted, and I realized where I was. I was in a dream. I made peace knowing the image around me wasn't real. The creatures left as soon as that happened, leaving only the black robes behind.

As I looked around, I saw the man was still lying on the ground, joining hundreds of lifeless bodies, all merged into one catastrophic moment I couldn't handle. So, I forced myself to wake up. Luckily, I didn't scream, so I didn't need to explain why I was wide awake in the middle of the night.

All I could think as I lay my head back on the pillow was that I wanted to hold it instead like I did when I was a little boy alone in the orphanage. Who were the monsters in my dream, I wondered? Who gets to decide they will crucify all those people? I wished I had someone in my life to explain these times of tragedy to me. Unfortunately, I couldn't talk about it, especially with Tyotya Valya. I knew she wouldn't care.

We didn't go to church often, but I did go to bible studies whenever I could. I remember learning the story of Sodom and Gomorrah. The bible said that divine judgment destroyed the cities of Sodom and Gomorrah as punishment for their sins. I wonder who decided what a sin was and what was okay.

I wondered if it would be the same for me if the people around me knew my secret. Would they react like the monsters in my dream? I didn't want my life to be a sin, but I couldn't deny what I felt when I was around boys like Zhenya. I couldn't resist spending time with him, maybe because I didn't know why it was wrong.

When the Nazis killed millions of Jewish people in the name of God, was that different than God destroying Sodom and Gomorrah in the name of love?

28

My Sweet Sixteen

This is me at 16. I took a picture for my passport in the same turtleneck sweater.

THE WEATHER USUALLY WRAPPED MY BIRTHDAYS in rain, fog, and cold wind, but my sixteenth year began with falling snow. It snowed for most of the day, not stopping until the evening sky sparked against it. Turning sixteen seemed like a massive number for me, though I already felt much older.

I always thought being born was a good reason to celebrate, but my life told a different story. It was too expensive to celebrate birthdays at the orphanage. Over three hundred children lived there, so I never had a day that was just mine, nothing to tell me I was special. I wonder, what could show better that not all life is important than a building filled with abandoned children?

Living with my foster family was a little different. Even though we didn't get to throw a party and invite friends, we did have a small celebration. Everyone in our house loved Lady Caprice cake, and Tyotya Valya made it for birthdays and other special occasions. We all got only one piece of cake per day, which annoyed me. It was my cake and my day, but Tyotya Valya's rules every time, but still, I was grateful. She did give me a bigger slice than the others. Also, Lady Caprice cake was very complicated to make. It had seven layers of honey dough smothered with boiled condensed milk, buttercream, and sprinkles of nuts and grated chocolate. It was one of the most delicious sweets I've ever tasted, and Tyotya Valya's was the best.

In addition to the cake, my sixteenth birthday was the first time I got something special. Dyadya Grisha and Tyotya Valya decided to buy me a water-resistant mechanical watch. I loved my present, but it also reminded me of my summer in Sweden. One of the many gifts they gave me during my visit was a Casio electronic watch. I liked it more than the mechanical version, but Dyadya Grisha decided that the first watch would look better on his wrist than mine and took it without question.

They took all of my gifts and dispersed them to their family, telling me I had to share. But I guess now it was my turn to have a watch of my own. I don't know if they were trying to redeem themselves, but I didn't say anything. I loved mechanical watches, and this was my first genuine gift from them that was not clothes or shoes bought to replace the threadbare garments we usually wore. So, I decided to treat it as a special gift from the first time I put it on my wrist.

Dyadya Grisha was happy to see me happy, smiling and patting my head before he went to work. While we waited for Tyotya Valya to make lunch, I laid my head on the watch and listened to its endlessly ticking. It was very soothing and gave me hope for better years to come.

After our lunch was over, we had our piece of cake and went to our room. That was it. Tyotya Valya didn't want more time with us than that. Still, we didn't mind. We had a Monopoly game in our room, so we decided to play it. We loved playing Monopoly. Everyone was highly competitive. So Monopoly made us fight a lot, as we were taking the game too seriously, but we had fun too. We cheated each other, looking for ways to own as much property as possible, filling them with tiny houses and hotels.

When we were near the end of the game, baby Sasha came into the room uninvited and began wrecking the board with his meaty hands and feet. I wasn't happy with him, so I pulled him aside, away from the game.

Though I didn't hit him and never meant to hurt him, he started crying in a high-pitched tone that made my chest pulse. "Sasha, come on...." I said, trying to make him stop, but it was too late.

As expected, Tyotya Valya appeared at the door to our room, her face swollen in rage, "What did you do?!"

I never had a chance to answer. Instead, she just yelled until her voice was the only thing you could hear in the entire apartment, saying, "... How dare you do that to my son?!!"

I boiled with rage in return, forgetting everything I ever knew about her. She didn't even know what I did. I jumped from the ground and fired back with my tone raised as never before, "He came in and started wrecking everything! Do we wreck his toys?!" I was out of my mind, feeling like I had left my body.

"Don't you dare yell at me!! Don't you dare even look at me the wrong way, got it!?" Though I thought it impossible, Tyotya Valya's voice became even louder.

"I don't see the difference between you yelling at me and me trying to defend myself!" I was still trying to make things right. I didn't see any reason for Tyotya Valya to be yelling. We hadn't done anything wrong.

Blinded by my rage and provoked by her merciless shooting, I couldn't hold myself back. I said everything I hadn't said in the last four years of living here, and finally, Tyotya Valya became quiet. Then, she marched out of the room.

I knew she couldn't afford to lose her authority. Our altercation couldn't be over so quickly. So I listened as she marched through the hallway and into the kitchen, where I knew she had been boiling linen. Everything was still and quiet for a moment, bringing my attention to the feeling of humidity in the air mingling with the scent of laundry powder.

When she returned to the room, she carried the stick she used for mixing the laundry. She usually used it to stir the boiling water and remove all the dirt and stains from our many adventures. Unfortunately, I knew she planned to use it for something else this time. Tyotya Valya always looked like she was ready to boil over, but the look on her face as she approached me with the stick was different. It was calm and clear, and I knew I had crossed a line. Nothing, not even the fact that it was my birthday, could save me now.

Everything happened in slow motion as I watched her raise the stick above my head, aiming to hit me. I managed to soften the impact on my body by crossing my hands over my head before she could bring it down for the first blow.

I felt red-hot welts forming along my arms, from the wrists to elbows. I didn't know how long her fury would boil inside of her, but I also wasn't in a place to find out. After several blows, my rage boiled again, and I took the stick out of her hands, breaking it in half across my leg.

I don't know why I was so angry. It wasn't the first time she hit me, but I think I had decided it would be the last. Maybe, I was in shock, or perhaps I had finally had enough. I couldn't believe she would do this on my birthday, ruining the whole day for all of us. Whatever the reason, before that day, I was unaware I dared to do anything against her.

Once she realized I had broken her stick, she started mumbling something and exited the room, marching through the hallway again. I knew she wouldn't give in. She was looking for something else to finish her task. So, I ran towards the door, rushing out of the apartment with only what I was wearing.

Tyotya Valya followed me, watching me make my way to the building's entrance, yelling at me the entire way. "Come here, boy! Don't make me chase you!" Her voice echoed across the empty hall as she lifted the new stick she had found in the air, waving it at me.

I looked at her, struggling between facing her and running away. Finally, I decided it would be wiser to run. So, I burst through the door and ran down the steps to the frigid streets, feeling exposed to shame, loneliness, and the stubborn snowflakes that were still falling from the sky.

I walked the streets for some time without a coat and with snow melting through my sneakers. Still, I didn't feel the pain. I didn't look for ways to excuse my actions or think of apologizing. Instead, the only thing I could comprehend was getting even. So I thought of serving my revenge cold without telling anyone about my plans.

As I thought of things that could hurt Tyotya Valya the most, the only thing that crossed my mind was the apartment where we lived. I knew she would do anything to have the apartment only for herself and her children. The fact that her family had to share a home that belonged to abandoned children was a thorn in her side. So she liked to forget the circumstances under which she got the apartment in the first place and plan for what she would get out of it.

She knew that we wouldn't be around much longer, as we would become self-sufficient once we turned eighteen, and I had no doubt she would find a way to put us out on the streets the moment that happened, but I had another plan. I was only two years away from the day when she could say "Get out!" without even blinking, so I had to do something to make sure that Nadya, Masha, Serhij, Slavik, and I wouldn't end up on the streets, and would ruin her plans the way she destroyed my birthday.

It was still early in the afternoon. So, I went to talk to the social workers. They claimed on several occasions that they gave us the apartment to keep us safe and sound even after we turned eighteen.

"Vitaly, what are you doing here and without a coat?" Vira Mykhailivna, the social worker who had visited our home several times, was surprised to see me in her office, but I think she was even more surprised to see me so poorly dressed on such a winter's day.

I didn't answer her. I had questions of my own. "You said you worked for us more than you work for Tyotya Valya, right?"

She looked at me, and I saw the realization in her face. I don't know if it was the welts on my arms or the puddle my wet clothes were making on her floor, but I saw Vira become determined to help me. "Sit down," she said, throwing me a donated sweater that was sitting on one of the office chairs. Then, she sat across from me, pulling my file from her desk. "The answer is in getting a passport and signing it with your apartment address as your residence. That way, you have proof the apartment is registered in your name when you become an adult. That would make it yours legally.

"As you are nearly...." She paused to look at the file and grimaced before she continued, "...already sixteen... Oh dear, today. Vitaly, I'm so sorry. I can help you get a passport."

She spent the next couple of hours with me, making my plan a reality. She took me to get a photo, finish the paperwork, and take care of everything I needed. The work was tiring, but I knew that the result would go in my favor, so I stuck with it.

That night, when I came back home, I was so grateful that kind workers like Vira existed. Thanks to her, I returned home knowing it was my house, and she couldn't take it from me. So, I felt no fear in facing Tyotya Valya, but I knew I had more to do to ensure it stayed that way.

Before going into the building, I started looking around, searching for a pebble or small rock. I knew that the windows of our room looked over the streets to the west of our building. I remember watching sunsets at night, so grateful we had such a view. I also knew that everyone would be in there playing, away from Tyotya Valya's rage. So I gathered several stones from the ground and started throwing them at the window.

Slavik opened it, saying, "Vitaly! You are here."

"Open the doors, please!" I whispered to him as loud as I could.

He disappeared from the window, so I rushed into the building to wait until he opened the doors.

I entered the apartment quietly, whispering, "Where is she?"

"In the kitchen," I could barely hear Slavik. He was so quiet. I don't remember ever seeing Slavik so afraid, but at that moment, he looked like he might have been the one she attacked. He almost was when he tried to defend me, telling her it was Sasha who had ruined our game and that I hadn't done anything wrong.

Tyotya Valya had turned on him, but I stepped forward again, taking the brunt of her rage. I couldn't let her hurt Slavik, but I could see that he was still afraid she might want to try.

I wasn't afraid anymore. So, I slipped into the room, trying to ignore Slavik's and Serhij's worried expressions, and put on some dry clothing.

Nadya was in the room. She was also worried. She was the first to ask, "Where have you been?"

"Shhh." Slavik's hush was almost as loud as her question.

I looked around to see if Masha was around. She wasn't, which was perfect. I could tell them about my plan. Masha was devoted to Tyotya Valya, so I couldn't afford the risk of revealing anything to her yet. I wanted Tyotya Valya to feel the sting of it, the way I was still feeling the sting of her strikes against me. Besides, if she didn't know, she couldn't make a plan. By the time she realized what was happening, it would be too late.

"I got my passport, guys. That means we can keep my part of the apartment without Tyotya Valya taking it away when the time comes. Once you are sixteen, I'll help you do the same. We won't tell Masha until it's almost her eighteenth birthday, or this won't work. So, you have to be quiet about this. If we do it correctly, we can't have our apartment taken. It belongs to us."

They looked at me silently, and I knew they understood the importance of what I was saying, and I knew, when the time came, they would do as I asked. Everyone looked up to me as the oldest, and they would follow my lead. Serhij and Slavik were next in line, so I knew they could get their passports in June. I eventually explained the benefits to Masha, and she went at the end of the summer. Nadya was the youngest by two years and would need to wait, but everyone would do what they needed to do when the time came.

Tyotya Valya did not leave the kitchen before Dyadya Grisha was home that night, probably because she thought I was locked out, standing in the cold. Masha stayed in the kitchen with her, helping with dinner, and I knew no one else would tell on me. By the time she saw me come out of the bedroom to eat, it was over. We both had time to cool off, and Dydya Grisha was there to stop her from continuing her assault if she tried. I knew there was nothing more she could do that night, but things never returned to the way they were between us.

I went to bed early, not wanting to think of the unfortunate circumstances that occurred or stoke the embers that were probably still burning under Tyotya Valya's calm demeanor. When I returned to my room, I saw my new watch was gone. When I asked about it, Slavik told me she took it back. I wasn't surprised, but I was angry. That was the only gift Tyotya Valya had ever given me that was all mine. I couldn't believe she had taken it back.

I knew that things could have ended differently. I could have remained silent and put up with her yelling. Still, I was glad I didn't. I couldn't let myself take another punishment I didn't deserve or believe that she deserved to take anything else from me. No matter how many times I went over the situation in my mind, I just couldn't make myself regret or change what had already happened.

I felt strange as I lay alone in my room, watching snowflakes fall from the night sky. Snow always gave birth to little butterflies in my stomach, stirring memories of cold fingers and snowball fights. It was always so comforting to remember what we did as children. But, this time, I knew my life would never be about playing in the snow again. It was time for me to make a plan for the future, to figure out a way to take care of my brothers and sisters before Tyotya Valya tried to take everything away.

29

Christmas Traditions

Traditional Christmas meal with my foster family left to right: My Babushka Halina (Tyotya Valya's mother), Dyadya Grisha's mother, Dyadya Grisha's nephew, Dyadya Grisha, Nadya, me, Nastya's daughter, Nastya, Masha, Tyotya Valya, and Sasha.

I LOVED DAYS THAT WEREN'T ORDINARY, days filled with a magical quality of importance and celebration. Of course, I never enjoyed facing the harsh realities of the following morning when the magic would suddenly vanish again, but that never stopped me from believing. When I woke up on the next holiday, I always felt that things could change, that everything would be alright.

One of the holidays I liked was on December nineteenth, when we celebrated Svyatyy Mykolay, who Americans called St. Nichola. Like Santa Clause in the west, Svyatyy Mykolay, or Father Frost as we sometimes called him, was a favorite of most children in Ukraine.

I remember celebrating the festivities at the orphanage. From the moment we opened our eyes, we knew it would be a great day, as there would be food and presents for us. The presents came from the donations of people who still had some kindness in their hearts. People would bring toys and clothes and my favorite, candy. I was grateful to the generous people, though most of my thoughts didn't stay with them long as I would rather guess what my gifts would be.

Like most Ukrainian families, we would have a big dinner, and our teachers would make bags filled with candy to give to us. As we received our bounty, our educators shared stories about St. Nicholas. Those stories were the reason I appreciated the holidays.

"The story of St. Nicholas goes hundreds of years back," one of our teachers would say. "He came from one of the few families who were rich at that time, but that didn't affect his feeling of empathy, as he always shared everything he had with those who were less fortunate. From him, we learn to share and help each other."

Though most of us had heard the story many times before, we sat with wide-eyed anticipation, waiting for them to tell us what St. Nicholas would do next.

I always thought that his life taught us something, so I was happy to share presents and gifts to honor him. Members of the Greek Orthodox Church were very generous, which made me think a lot about how communism tried to take their religious beliefs away. I didn't experience a lot of religion, nothing more than what Martha taught me. So, I often didn't know what to believe, but I always felt that God was there, giving me strength and supporting me when I needed help, but God could not hold me as a Mother could. I was grateful to have Him in my life, but He couldn't wrap his arms around me or make me feel like someone special.

Still, having faith helped me feel like I was a part of something greater, some bigger plan that included everyone. Not having much as a child, I often put the abstract above the material, so my wishes usually revolved around those things you couldn't buy. I believed celebrations and holidays brought people together, summoning the kindness I knew we all had buried deep inside. I thank my educators for teaching me that.

Despite the many people maniacally indulging in Christmas and New Year's sales and discounts, I was at peace whenever I walked along busy streets decorated with holiday cheer. I loved the holidays and how everyone wanted to greet January first as a better and more generous version of themselves than they were the rest of the year. So, here I was, part of a massive movement of great expectations and wishes for the coming year, having some of my own, as well.

St. Nicholas Day, New Years Day, and Christmas Eve celebrations were great distractions from everyday dullness. However, they also stirred the desire to be loved. I often wondered what my mother was doing during the holidays. I dreamt of family celebrations with her and Roustam, all of us sitting around the tree laughing and loving each other. The thoughts stirred a dull ache in my chest and questions I didn't know how to answer. Was she alone? Was she lonely? Did she think of me, at least for a moment? I didn't know, and I wished I didn't care, but sometimes I did.

My dreams of Roustam slowly died the longer we lived with Tyotya Valya. She didn't do much to make St. Nicholas Day memorable for us.

Except to prepare a nice dinner and give us the chance to eat meat, to her, it was an ordinary day. We didn't receive presents or tell stories. I never knew if she wasn't aware of the importance of St. Nicholas or if she just lacked the will to make that day special, but St. Nicholas Day was just like any other day of the year.

We still had our New Year festivities to look forward to, although it wasn't as fun as our educators made it at the orphanage. We didn't dress up in costumes to showcase our talents or open our presents under the big tree. Instead, Tyotya Valya prepared tasty dishes, including cake, sweets, and even more meat. She cooked the entire day so that we could all spend our evening enjoying the spirit of the New Year celebration, but it wasn't just for us. The biggest celebrations in our house only came when Tyotya Valya and Dyadya Grisha had their friends and family joining us.

Tyotya Valya would always prepare the best meals when they would come, and we would eat together as we watched the New Year's celebrations on television. Then, we would talk until early morning with her and Dyadya Grisha's family members and friends.

After the New Year's celebrations were over, most Ukrainians began preparing for January seventh, the day we celebrated Christmas. As the Greek Orthodox church uses the Julian calendar to recognize Jesus' birth, our Christmas Eve was not on December twenty-fourth, but on January sixth instead, making January seventh our Christmas Day.

No matter the day, the spirit of Christmas was the same as it might be in any Christian home. For us, it also meant we would spend the day with Tyotya Valya's mother, Halina. Babushka, or Grandmother, Halina loved talking about Christmas. It reminded me of listening to the stories of St. Nicholas told in the orphanage, but she was not quite as cheerful.

She asked us to sit around her as she inflated like a balloon, full of pride like she was the only one worthy of sharing the story of how

Christmas began, "We count our days on Earth from this day forward. On this day, hundreds of years ago, the Son of God was born as our savior...." She sighed and made a significant pause to observe our faces, inexplicable pride written on her wrinkles as she continued, "Jesus' mother, the Virgin Mary, and her husband Joseph lived in Nazareth. Although Mary was pregnant, they traveled the long journey to Bethlehem to oblige the Roman Emperor Augustus' order. But as they arrived, Bethlehem was swarming with people, and Mary and Joseph couldn't find a place to sleep."

Even though I read the story many times in bible class, I listened with great dedication, waiting for her to continue. It seemed she enjoyed having all the eyes in the room on her as she spoke. "They finally stopped at a house, asking the landlords to give them a place to stay for the night, but the owner of the house said that there is no place for them. As his wife saw that Mary was pregnant, she felt sorry for her and offered to let them spend the night in the stable.

"As they entered the stables, grateful for the woman's generosity, Mary saw three bright stars shining upon them from the sky, and she knew that she would give birth to the Lord's son that very night.

"And so it was... Mary gave birth to Jesus, and that night the angel descended from the Heavens to tell all the shepherds that their Lord, the son of God, was born. They hurried to the stable to kneel and worship. Following the same star, the Three Kings, also called the three wise men, came to give their gifts to the son of God.

"One of the Kings gave him gold as a symbol of royal power, to wish him to rule righteously and with might. The second gave him incense as a symbol of God's will and as a reminder to let God rule his life. Finally, the third King gave him myrrh to express his faith that God had sent us His prophet." Her eyes sparkled, as ours did, too, lit up at the thoughts we were having of the presents Jesus received.

"Thousands of lamps were lit that night by the believers to shine the way for their savior. We put a candle in the window to this day to remember and share our faith with the world. Our candle also welcomes wanderers without families to join our celebration of this special time." I didn't know how many people Tyotya Valya would invite into her home. Still, Babushka Halina's words reminded me of walking the streets and seeing all the windows lit with candles and how some of those people probably would welcome strangers into their homes.

"Jesus performed many miracles in his life, and that is why we celebrate this day with devotion and faith." Babushka Halina ended her story here, nodding her head continuously to prove her point. Her last words erased the pleasant memories I was having of love floating like stars through the streets of Chernivtsi and brought me back to the room.

Listening to the stories of Jesus reminded me of Martha again, and the night she introduced us to the God our families weren't allowed to worship. I thought of Jesus and how faith in him put love in the eyes of those who believed. Even long after being gone, he helped people feel better about life and who they could be. It was remarkable to me that we had teachers like Jesus and St. Nicholas to help us be the best we could be, but still, people could be greedy. At times, the holidays did have the smell of hypocrisy, as everyone was not always so generous. It would be nice to have Christmas every day of the year, not just for the presents, but for our feelings when giving them. Still, I guess that feeling special for one day was still better than not feeling special at all.

After listening to Babushka Halina's story on January sixth, we all went to the church to honor the Christmas Eve celebration. Although it was Christian, our church had a lot of different ways of worshiping God. For instance, in Ukraine, Orthodox Churches have no seats. Instead, believers stand during the liturgies. Every time Tyotya Valya took me to church, she stopped me on the front steps, telling me to take off my hat, cross myself three times, kiss the church entrance doors, and then enter. Inside, there was more kissing to do, as I also had to kiss the icon standing in the middle of the church, the bishop's hand, the sacrament bowl, and too many other things to count.

I always wanted to ask why we had to do all these things, and Tyotya Valya always had the same answers, whispering fervently, "You desecrate God's name. He died for our sins, and you are born as a sinner. You live as a sinner, and without redemption, you will die as a sinner."

I always thought she didn't like me very much. Well, I guess she didn't like anyone, as she was always grumpy and complaining about everything. Still, I had to buy a candle and kiss it before lighting it to remit my sins. I didn't understand the meaning of redemption, as it wasn't clear to me what I did that was so wrong that I should need to redeem myself, but I followed the rules.

During the ceremony, Babushka Halina never took her eyes off me. I was bored and struggled to stay upright as we stood for hours listening to the liturgy spoken in the Old Slavic language. I didn't understand a word, although I tried hard to understand it and keep myself awake. After coming to the church services a few times, I set a goal to read the old Orthodox books that Babushka Halina brought with her from her village to learn how to pray in the Slavic language. I always felt empowered when I spoke the original language of the first apostles and saints of the church.

After the sermon was complete, Babushka Halina silently approached me, sparking memories of a shadow from a long-ago dream. Her motion was barely visible, like the movement of a rolling cloud as she leaned to whisper in my ear, "You have evil sitting upon your shoulders. That is why you get tired. In the church, the Lord saves us." Tossing a final glance at me, she frowned towards the spot where I was standing. Uneasiness overwhelmed my limbs as I tried to get the sound of her voice out of my head.

It lingered for some time, like the smell of incense that now filled the room. Then, her cloud-like presence left me as we lit our candles, and the church's hall exploded in a pleasant blast of a hundred fireflies. The room sparkled, purifying us as the choir started to sing, and one by one, our voices joined the celebration. I loved the feeling of all the different people, who were not more than strangers, coming together to join their voices in harmony. At that moment, we were one word, one faith, all sharing one song.

As the words of our carol sank into my heart, I realized that Babushka Halina was a saint. Though she may sometimes seem old and resentful, her anger was not about me. So I let the freedom fill my heart as I joined the chorus, "On earth, peace reigns, and hearts filled with goodwill...." That is when I remembered I was a part of something bigger, feeling the power of belief coursing through the room, the city, and maybe the whole world.

30

Carol of the Bells

Carolers in Kyiv, celebrating the Christmas Season.

WHEN WE ARRIVED HOME, Tyotya Tyotya Valya had a lot of work to do. During the Soviet occupation, Ukrainians did not officially celebrate Christmas. The communist government insisted they ignore it and celebrate only the New Year, but people secretly kept their traditions. One of the essential religious customs we still celebrated was Christmas Eve dinner.

When we were allowed to attend church again, we did not each until after the church services, as it was customary not to eat it until the first star appeared in the sky. We did this to honor the journey of the kings to Bethlehem.

Our Holy Evening or Sviaty Vechir began with a Holy Supper called Sviata Vecheria. The meal commenced by placing garlic at each corner of the table. After the garlic, we created a centerpiece with hay to symbolize the manger. After adding salt and a candle to the centerpiece, Tyotya Valya set the dishes, adding an extra place setting to remember those who have passed. The entire family gathered around the table, waiting to dig in, but before anyone could eat, we had to recite the "Lord's Prayer." I couldn't help noticing that the grownups were eager to start their dinner even though the children were most excited.

Greek Orthodox homes prepared twelve unique dishes to honor the twelve apostles as part of our Christmas tradition. The meal didn't have meat, dairy, or any animal fat. The only protein in the traditional meal was fish. So, this time it wasn't Valya's stinginess that meant we wouldn't have meat dinner. It was the holiday.

I didn't mind not having meat, as we had so much food to share. One of my favorite things to eat was a traditional dish called kutya. Kutya was the spotlight of our holiday dinner. Tyotya Valya prepared hers with thick wheat, poppy seeds, raisins, walnuts, and honey, and I loved eating it. We would usually eat it until the end of Christmas as Tyotya Valya always made a lot of it.

Along with tasty kutya, there were other delights set out for us to enjoy. Tyotya Valya put a lot of effort into making everything perfect. We had pletenka, a bread roll woven into a braid and sprinkled with poppy seeds. For drinks, we had uzvar, a sweetened compote style drink made of a mixture of dried fruits. We also had mashed peas and beans. Two dishes topped with roasted onions. I didn't like them very much, but she made them taste good, so I ate them.

After the first round of courses, Tyotya Valya served cabbage rolls stuffed with boiled rice, fried carrots, and onions. Atop those dishes was another of my favorites, vareniki, dumplings stuffed with potatoes and mushrooms, cherries, or cottage cheese. We also had marinated mushrooms, various salads, and then the dessert. The desserts were often served with rose jam or sometimes with cherry or poppy seeds. Finally, we finished the meal with donuts and cakes, though there wasn't much room for it.

Tyotya Valya didn't move any dishes as she continued to bring more to the table. When Masha asked why, Babushka Halina stared at us as if she wanted to scare us with her next words, "The dead souls might come tonight. They are hungry too. It wouldn't be nice of us not to offer them some food as we get our bellies full."

That night, when we all went to our beds, I listened carefully to hear if any hungry souls had come to eat the rest of our dinner, but I didn't hear anything. Maybe the souls were quiet, or just a figment of someone's imagination. Unfortunately, there was no way to find out if they were there, as there were no dishes on the table by the time we were up the following morning. I also knew it wouldn't help to ask Tyotya Valya if any food was missing, so it seemed, Babushka's story would remain a mystery.

On Christmas morning, everyone greeted each other with "Jesus is born," to which anyone would reply, "Glorify him." Many people greeted each other this way for the entire day and even a few days after the holiday. The holiday spirit was present everywhere I looked, and everyone seemed more cheerful than they were on other days. Maybe it was the food that made them so generous. Perhaps it was that many people took their vacations for the holidays, or it could have been the good tidings going around in a big circle, reminding us that we are human, even if it was just for a couple of days.

As evening came, Slavik, Serhij, and I continued the tradition of caroling we learned at the orphanage. I found a book called "Ukrainian Koliadky" filled with dozens of celebration songs. We sang "Joy, Earth, Joy. The Son of God was born" and "Good evening, Holy evening. To good people for good health." I didn't know how to read the notes and music sheets, but I tried to keep up with the lyrics, combining them with what I remembered from years past.

Slavik and Serhij didn't know the words to every song I knew. So, we always began our performance with the tune that would bring people to their doors with bright smiles to sing with us. Everyone in Ukraine knew the world-famous "Shchedrivky" called "Carol of the Bells" written by Ukrainian composer Mykola Leontovych and lyricist Peter J. Wilhousky, so we liked to use that song to warm their generosity.

Hark how the bells,
  sweet silver bells,
  all seem to say,
  throw cares away

Christmas is here,
  bringing good cheer,
  to young and to old,
  meek and the bold.

Ding dong ding dong
  that is their song
  with joyful ring
  all caroling.

One seems to hear

words of good cheer
from everywhere
filling the air.

Oh, how they pound,
  raising the sound,
  o'er hill and dale,
  telling their tale.

Gaily they ring
  while people sing
  songs of good cheer,
  Christmas is here.

Merry, Merry, Merry, Merry Christmas,
Merry, Merry, Merry, Merry Christmas.

On, on they send,
  on without end,
  their joyful tone
  to every home.
  Ding dong ding... dong!

I felt warm inside as I sang those words for the hundredth time that day. I was grateful for the donations we received. They were great tokens of appreciation from the people. So, we enjoyed another long tradition together, and I was always happy to get money.

I was a little upset sharing my money with Serhij and Slavik as I was doing all the work, but I made peace with the situation as it was nice having company. I was glad they were there to back me up since I wasn't sure if I would have enough courage to sing on my own in front of so many strangers.

A few days later, everything was back to the way it was before Christmas. Babushka Halina returned home, Dyadya Grisha returned to work, and Tyotya Valya was yelling again as we prepared to go back to school. It seemed everyone was packing their smiles in some dusty boxes to wait again until next year. Still, I wasn't worried. My new year was about to be the best yet.

After Tyotya Valya took my watch, I decided I needed a Christmas gift of my own and had the perfect plan to get it. We loved going to Uncle Lonya's house best when we were caroling. So the one gift I could say I received from Tyotya Valya was my Uncle Lonya. Even though they were not related, Valya christened him and my Aunt Lena as our godparents when we were still young.

I remember I was twelve and everyone else was eleven. It was a year after she took us into foster care. She said she needed help to raise us. So, Aunt Lena and Uncle Lonya were our godmother and godfather. Uncle Lonya was always taking care of us. He would bring us money to buy candy and babysit us when Tyotya Valya and Dyadya Grisha traveled. He also owned a barbershop, and his wife Lena did our hair for free. Aunt Lena was so kind to us. She loved to have us around, and I often wished I could live with them instead of Tyotya Valya.

At Christmas, he would feed us until our bellies were full, and then, he would give us extra donations for our songs. Thanks to Uncle Lonya, I had earned enough money from caroling to buy my first television.

A friend of mine from school had a television he agreed to sell me for fifty hryven. I was so excited by the deal. I bought it instantly. That was the moment I knew I didn't need Tyotya Valya anymore. If she didn't want to take care of me as a mother, I would care for myself.

With Slavik's help, I carried the TV to our room. We did it secretly so that Tyotya Valya wouldn't see it. I knew she would try to find a way to make it something to keep if she did.

Of course, my secret didn't stay a secret for long. As Tyotya Valya called us to dinner, she looked into my bedroom, saying, "Where did you get that?"

I could tell she was angry. I waited for her to accuse me of stealing it or even punish me for having something she couldn't take away, but she just stood waiting for my answer.

"My friend gave it to me," I answered defiantly. I didn't tell her I had money. I knew there would be a consequence if she knew how much we earned, so we all agreed to keep it secret. Still, she couldn't let it go.

"Well, you won't be watching it without my permission," she shot back. Her comment didn't surprise me. She liked to monitor us and control what we did. We often said she spent her days with her ear to the wall, waiting for a reason to strike. It felt as though she heard everything we said, even when we whispered.

At Tyotya Valya's house, every step I took had been on tip-toes until my birthday. That day changed me. Tyotya Valya could not control me anymore. I didn't respect her, and I couldn't stand her telling me what to do. So, I spent many nights hiding under the covers and watching images float across the screen. I didn't care that I had to have the volume down or even when I was tired the next day. I loved having the freedom to do what I wanted to do.

Tyotya Valya's angry voice no longer overshadowed the Carol of the Bells. The song rang loud in my ears all year long. I believe in joy and positivity, and I knew I would find a way to be successful with the help of people who cared about me.

III

Into Adulthood

Nothing in life is to be feared, it is only to be understood. Now is the time to understand more, so that we may fear less.

—Marie Curie

31

Much Needed Help

This is a high-school graduation picture. In Ukraine, we have the option to continue to grade 11 or graduate after the 9th grade and attend vocational school.

NEAR THE END OF SECONDARY SCHOOL, we got out of the house to adventure with a social worker. As part of the foster program, they invited us to visit the Vocational

School just down the street from the same University Tyotya Valya told me I could never attend.

Chernivtsi National University sat above Ukraine's city on a natural pedestal. It stood like a beacon of possibilities to Chernivsti's young minds. The University was founded in 1875 when Chernivtsi was the capital of the Duchy of Bukovina. It is one of the best higher education institutions in Ukraine, teaching around twenty thousand students a year, and I was determined to be one of them. If I worked hard, I knew I could impress them, and they would let me into their school. I could build a different life than the cold and empty experience Tyotya Valya believed Ukraine's poor children deserved.

There was a marked difference between the University neighborhoods and those around the orphanage on Fastivska Street. Chernivtsi is a beautiful city full of hand-crafted buildings, cathedrals, and colorful architecture. The city center shines brightly against the monotonous slate gray boxes, where I began my journey. The tiny, beat-up apartments stacked row by row in the city's poorer sections were a far cry from the new apartment given to us for being orphans. Not only was our apartment better, but the streets near the University were wide and clean, with buildings painted in many exciting colors.

The social workers guided twenty foster kids I recognized from the orphanage to go on the field trip. Though some of us had passed the school a time or two, we had never been inside. The architecture was inspiring. The building was gigantic and divided into large classrooms, much bigger than we had at our school. Though Chernivtsi was still decades behind in fashion and technology, the education was top-notch. Visiting the vocational school felt like I was joining the center of the action, and I felt more inspired than ever to make the University my way of life. We listened to the facilitators as they talked to us about their classes and the fantastic career opportunities that awaited us after attending their school. I knew this was where I could pave the way for a life filled with success. My mind was spinning with possibilities.

While we were there, the social worker told us a generous donor from Germany donated five hundred American dollars to split between us to help us prepare for vocational school. It was inspiring to know that the government wasn't the only one sending money to support us. Sometimes people from nearby countries like Germany were looking for ways to help our little town. We were always in the middle of some war or disagreement between nations. So they would offer money to the orphans, especially during the holidays.

The holidays were full of generosity. Everyone had so much to give, and for orphans, it was like a miracle every day. Of course, I wished they would remember us other times of the year as well, but I was grateful. Presents and donations like new shoes and coats always made life a little better for us, and it was a treat to see they still cared, even after we moved to foster care. Because of them, our bodies could be warmer, and so could our hearts. I think that is what makes Christmas so exceptional. Everyone gets to feel loved.

The social worker told us the people donating the money insisted they give it to the children. So, the teachers didn't want us to tell our foster parents we had it. If our foster parents found out, I guess it would be their money and not ours. It seemed like everything that was ours wasn't really ours. Tyotya Valya believed we had enough, taking what she wanted. Still, it never felt like enough to me, so I was always grateful for gifts when they arrived and was happy not to tell her.

When they divided the five hundred dollars, I got forty, like the rest of the boys. The girls got twenty-three. I'm not sure why they got less, but we didn't think much about it then. It's just the way it was, I guess.

I was excited to have some money of my own. I didn't have a good coat, and the rain and snow always worked their way through the holes in my shoes. It rained and snowed a lot in Chernivtsi. So I felt like

I was always cold and had wet feet. On the worst days, I doubled up on sweaters, wore as many socks as I could, and wrapped my feet in plastic grocery bags before putting on my shoes. Now, I could buy a coat and a new pair of shoes with this money. I was happy to have relief.

Still, I didn't just buy clothes with the money they gave me. I knew that day I would be attending Vocational School. It was my first step to creating a life of my own. So I also bought the supplies I would need to attend the classes I wanted to take.

I left the school that day faced with a gray and cloudy afternoon. The light outside wasn't much different from most days in Chernivtsi, but my life was looking brighter than ever.

32

Family Reunion

My brother and I met in Los Angeles many years after I came to the United States.

WE WERE ONLY DAYS INTO SUMMER, and Slavik and I were already facing utter boredom instead of long-awaited adventures. When we were younger, we filled out our long summer months with camp activities, but that July, Serhij,

Nadya, and Masha went without us. So, we had to make peace with staying home and finding something else to do. The steaming hot days seemed as though they would never end, and every time I looked at the window, watching the sunset from my room, unwelcomed melancholy nested in my chest, filling me with remorse even though there was nothing to regret.

July and August eventually dragged themselves through the stone streets of Chernivtsi, and I was somewhat at ease, knowing that September would soon arrive. I was looking forward to getting back to school and out from under Tyotya Valya's constant watch. So we spent as much of our time as we could preparing to apply to Vocational School.

After taking our grades into account, we endured a lengthy application process. My grades were worse during my final year of secondary school. I could have made a hive out of all the Bs I had, but still, I did far better than Slavik. So, he applied for Culinary Classes as a station chef, which meant that, upon graduation, he would have the skills to prepare food in general. He was learning to check food for freshness. Then, wash, cut, peel, and create dishes that would look artful and taste delicious.

I decided to enter the program to be a Pastry Chef. The courses I took would qualify me to do what he did and more. I learned to create appetizers, first and second courses, confectionery, beverages, and desserts. I also learned the nuances of more refined flavors and smells.

On the first of September 1996, Slavik and I officially started attending Vocational School. I knew I would enjoy attending Culinary Arts classes, as I enjoyed helping around the kitchen. I was finally looking forward to building my future, but I had no clue how it would look.

Just as we began school, Yura, Tyotya Valya's oldest son, returned from military service. Growing up, I thought of him as my older brother and was thrilled to see him again, but no one could be as excited as Nastya. She was ecstatic to have her husband returning after so much time away. Her entire body trembled as she occasionally caressed the child she held, possibly trying to tell them that their father was finally coming home.

I never thought our state system was fair as it required all boys to give two years of their lives to military service after they turned eighteen. I couldn't understand their ability to force us to defend ideas that weren't even ours to protect. Still, it wasn't the worst it had been. When the USSR inhabited Ukraine, military service was more demanding. The Russian Empire required twenty-five years of service. Over time, the requirements dropped to twenty. However, with the end of communism, a new law reduced it, requiring all twenty-year-old males to serve at least two years in the military.

The patriotic spirit of serving their country brought pride to many. Still, with the amount of abuse from the co-cadets and the leaders, many young males did everything possible to avoid service. Some had fake documents saying they couldn't serve or bribed leaders to make the requirement go away for them. There was always "a way out" of the military service, but it came at a cost, which meant most of those serving were poor. Yura, like many young men, had no other choice.

When Yura walked in the door, I looked at his face, wondering how much he had changed during his service. He was taller than all of us, hidden under a bush of wild dark hair. He was neatly shaved, had a sizable nose, and wore a smile that beamed from across the room. Still, I couldn't concentrate on his face. Instead, I was distracted by how he was breathing. His nostrils made a loud sound every time he inhaled air.

Tyotya Valya was distracted in the other room, making lunch for us, so Slavik and I were somewhat free to ask anything we wanted about what it was like in the military. So, we gathered around him as he sat next to Nastya, asking everything we could think to ask.

Yura was controlled and cautious as he recounted what it was like to be in a military camp. He didn't give an opinion about what it was like to serve two years away from his family. He told the facts.

I watched him closely, absorbing everything he had to say. I didn't like what I heard, and I couldn't imagine myself holding a rifle and rolling in the mud. I tried to imagine doing anything Yura was saying until he spoke words that struck me like a clap of thunder, forcefully dragging me from my thoughts. "Vitaly, did you know that your brother's wife is Nastya's best friend?"

I opened my mouth, trying to give some answer, trying to acknowledge that I understood his question, but I couldn't make myself speak.

Finally, after several seconds of searching for words, I turned to Nastya, "You know Roustam?"

She bobbed her head casually as if years of never telling me was nothing to her.

"I actually met him during my service in the military, but I didn't have a clue that you made relatives of us...." Yura said, smiling. He had the same casual air. It was like the relationship between my brother and I meant nothing to any of them.

Nastya leaned forward, saying, "He wanted to see you, you know? But when they transferred you to foster care, he wasn't allowed."

I was trying to piece together what she was saying. Why hadn't I heard this from anyone before? I knew it probably had something to do with Tyotya Valya, but I didn't understand why. At that moment, I didn't care. I had spent years setting aside expectations of my brother. Still, I never stopped thinking about him, especially with everything around me, reminding me how happy I was when he was in my life. I remembered the day we had watermelon and how he gave me the larger piece. I remembered when we went to the movies or sat on the grass at the orphanage.

I missed Roustam every day, and now, I was finding out everyone knew my brother. They were still spending time with him, but no one told me.

"I could give you Ludmila's number so you can get in touch with him," Nastya said compassionately. "I think he would be glad to hear from you, as you two probably have a lot of catching up to do."

"Really?" was all I could say. She was still very indifferent, and I felt stupid not asking more questions, but I couldn't make myself say anything else. I can only imagine the look I must have had on my face. Disbelief, fear, hope, and pain all pooled together into a moment of utter confusion.

"Yeah," Nastya was smiling, like the moment was an exciting adventure. "I could get it for you. It would only take a second."

"Yes, please!" was all I could muster. Joy overtook me. I could almost feel it bouncing off the ceiling to radiate throughout my body and make me forget all the years they kept him from me.

Nastya went to her room and returned, carrying a piece of paper in her hands. She handed me the note with Ludmila's number neatly written on it, and as I took it, it felt like being given a piece of gold. I couldn't stop looking at it. I was reading the numbers, repeating them in my head, afraid the digits might suddenly disappear if I diverted my eyes, even for a moment.

I was sweating as I walked to Tyotya Valya's room and dialed the number.

I saw him not long after. He invited me to dinner with his new family, but the experience wasn't anywhere near what I hoped it would be.

"Hey, little bro!" he said, hugging me and tapping my back as I walked in the room. My brother did seem happy to be reunited, but the smile he wore held no reflection of the one I remembered.

Although I hugged him back, there was an odd feeling floating around us like a mist of uneasiness that discouraged me. I felt like something terrible was about to happen, and as it turned out, I wasn't far from the truth.

"So, how are you doing? What have you been up to?" he asked me impatiently.

I thought the impatience might signify his interest in me, but the questions were just conversation starters. He didn't even wait for me to finish my answer before he started talking again. "So, our mother is moving from that old apartment where I took you. Do you remember? Well, I have to help her out with that. This new owner needs some testimony for the government and the social workers, and since we are both her sons, I would need you to back me on this."

"To help you out with what exactly?" I asked, confused. I didn't know why he would need my help. I only ever saw my mother once. What testimony could I give? It all seemed rather odd and unnatural with Roustam's entire family present at the dinner table. I wondered if he was hoping that their presence would influence my answer.

"You see, for our mother to safely move into her new apartment, which looks far better than her current place, by the way, we need to testify in front of a committee... which is not even half as scary as it might sound." His smile was artificial, and his words anxious. He was nothing like the brother I knew.

I stared at him for a moment, watching him pet the black poodle the family had. I thought about how I never had a dog. It seemed I never had a lot of things. I was frustrated, finally saying, "Sorry, but I still can't see my part in that. What is my role in her life, anyway?" I was trying to remain calm, clinging to some common sense, which was slowly slipping through my fingers in the face of what he was saying.

Roustam wouldn't give up, insisting and trying to convince me that he needed my help. In the orphanage, I had developed a weakness for my brother. He was the only family I had.

Finally, I agreed to help him, but I knew I would never see him the same way again. Like the day Tyotya Valya walked into my room with that stick, my spirit left my body. I forgot everything about reasoning and thinking clearly. I just wanted to move on with my life, "All right," I said.

On the day we went to the committee, Tyotya Valya told me she would be coming with me. I didn't trust what was happening. She never came to support me in anything I did, and she never did anything that didn't benefit her. Now, when I agreed to help my brother, she would be there, in front of the committee with me, listening to everything I said. Something wasn't right, but I didn't know what it was until it was too late.

The committee asked me various informational questions about my mother that I didn't understand. It wasn't until Roustam testified that I could finally see how everyone was about to gain something again, everyone but me.

"So, you have agreed that it is in your brother's best interest for you to take care of him once he is out of the foster care program?"

"Yes, sir. I do." Roustam shot me a look to remind me to agree.

There was a time in my life where that question would have meant everything in the world to me, but now I understood what I was losing.

"Would you like to add something, young Vitaly Magidov?" one of the committee members asked me.

"No," I said plainly with mechanical coldness in my voice. "I agree with Roustam." I don't know if I hoped they wouldn't believe me or not to trust a word I was saying, but I agreed. I didn't know how to do anything else.

The apartment our mother received from our testimony was more considerable than where she lived before. She had her own bathroom, hallway, bedroom, and a slightly bigger kitchen than her previous apartment. So, it seemed she had gained something from our effort. So, had Tyotya Valya. I didn't have the same claim on my apartment as I had just an hour before.

Later, I heard various stories about how my mother's previous apartment owner promised to pay my brother if he could get my mother to move. I didn't want to believe the rumors. I wanted to have faith my brother was the way I remembered him, as the one who said he would always have my back. However, a few months later, I saw Roustam pushing a new car down the road, a car he didn't own, before speaking to the committee.

I pretended I wasn't there, that I couldn't see him. I was disappointed by my brother. He sold me out as if I meant nothing to him. He treated me like I wasn't his brother and as if my future didn't count at all. I wished he cared. I wanted any of them to consider my feelings. But more than anything else, I wished I didn't have to live with the memory of seeing him betray me in front of that committee. That was the day I saw who my brother had become, and it soured all those sweet memories of my time with him.

33

Impossible Dreams

High-school Graduation picture. I am in the middle at the bottom, and Slavik is on the second row at the top left.

TIME FLEW BY. STILL, nothing changed much around our apartment. Masha, Nadya, Serhij, Slavik, and I were still living together, and Tyotya Valya continued to find shouting and making orders more comfortable than silence. As Slavik and I were preparing to graduate from high school, the school asked everyone in our class to gather money to buy chocolate and flowers for our teachers to show our appreciation for their efforts. We also had to collect money for class graduation photos to remember our time together. Unfortunately, we didn't have enough, which meant only one thing. I needed to go to Tyotya Valya and ask her to give it to us, which she didn't like doing at all.

Since the incident on my birthday, Tyotya Valya didn't bother talking to me unless she had to. She even went as far as to get more involved with the others to isolate me further and mark me as unnecessary and unwelcomed. I knew she thought the situation between us was my fault, just as I thought she was the one to blame. I could see we both had our opinions. She thought, if she could keep me here for two more years, our apartment would be hers. I looked forward to telling her it was mine and that it had been since the day she hit me with that stick.

After several weeks of the kind of silence you only hear when passing through a graveyard, I decided to take the first step towards talking to her. She responded, but the answers, statements, and questions were spoken mechanically and soullessly, without any sign of affection. Things were never the same between us after that.

"Why do I always have to ask her?" I asked Slavik, frowning. "She would rather give someone her right arm than open her wallet, especially for me."

"But you know how to talk to her. She gives me that stare, and I don't even ask her what I want in the end! I get all sweaty, and my hands start shaking. So, I just stand there, afraid to speak." Slavik visibly shook off the memory of trying to ask Tyotya Valya for something.

"I hate doing it as well. She is always so cold to me." I tried to think of ways to get out of it, but Slavik was relentless.

"Here. Let me put it this way. I have a candy bar that I got from

Oksana." Slavik was smiling at me, trying to bribe me with chocolate as if I were a ten-year-old. "It's yours if you ask her to give us the money for school."

"Okay, fine. I'm going." I couldn't say no to him. Still, if I was going to do it anyway, I might as well have some chocolate for my trouble. I knew that he was far less comfortable than I was, so I pretended I cared for that secret candy bar and smiled back at Slavik.

Earlier that day, Tyotya Valya had bought Masha a new pair of shoes, a pair of pants for Serhij, stuffed the fridge and covered our dining table with all sorts of fruits and vegetables. So, I knew she had received the check the state sent her every month for taking care of us.

'If I ask her now,' I thought, 'she won't make a big deal out of it.' Also, I knew that Tyotya Valya was in front of the television, watching her favorite daytime drama, a novella from Mexico that became very popular in Ukraine called "The Rich Also Cry." Tyotya Valya loved it. So it always put her in a good mood. Talking to her while she watched it was my best opportunity for success.

I approached the door slowly, thinking of the irony of asking my question during a show with a title that indicated life was not all about money. But, of course, Tyotya Valya didn't see it that way. So I knew that I still needed the proper intro to boost her mood a bit. I watched her for several minutes, trying to read her emotions from the expression on her face. Over the years, I learned it was better to talk to Tyotya Valya when she was in a good mood. So, I had mastered the art of reading her temper.

She was enthralled watching the show, and once I saw her smiling at the destiny of her favorite heroes and heroines, I knew that something positive had just happened. So I took advantage of the moment and entered the room to sit on the floor by the couch. The timing was perfect as a commercial break was just about to start.

Tyotya Valya noticed me as I leaned against the sofa. "Is your homework done yet?" she asked with unquestionable authority. Of course, she knew that I always finished my homework before starting anything else, but I guess that was another way for her to state her position.

"Yes. It's done. I finished everything," I replied, waiting for her to ask about my day at school.

She didn't say anything further. So, I tried to push the conversation in that direction.

"We had some tests today," I continued with a smile.

She wasn't interested in what I did, but she looked as she felt obligated to ask for details, "Yes? How did you do?"

"I got an A in literature and Bs in math, physics, and Ukrainian language." I was almost afraid to tell her about the Bs, but she seemed okay with my grades if I didn't fail. I sometimes felt she didn't worry about my work because she knew I was doing my homework and was highly praised by my teachers when she talked to them at the parent/teacher conferences. She only came to a couple of events, but it seemed enough to satisfy her expectations.

"Great. You did fine. Way to go, Vitaly," her tone was dry, like the mechanical subway voice I saw in movies. Still, when she praised me for my success at school, my lungs filled with pride. Even with her yelling, I enjoyed Tyotya Valya's attention. I always used her positive reaction to my good grades as motivation to do better at school and be among the best.

Her tone lifted a little as she continued, "... and how did Slavik do?"

I knew that she didn't have high expectations for Slavik as I helped him with almost everything in school. So I wasn't sure if I wanted to talk about his achievements. Still, since she asked, I gave her the most positive answer I could. "Lyudmyla Ivanivna told us that Slavik is making real progress in algebra. He got a B- and she encouraged me to continue helping him with math, so I think he is doing well." I was careful to keep a positive tone.

The conversation had gone as well as I could have hoped, and I finally had enough courage to ask her. So, I took a deep breath and just let the words flow, "So, our class is collecting money for the group photo." I was breathing heavily with my eyes wide and blinking as I waited for her adverse reaction.

"How much?" she asked coldly.

No eyes were rolling, and there was no shouting. My hopes began to rise.

"Ten hryven." It was equivalent to about two American dollars, so I wasn't asking for a lot.

"That much?!" She raised her voice a bit, and I could see her mood shifting back to her usual hostility.

I became insecure again, but I kept talking, "But, as Slavik and I wanted to have separate photos, that would mean that we need twenty hryven to buy two...."

She was looking at me coldly, and I knew she wasn't pleased with my request. Even though the state gave her plenty to handle little expenses, she never spent a dime on us if it was up to her.

She blinked, biting her lip. She didn't have a good reason to decline. I could tell. "I will leave twenty hryven on the dining table for you in the morning before you leave for school." Her voice was tense and trembling uncomfortably. "But, don't expect anything else from me from this point on."

My fears had come true. I knew that everything she gave us had its price, and my price today was never to ask her for anything again.

The room went silent as Tyotya Valya went back to watching "The Rich Also Cry." I was still sitting on the floor, leaning against the couch. I felt like someone had glued my legs to the floor. Even breathing felt uncomfortable. I wanted to leave, but I didn't dare move. I didn't want to do anything that would give her a reason to change her mind.

So, I stayed and watched the entire episode with her, trying to be as invisible as possible.

When the show was over, I stood up and went to my room. I couldn't wait to tell Slavik that we had gotten the money and that his chocolate bar was now mine.

"I can't believe you did it! Did she yell?" Slavik asked.

"No. She was pretty much calm, as Tyotya Valya could be anyway. Now, give it up!" I finally released the tension I was holding and began laughing.

"Give what up?" Slavik asked.

"Your candy bar."

"Oh. I thought you were not going to do it, so I ate it." Slavik was embarrassed. He could never help himself if he had candy to eat.

I started laughing, "I still want my reward."

"All right! You can have my dessert on Sunday when we go to the movies. Deal?"

"Deal!"

Two days later, we were back at school for our final day and getting ready to take the class photo. Everyone already knew what they would do after the ninth grade. Some of them decided to stay in school for further education. Others thought it would be better to go to vocational or technical schools, learning about computer science, electronics, construction, and similar degrees. Zhenya decided to leave early and go work in construction. It was our last day together, but I knew that in advance, so I was ready for it.

Oksana, the clever girl from my class, wanted to study at the University to become a math teacher. She was a brilliant and kind creature and was always there whenever I needed her help, so it made sense. I could see her being a teacher. She remained at school for two more years to get her high school diploma, and then, she continued to get her degree and follow her dream. All of my new friends were going in their directions. I considered my options for a long time, and I was already thinking about going to University like Oksana, but I wasn't sure.

While Dyadya Grisha was at work, Uncle Lonya and Aunt Lena often visited us at our apartment for lunch or occasionally asked us to their home. Tyotya Valya was a close friend with them, so she didn't mind their visits, and she probably enjoyed the break from cooking when we went to their house as well.

It was only a twenty to thirty minutes walk from their house to ours. So, after one of our visits, we decided to walk home. The road we took led us through the University's beautiful grounds. I was in awe of the multiple buildings with different departments where they held lectures on economics, business, history, geography, biology, finance, and art. I was so inspired, I forgot myself and expressed my desire to attend classes there to Tyotya Valya.

She laughed aloud in response, mocking me with her condescending tone. "University is for rich kids, Vitaly. It's no place for you. People in high places go to University. Besides, even if you tried, they wouldn't let you in. It takes money to bribe the testing officials? You don't have the knowledge or money to pass those tests, and I'm not giving it to you. You are my responsibility only until you are eighteen. After that, you are on your own.

"For once in your life, be happy with what you have. You must learn to accept life as it is, or people will think you are ungrateful. "

Without even a pause, she turned to Masha, saying, "We need bread for dinner."

She always knew what to say to break my heart. She seemed to enjoy reminding me that my dreams were impossible to achieve, planting seeds of doubts in my mind. All I ever wanted was her love and understanding, and she used that desire to hurt me, leaving scars in me. I couldn't help but wonder what she might do to someone if she ever had a mind to cause real harm.

She gave me the exact amount needed for the bread and sent me to the store. As I continued down the street, I felt defeated, counting each step as her words rolled back like a tape recorder in my mind. I tried to think of anything but Tyotya Valya's harsh voice, but she had a way of drowning out everything else. Then, just when I felt I couldn't take one more second, I heard a familiar voice coming from my left.

"Hi, Vitaly!"

I turned to see who it was. It was Vanya, the boy from my building. I was surprised to see him and replied clumsily, "Hey, Vanya! What's up?"

"I was wondering if you know what you are going to do after we graduate. I mean, I am not certain what I am going to do. So, I wanted to see if you felt the same."

"I think I will stick around until ninth grade and then apply to the Vocational School of Culinary Arts. I'm hoping to become a chef and finish high school while getting my degree," I replied, not knowing what else to say.

I liked to cook the essential foods that Tyotya Valya usually made for us: mashed potatoes, boiled pasta, fries, eggs, and some celebrational dishes she made for birthdays and holidays. I also remembered the various summer camps I visited. I spent a lot of time in the kitchen with other chefs who were kind and willing to teach me some of their culinary skills. They fed me well with various treats before other kids could taste them, making it easy to decide what I wanted to do after graduating from high school. It felt so good to have my belly full.

"It will give me a job I could enjoy as a profession and provide the necessary skills to keep me full." I continued, laughing. "What do you think you will do?"

"A chef, huh?" Vanya said with an honest smile on his face. "That sounds great!"

"Yeah, I guess it is something I could be great at, and as a big plus, I will learn to find my way around the kitchen. Tyotya Valya wants us to become self-sufficient and have enough money to support ourselves when we become adults."

"I will probably become a state lawyer," Vanya replied, dropping his head. "I mean, as my parents are so familiar with politics and law, I would probably need to do one or the other, but I am more optimistic about the law."

"Really? But I thought you were going to become a surgeon. I remember you talking about it with quite a lot of dedication."

"Yeah. That's true. I love doing good for people, and everything related to medicine is so interesting, but my mother wants me to become a lawyer. She said I would be able to earn a lot of money that way." Vanya frowned, trying to justify his mother's motives.

I looked at the ground and back at Vanya. I wanted to do something to help him. "Well, I hate to break your mother's dreams, but I heard lawyers were maybe earning big cash years back, but now there's a surplus in law. So, there aren't many positions for that profession."

"Really?" Vanya was surprised. I could see him rethinking his options.

I paused, waiting to see if he would say anything, but he didn't, so I continued, "You know Natalia? Well, she finished Law School, and now, after two years, she can't even find a job."

"Wow. I didn't know that. Maybe I should reconsider my options." Vanya was surprised, but an expression of peace mingled with the previous disappointment on his face, letting me know that he was content with the information I was giving him. He paused for a moment, looking at me as if he were still listening to statistics or contemplating another argument. Then, it clicked. I saw it. His face lit up as he continued, "Well, thanks, buddy! Thanks! Really! Bye, Vitaly! See you around...."

He raced away like he knew his direction, the light of conviction shining in his eyes.

"Bye, Vanya...and good luck!" I replied, leaving in the opposite direction to buy bread for Tyotya Valya.

I believe my conversation with Vanya helped him see what he wanted in life, but it also helped me. So why would I let Tyotya Valya talk me out of my dreams if I didn't want Vanya's mother talking him out of his?

My conversation with Vanya reignited my desire to attend University and get the degree I wanted. Tyotya Valya's words would have the opposite effect of what she hoped and decided that she couldn't hurt me anymore. I would use her judgment to increase my desire to study and be better so I could be one of the people who had vacations and ate meat on more than just special occasions. Education was my opportunity. Knowledge would give me freedom, and no one could take school or the opportunity it presented from me, not even Tyotya Valya.

I would show her my capabilities, and she may not be happy to see me go to University, but I would go anyway. This was a chance to show her what I could do without her help. I would go to Culinary School, but I would not stop there. I would go all the way.

The next time we decided to walk home from lunch with Uncle Lonya and Aunt Lena, I knew I would not just attend classes in those beautiful buildings. I would get a degree from that University, as well.

34

Vocational School

I spent a lot of time in the kitchen practicing to be a chef. Mariya Omelyanivna is located at the back wearing the long, narrow hat with a stripe on the bottom. I am in the front, on the left, sitting with two of the six boys we had in our class.

EVERYTHING ABOUT TAKING CULINARY ARTS differed from what I had experienced so far. At Vocational School, there was no lining up to meet our teachers. We watched welcoming lectures held by several instructors instead.

Before we headed to the welcoming, I met everyone in my class, and then we went together as a group to watch the lectures.

Our principal Yuliya Dmytrivna was the first to speak. She always made us do better than we thought we could. No one dared ask her a single question or even whispered during her class, and I could swear that some of us didn't even dare to breathe loudly. She was strict and criticized us when we made mistakes. Still, as she taught physiology, hygiene and sanitation, I realized that she made sure that we learned everything we needed to know to keep the people eating our food safe and healthy.

It was almost impossible to get an A in her class. Still, I knew for some reason that I could talk to her, and she would not mind. I could tell she appreciated my efforts and noticed I studied because I was always willing to speak up while learning. I was never afraid to say what I felt, even though I was usually the only one who did.

Our principal wasn't the only one who expected the best from us. I had the most formidable teacher I ever met while taking culinary arts. Her name was Mariya Omelyanivna. Most of the students were afraid of her, but she never scared me as much as she challenged me. She yelled when we made mistakes, but she always made her classes enjoyable and taught us well. Though most students said it was hard to get a B in her class, I always aimed for an A, and I got it. As I remember, I was the only one in her class who had ever gotten an A. Of course, she made me work for it, but I always admired her because she was helping us grow.

Over time, we became close. Mariya oversaw all of our education. She made sure we understood the hygiene lessons we learned from Yuliya Dmytrivna and knew how to apply them in the real world. She taught us everything related to cooking. We learned to make dishes, wash pots, clean the kitchen, bake and cut meat. During Mariya's lessons, we would cook for the entire school the whole month. We all had a turn at practicum, having a chance to use our knowledge at that school's dining area. Mariya's job was to set us on the right path towards getting our degrees.

Mariya understood the conditions I was living in, and she did everything she could to help me be successful in school. I appreciated her immensely.

I knew the teachers here expected the best of us, but they were willing to give the best in return. So, as my classes began, I decided to focus all my attention on school instead of thinking about the things I wanted to change in life but couldn't. Instead, I chose to look forward to the new skills, new people, and new knowledge I was gathering to build a life of my own, away from Tyotya Valya.

Soon after our first year at vocational school started, they put us to work practicing the culinary arts. There were only six boys in the group, including myself. The rest were girls, almost twenty of them. I was not used to being around so many women at one time. I wasn't sure what to do. Most of my schooling separated boys from girls, and if the school didn't do it, our interests did.

Though I got along well with all the boys in my class, I didn't appreciate one boy I met named Sasha. I would have been fine if he was never in my class. He was a cocky boy who was always trying to be the best. Usually, that wouldn't be a problem, but Sasha was always bragging that he was the best at everything, and he wasn't. From what I saw, he excelled at cutting meat, and that was all. Of course, he usually worked cutlery since he was good at it, but I thought he should notice that he only did one job well and not believe he was better at everything he did.

The only thing that made me want to tolerate him was that Oleksiy worked in cutlery with him. Oleksiy captured my attention instantly with an enchanting smile and almost contagious laughter. He made putting up with Sasha worth it on most days.

I got out of my bed at four a.m. every day, so I could be in the kitchen by five and start making dough for baking bread and rolls. Mariya was already there beating dozens of eggs with sugar, salt, and other ingredients when I arrived.

"Vitaly, I already started the mixing. I want you to knead the dough."

"Yes, Master." Each day, we fed over three hundred students and various bakeries, and many of the kitchens we used for practice didn't have automatic dough mixers. So I kneaded the dough by hand. With so many mouths to feed, I felt like I was becoming an expert. I was also getting strong. It wasn't easy, but mechanical action helped me clear my mind and loosen up a bit, even if it was for just a couple of hours.

When Mariya saw how well I was doing with kneading and baking, she decided to put me in charge of the baking department. She also sent one of my classmates, Nelya, to help me. I was glad to have Nelya by my side as I always thought she was the cutest girl in our class. There was something about the way she observed things. Her eyes glowed like she saw even old and boring stuff for the first time.

Over time, we developed somewhat more of a personal relationship, and I pretended to be her boyfriend. There was something attractive and amusing about playing make-believe games, and this was a chance for me to show everyone how I could have a pretty girl to be my girlfriend.

She always blushed a little as she came in, seeing me there mixing ingredients.

I smiled at her. Being her boyfriend felt like having another best friend like Slavik, "Good morning, Nelya."

"What are we making today?" she asked playfully.

As I got to work with someone I liked, baking came easy, and kneading the dough soon became an unconscious act. The better I grew to be, the faster I was, and the dough was starting to look and feel better as well. After waiting for the yeast to rise and a little more kneading, the most exciting part of the process would come when Nelya and I would make it into different shapes. We had three patterns we used, but Nelya and I often finished our work before noon, so we spent a lot of time expressing our creativity and trying things we hadn't tried before. Nelya was not just cute but was very creative with dough. I liked her adventurous spirit.

"Let's see. Yesterday, we made trees and flowers. What if today we tried making animals?"

Nelya smiled, "Yes! What do we want to start with?"

"How about a bear?" I answered, excited to try something fun. Of course, we had made animals before, but I always liked a challenge, and so did she.

"Wow! That's a good one. Okay, let's see who makes the best bear. Go!"

I giggled as we played with the dough. It was a new experience for me to have a girl as a friend, but it was excellent. She was sweet and never wanted anything more from me than holding hands or a kiss on the cheek. Plus, I could invite her to dances, and we would do things together that Slavik and I couldn't do.

"Nalya," I stifled my laugh and returned to kneading as Mariya approached. "I want you to finish the dough. Vitaly, I need you to help in cutlery."

"Yes, Master!" Nalya and I spoke in unison.

Mariya didn't stop to record the confirmation. She just gave us the order and moved on to her next task. On days Mariya was in, she would sometimes send me over to the other departments as an extra pair of hands. I didn't mind preparing vegetables and meat for lunch and dinner, but I wasn't always comfortable when she would send me as a messenger. Passing on her assignments wasn't hard itself. I would always start the sentence with, "Mariya asked me to tell you..." which worked for most stations, but going over to cutlery where Sasha was working was never pleasant when I had to tell him what to do.

Sasha and Oleksiy worked together at the meat department, and they got along well. However, I felt mixed emotions whenever Mariya sent me to help them. I liked to see Oleksiy and often watched him from across the kitchen as he worked. So it was exciting to spend time at his station, but Sasha created tension for everyone, and as he liked to be the only one bossing anyone around, I knew he would make it difficult for me to enjoy myself.

"Hi, Vitaly!" Oleksiy's smile made me smile in return.

"Hi, Oleksiy... and Sasha. How are you today? Mariya sent me to help."

"Good. Prep the fish," Sasha said, never acknowledging my greetings. I knew he wouldn't, but I insisted on giving them anyway, even if he gave me the fish. I didn't appreciate working with fish, and Sasha knew it. Still, it was his department, so I did as he asked. I scraped gills and scales and cleaned the workstation afterward, which was even worse. The scent wasn't as pleasant as the freshly-baked bread I enjoyed at my station, but I did what I needed to do and was grateful for the opportunity to do it.

I learned a lot and mastered many skills in the kitchen with meat, fish, vegetables, bakery, and more. I knew I would need every skill to pass the final culinary exams, but I think the thing I liked most in the kitchen was the family I was growing there. I wanted more than anything to be a successful chef and now was my chance to do not just that but have new and exciting relationships. These relationships would eventually change my entire perspective of life.

35

My First Job

I am sorting and cleaning the vegetables and fruits for cooking at the summer resort.

EVENTUALLY, ALL OF US WERE ATTENDING Vocational School. Nadya and Serhij went to the construction vocational school, while Slavik and I took culinary classes together. After about a year, Masha joined us. She applied to become a candy maker, which suited her very well, as she loved eating candy. I also felt like she needed it most as she was so skinny some of our teachers thought that she didn't get enough food from Tyotya Valya. Getting accepted to the Confectionery Courses was easy, so she started soon after applying. It was nice having both Slavik and Masha in school with me. They helped me with my confidence and inspired me to be surrounded by the people I love.

As part of our culinary training, we also worked in a restaurant. Slavik waited tables while I bussed and washed dishes. I also took every opportunity I could to make food. My favorite part of my job was when they let me make dinners, prepare the salad, and even eat sometimes. Still, not everything was perfect. Periodically, they would send me out of the kitchen when there weren't enough waiters, and I hated it. I would rather wash three sinks of dishes in vomit-like water than serve. I was worried about spilling on someone or serving them the wrong food. I didn't know if they would be aggressive or verbally abusive for poor service. In the kitchen, no one saw me, only the success of my creations.

Slavik didn't care much about what people thought. He liked being a waiter because he didn't want to get food on his hands or clean up after others. In addition to culinary classes, Slavik was also attending modeling school. So he did everything he could, never to feel like a busboy in front of the girls there.

Overall, getting experience in a restaurant was great for both of us. We learned how to make a lot of great food, but we also learned what it takes to make a restaurant successful, but it was more than that. We were building a whole new life at Vocational School.

I worked with teachers who were always happy to help me with my studies, and the students enjoyed spending time doing fun things between classes. Nelya and I were good friends working side by side in the bakery, and I was getting to know Oleksiy though I wanted to know him better. I thought about Oleksiy a lot. I loved watching him from across the kitchen and became so excited when he brushed against me on the line. I liked to try and match when he was in the backroom, changing into his chef coat so I could be with him. Everything about him inspired me, but I never told him. I watched and pretended that I didn't feel the way I did. I couldn't risk it.

I knew we wouldn't be in Vocational School forever, and Slavik and I needed to make our plans for the future. As they were still doing everything they could to help us, the social workers also introduced Slavik and me to Olexiy Nikolayevich. He owned the Cherniy Piven or Black Rooster restaurant, where we eventually started to work during our internship. He was a good man and wanted to help people. He first met Slavik through a fund that helped orphaned children. So Slavik worked as a waiter. I asked if he could help me get a job, too, as a sous chef. They agreed to let me work for a trial period, but I proved myself and ended up staying for a year or more.

When we started, he gave us money to buy clothes, and then we worked as interns. He paid us a little each month. He didn't need to. The fund was there to help us learn skills, so he could have had our work at the restaurant in exchange for what we were learning, but he didn't want us to work for free. When he did well, he shared. It was barely enough to pay the utilities, but we were grateful.

Besides having the job, the chefs always made delicious meals for us. We would have soup or maybe a quick sandwich at lunch, but we had food as good as the restaurant guests at the end of the day. Mykolaj was the head chef in our kitchen. His mother graduated with a degree in Electronics Engineering but then left the field to join her son in the kitchen, where she advanced to a chef position. Vera was a little strict, but she and her son Mykolaj made excellent meals together.

Knowing Vera had changed careers and still became so successful made me realize I could do anything I wanted. Mykolaj taught me the same, but it had less to do with success and more with vodka. I was still seventeen when I had my first drink, but it carried forward into how we lived life. It was the way everyone in Ukraine lived.

I still remember the day. It was late, and we were tired after catering a big banquet for sixty people. It was common for us to sit down and eat leftovers after a big job. We still had a lot to do, but we all enjoyed having a break and some food after a long day of serving, and I was happy to be away from Tyotya Valya. Some nights I would sleep on a bench at the restaurant, so I didn't have to go back to her apartment at all.

Mykolaj and his mother, Vera, owned a big dalmatian dog that they would bring to the restaurant on the nights I stayed to keep me safe and entertain me while I did my work. I usually put food away in the evening, and the rest would wait till morning.

That night, I sat at a table counting tips when Mykolaj sat across from me, pounding a bottle and two small glasses onto the table in front of us. "Here, Vitaly. You're man enough to have a drink with me. Especially after a night like tonight."

He poured about a finger's worth of vodka into one of the glasses. The liquid was as clear as its container. It rippled, reflecting the dimmed lights of the kitchen as it settled in the glass.

When I took my first drink, I hated it. It was bitter, and it burned like a river of lava. I felt it run down the back of my throat and through my chest to settle in my belly. I coughed and even gagged a little, passing the glass back to him.

He laughed in response, "That's not how you drink vodka! So, here, try it again, but this time close your nose and gulp it. So, you don't taste it."

"Why am I drinking it if I don't like the taste?"

He laughed for some time before he answered, "Because it feels good." Then, he threw his head back, downing the contents of his glass in one swallow before filling it again.

I followed his lead and the burn soon spread to make me feel warm all over. He was right. It did feel good. I guess he was the one who prepared me for even longer nights and parties with my friends at the vocational school. We spent many late nights cleaning the kitchen and having family dinners. I knew family dinner didn't mean spending time with our families. Most of us were at the restaurant for so many hours we barely saw our houses. Family dinner was when we all gathered in the kitchen and shared leftovers from that night's menu.

The family meal was my favorite time of the day. The food was delicious, better than any I had. Tyotya Valya was an excellent cook, but the food we served at the restaurant was for people who had a lot more money to spend on dinner, and it was exquisite. Still, it wasn't just the food I liked. The food was always good, but the company of friends all working together was even better. It felt more like a family than any family I had growing up as an orphan. Except for with the friends who traveled this sometimes difficult road with me, I had never been allowed to laugh and talk and sometimes even sing at the dinner table.

I was grateful that Slavik and I had a chance to spend our time together in the restaurant. It was good to know I had people I trusted and who knew they could count on me, but now we also had friends at the restaurant and the vocational school. Our friendships were growing just as I knew they would when we finally found our way out from under Tyotya Valya's ever-present thumb.

36

Valya's Greed

With my foster family as an adult. Left to right: Luda (Slavik's wife) with Slavik,
Tyotya Valya, Serhij, Sasha, and me.

MY YEARS ATTENDING VOCATIONAL SCHOOL passed quickly. Before I knew it, the flower buds were already opening, spreading a good mood to everyone. I loved spring, and although it hadn't rooted itself yet in Ukraine, March 8, 1998, was a remarkably fresh and sunny day, giving a glorious hint to the coming season.

Spring always made me dreamy, and since it was Women's Day, I also wanted to make it exceptional for Tyotya Valya. Much like Mother's Day in the United States, we celebrated honored traditions every year. All the women in our home enjoyed a day off while the men did all the work. Though I often felt we did a lot of work every day, it was a special gift to give them the day off.

My life changed when I moved into foster care, but many of my habits remained the same. I still found the intimacy I could and continued the discipline I was taught to embrace, which meant following the rules Tyotya Valya taught. I think she appreciated my efforts, especially on Subotnik.

Having a family made Subotnik easier. The entire family would gather and get to work, cleaning grease out of the kitchen, dusting, and scrubbing so everything would shine and glow for the next couple of days. It was a never-ending cycle of unwanted commitments from cleaning the toilet and bathroom to dusting, doing dishes, and washing clothes. The kitchens in our new apartment lacked the familiar smell of grease stuck on the walls and ceiling, so there was less scrubbing, but we still had much to do.

One day cockroaches attacked our kitchen. The issue started with one bold adventurer running across the floor like a rocket. Still, we didn't realize how bad it was until the morning came, and we turned on the lights earlier than they expected. We had a massive invasion of tiny legs running for their hiding spots. Tyotya Valya sprayed poison on them and made us clean the kitchen every day, paying particular attention to every corner.

I knew Women's Day would be a lot like those days. We had a lot of work to do. Still, I wanted to do something memorable for Tyotya

Valya. As I was attending culinary classes, I decided to make one of her favorite dishes to celebrate her day; fried potatoes with onions, eggs, and sausage chunks. I was cutting, stirring, and frying most of the morning. I thought of presenting my gift to her the whole time, imagining the look she would have on her face when she saw what I had prepared for her. However, unlike my dreams of the mesmerizing spring day, the reality of who Tyotya Valya was didn't change,

"What have you done?!" She screamed as she burst into the kitchen, just as I put the finishing touches on the dish I prepared and decorated for her. She frowned instead of giving me the smile I always hoped I could get from her, "What were you thinking? Look at all this mess!"

As it was Women's Day, I was planning on cleaning the kitchen for her as well. I hoped to do it while she enjoyed her excellent breakfast, but she didn't give me time to explain the gift. Her rage grew instead, and I could feel that she was about to have another hysterical attack.

"Now, I have to clean everything!!!" She yelled, trembling in anger.

"The boy just wanted to make something nice for you, Valya," Dyadya Grisha said quietly.

She didn't listen. I don't even think she heard him. When Tyotya Valya thought something, that was it. Nothing could change her mind.

I didn't cry while she stood screaming at me, and I didn't say anything as there was nothing left to be said. I wasn't angry at all. I just felt cold inside and rigid, like something had died in me.

Everything was quiet in the room around us as I calmly waited for her to finish. When she did, I quietly walked to my room and sat on my bed. Then, moving my pillow slightly, I retrieved a handwritten card I made to celebrate Women's Day and thank Tyotya Valya for everything she had done for us as a mother. I opened it, thinking about everything I had in mind when I made it for her. Then, I closed it and put it back where it belonged, under my pillow. I never gave it to her as I didn't want to get the same awkward reaction or feel acid bubbles boiling in my stomach when she rejected the words I created. Later that day, Dyadya Grisha brought her flowers and champagne. He knew how to please her. His five minutes at the market made her happy. She loved his gift. I spent hours. I could have spent days, but she already decided she would hate anything I gave her. From that first day, when I asked for a second piece of watermelon, she never forgave me for that, for wanting something more than she was willing to give.

For years, I hoped living with Tyotya Valya would finally be like having a mother, but she never thought of us as her children. I remember asking her and Dyadya Grisha if I could call them Mama and Papa not long after moving in with them. Their answers were vague, with Dyadya Grisha saying nothing and Tyotya Valya saying, "If you want to, I guess you could, but we would have to live together longer." I was so excited for the day to come where I could use those words, but it never did. Tyotya Valya never said, "Yes," and eventually, I stopped asking.

I spent my entire time with her trying to please her, making every day her day, which usually meant being unseen and asking for as little as possible. I was afraid to ask her for anything, even the things I needed. Instead of asking her for food when I was hungry, I would sit with a jar of jam and a spoon to eat under my bed. When I asked for money to buy supplies for culinary exams or confectionary classes, she made it as if I did nothing but take from her.

Early in my first year of culinary classes, I asked her for a few hryven to get ingredients. She responded with acid-spitting from her mouth, "Two weeks ago, you asked me for help, and I gave you some money, and now you're asking again. I don't know what they do at that school, that they expect poor parents to pay so much."

"But Tyotya Valya, it's only a couple of hryven," I was asking for less than a dollar, but still, I was careful with my tone. I didn't want her to think I was demanding. I was hoping maybe she would see it was not much money.

"I told you this would happen. School is for rich people, and we're not rich. I told you that from the beginning. They only give me a hundred hryven a month to feed you. I also dress you and pay utilities." She expected me to do well in my classes and sometimes complimented me when I was successful, but she didn't care anymore if it had to do with her giving money. She only cared about my grades when she could use them to punish me. If my scores were ever low, it was "No television until your grades are better." Still, she didn't think of that. She just kept going, "I just gave you money last week for your test. You need to figure it out for yourself. I can't keep doing this."

She always went back to the same excuse of being poor, but she never made efforts to change anything. I didn't want to be poor and struggle my whole life like the people in my family. I knew that if I wanted to succeed in life, I needed to take advantage of the opportunity in front of me and learn as much as possible. It was a risk, but I decided to keep going, "You didn't give me money for that test. You said you didn't have it to give." I was all in now. Tyotya Valya remembered every time she spent anything on us, but she never remembered when she said "No."

I was silent for a moment. I knew I was playing with fire, but I needed the money to take my tests. So, I wasn't ready to give up. It was my last chance to make her understand. I needed to go as far as I dared. When I spoke again, I was pleading, "My grades won't be good if I can't pass my exam. I know how important my grades are to you."

It was a thing she could not argue. Still, when Tyotya Valya thought something, that was it. Nothing could change her mind. So she responded the way she always had when there was no reason to refuse. Anger boiled in her response, "Don't talk back. I help you every chance I get. You are ungrateful."

That was it. I knew it was over. That was the last day I ever asked Tyotya Valya for her help. Some parents will tell their children, don't ask again because they are upset, but they don't mean it. When their children come back to them for help, they give it gladly. Aside from the single serving we were allowed at each meal, Tyotya Valya never gave me another thing.

I knew I needed to make a meal to show my culinary skills to my teachers and everyone in my class. Every student had the assignment to cook the meal as a final exam for graduation. Nelya often asked if I wanted to make meals with her throughout the year, and she would supply food. I was grateful. We did many meals together, but I couldn't ask for her help all of the time. So, I talked to my teacher, trying to see if there was another way for me to pass her class.

Maryia understood my situation and helped me by providing ingredients for my exams. She also invited me home and fed me sometimes. She gave me pickled food and jam to take home and hide in my room. I will always be grateful for the teachers in my life who were kind to me, being the parents my parents weren't willing to be.

As I grew, I learned the kind of person Tyotya Valya was. She believed she was the one who had sacrificed for us, and we would never be able to do enough to pay her back. She spent all her time searching for the next advantage, regardless of who she used. She exchanged children like they were a commodity to be bartered, returning them to the orphanage when they weren't what she wanted. Then, every step we took was an insult to her. Our meals were a gift to her, though they paid her to feed us. We owed her for living in apartments that belonged to us. Everything she had was because of us, but she resented us for it instead of being grateful.

Before we turned eighteen, she knew she would need to do something to get the apartment from us. So, she divorced Dyadya Grisha without letting anyone know to get another apartment. They stayed together, but their marriage was not sacred to her, not if she could get something for herself. We never knew about the divorce until the time came for us to separate and live independently. We found out about it when she had to sign papers for each of our apartments.

She also used my relationship with my brother to try and take my apartment from me. I don't know how involved she was with Roustam's plan to sell my mother's apartment, but she had taken advantage of it. I was so surprised to discover that Nastya had known my brother all those years I lived at Tyotya Valya. Tyotya Valya must have known about him, but none of them said anything until Roustam needed me to testify, and then she was there, watching and waiting for her chance to strike.

When they placed us in Tyotya Valya's care, she told us that we would only live with her until we turned eighteen. After that, we needed to find a place to live and survive without help. I knew that wasn't true. The government program Tyotya Valya used promised each orphan an apartment. But, of course, it didn't work that way when the time came for us to take over. Tyotya Valya worked her magic and found a way to make what was ours, hers again. Slavik, Serhij, and I received one two-bedroom apartment when we turned eighteen. Masha and Nadya received another two-bedroom, but it was much smaller than ours, and Valya kept the other three for herself. With Rulan's help, she convinced a committee that I didn't need anything, that my brother would be taking care of me. Then, she took one apartment for her husband, one for herself, and one for her children, saying that she had earned them by taking care of us.

If I hadn't helped my foster siblings register and obtain passports to prove residency when they were sixteen, I'm sure we would have been in the streets. Unfortunately, I lost my right when I testified for Roustam, so Tyotya Valya had her way against me. Still, legally, I knew four of the apartments should have been ours, but there was no point arguing with her. Some of Ukraine's poor people adopted children not because they wanted a family but because they would get money and apartments. Tyotya Valya was one of those people. She was always right and would look out for herself and her children first. So, I let it go.

I will always be grateful to Dyadya Grisha and Tyotya Valya for giving us something better than the life we had at the orphanage. Still, they weren't a real family to us. I never did find the kind of family I knew we deserved, not from Valya. She never accepted us, not as a mother should think of her children. We were a means to an end for her. Only my friends and teachers were my support, but never anyone to call Mama. My mother wasn't it. Roustam wasn't it, and Tyotya Valya definitely wasn't. So, I gave up faith in them, but I didn't give up on myself.

My whole life, the person who took the best care of me, was me, and I was beginning to believe I could do anything. Though I never stopped wanting a real family to give me the love I knew I deserved, I decided to end my constant searching for them and focus on my achievements instead. I knew I could be successful. So I concentrated on my studies, excelled in my classes, and decided to take things into my own hands. And who knew; maybe, in the end, I could use that success to create a family as well.

37

Girls

This is my beautiful girl, Nelya, who was my best friend. This picture was taken
spending time together at the Primorsk resort.

OUR LAST DAYS OF CULINARY SCHOOL WERE NEAR. We were all getting ready for our final internship at the beautiful Primorsk Resort near the Azov Sea. This trip was our last opportunity to gain practical skills and apply the industrial, educational, and undergraduate learnings we acquired through our three years of study at the Vocational School. After taking our final test to perform professional work, we would all get minimum wages for the first time.

Everyone was looking forward to the upcoming summer because most of us had never been to a summer resort. We underwent a lot of necessary medical check-ups and preventive narcological and psychological examinations to prepare for our internships. We also had to get a passport, a copy of the document on education, a copy of the registration number on the taxpayer's account card, and a copy of the internship employment contract with the timeline of how long the employment would last.

I knew it was important to be ready early rather than late. Things could change, and I didn't want to risk not having everything prepared for an exciting summer with my friends. A nurse at the vocational school who was like a friend to me helped me get all necessary medical documents without paying a penny out of pocket for those tests. She helped me schedule blood and urine tests. She also had connections that moved me to the front of very long lines at various medical centers. I was grateful for her help. I don't think I could have made it without her, knowing that Tyotya Valya wouldn't help me pay for anything. I've heard, "it is not what you know, but who you know that matters." I guess I was going on with life without realizing that relationships were essential to get things done.

This year, eighty-five students were going to practice professional skills at various recreation centers. My group went to the Primorsk Resort, a recuperative climatic resort in the Mariupol region. I didn't know much about Mariupol, the Azov Sea, or the summer resort where we would spend our internship. Still, I was excited to travel away from Chernivtsi. Our journey began by taking a twenty-seven-hour train ride through Kyiv to Mariupol. Our master Mariya Omelyanivna came with us.

The Azov Sea is an inland sea in the Atlantic Ocean basin connected with the Black Sea by the Kerch Strait between Ukraine and Russia. It is the warmest in Ukraine and the shallowest near Primorsk Resort. Arriving there was nothing like being in Chernivtsi. Trace elements and mineral salts saturated the air, inspiring people worldwide to spend their summer vacations there. The resort's guests enjoyed relaxing by the sea and visiting museums, temples, and churches.

We worked fourteen-hour shifts to ensure the tourists had their freshly made healthy food every day. Then, after a hard day working in the kitchen, we spent our night having fun like any other night after work. Because we worked only one day and had the next day off, we knew it would be a day we could do whatever we wanted.

We spent most of our day off at the beach. We would sometimes go sightseeing or hiking, but we would usually swim or sunbathe. Then, after an enjoyable afternoon, we would go to someone's room, so we could drink, talk, and maybe play a few games.

One night, a few of us decided to play Durak, or The Fool, a card game where the first player lays down a card. After their turn, the next player tries to beat their card with a higher card. If the next player is unable or unwilling to top the exposed card, the defender has to pick up the cards. We continue until the person with no cards is declared the winner. There were maybe ten of us in all, but the people who made the night most memorable for me were Slavik, Oleksiy, and two girls from our group, Olena and Leeda.

I got used to being around many girls at the vocational school. Some of them were nice to be around, like Nelya, but sometimes other girls weren't as sweet. Olena and Leeda were two of those girls. They wore tight dresses, lots of makeup, and flirted with everyone, even their teachers. In geography class, Olena liked to tighten up her bra and show a lot of cleavage to get good grades. She was not afraid to misbehave because she knew that Anatoliy Panasovich, like many other teachers, enjoyed it and would let her pass their classes.

I tried to be nice to them, but I didn't like that they were troublemakers, and I wished they didn't have to be with us tonight. They laughed, making fun of me and trying to get me to respond to their silly sexual comments. I tried to go along with them sometimes or pretend I didn't care. I didn't want to look like a fool or give any impression that it was okay to joke like that, but I was also afraid of having my secret discovered by not responding to their jokes. So I tried to stay as far away from them as I could.

"Hey, Vitaly," Slavik said, pulling all of the attention to himself. He loved enticing people with his stories, and I was grateful to have the girls' attention on him when he did it. "Remember when we had that broken couch at the apartment, and we had to sleep in the room with Tyotya Valya and Dyadya Grisha. The room was so small, and we all somehow fit in it, but it came with its consequences."

I began to laugh, knowing where he was going with this one, "Slavik and I slept in a room with Tyotya Valya, Dyadya Grisha, and their three-year-old baby while we were waiting for Dyadya Grisha to fix the couch where we would sleep. Sometimes, Tyotya Valya said she could hear Slavik or me fart. She would wake up the next morning, saying, 'Last night, you boys made me think that there was an earthquake!' We would all laugh so hard about it, but I don't think Tyotya Valya thought it was that funny."

"Yeah, Vitaly and I farted most of all the kids. Tyotya Valya probably regretted putting us on a couch in the same room where she tried to sleep. I wonder how she didn't suffocate from our farts."

"The food she cooked for us is what most likely created the gas," I added, laughing. It was primarily carbs, no proteins, and fats. "If you think about it, it was a problem she created for herself."

All the boys were laughing. Slavik was laughing so hard he was almost crying. "Well, to be honest, I was happy to know we caused her problems with our farts, especially when she was angry with us. Being angry seemed to be her favorite daily activity, but we got even at night."

Everyone burst into hysterical laughter at Slavik's last statement, except the girls. They stood up and left for the adjoining room. I thought maybe they needed to use the bathroom. I know girls like to do that, go to the bathroom together. Or perhaps it was because we were talking about farts. Girls didn't seem to want to talk about farts as much as boys did.

I didn't pay much attention to what they were doing. I was kind of glad they left. All I wanted to do was watch Oleksiy, with his bright eyes and perfect smile. I wished I could be alone with him, just the two of us, so we could talk without everyone else having so much to say.

I liked Nelya, and I wanted to like her more, so I tried. I dreamed of having a family of my own, with children I wouldn't abandon, and Nelya was the perfect girl for that. We did many things together, and I thought of her as my girlfriend, but I wasn't sure what that meant. I never knew how to act like a boyfriend, so I mostly thought of her the same way I felt about Slavik, like a best friend I wanted to be around. She wasn't with us tonight because she didn't like to drink, and even though I liked her, I was glad. I was happy not to be distracted, pretending to be her boyfriend. I wanted to put all my attention on Oleksiy and build a friendship with him as well.

"Vitaly," I turned from my thoughts of Oleksiy to see who had called me. The girls had been gone for a while when I thought I heard one of them calling me from the bedroom,

"Vitaly, come in here. We have something to show you." I could hear them talking and laughing. I didn't want to go, but Slavik and Oleksiy were deep in a conversation about the game, and I didn't want anyone else to notice I was avoiding them. So, I went to see what they wanted.

Olena was sitting on the bed topless, and Leeda called me from the door, "Come here, Vitaly. Come and sit with us on the bed." They were drunk and smiling.

I smiled back, nervously looking between them and the door, not knowing what to do. Unfortunately, I didn't have a chance to decide as Leeda decided for me, pulling me into the room and closing the door behind me.

"Don't you like us, Vitaly?" Leeda's bottom lip stuck out, reminding me of a kid I knew at the orphanage who used to pout like that when he wanted something from the teacher.

I was afraid she would tell everyone there was something wrong with me if I didn't agree to sit with her. So, I decided to stay while my brain turned in circles, figuring out what to do.

The moment I sat down, Leeda started to undress me, taking off my t-shirt while Olena removed my shorts, leaving me in the swimsuit I wore that day at the beach. I sat, mostly confused, letting them do what they wanted. I didn't know what else to do. I knew they flirted a lot, but I had never seen girls do this before.

Olena started rubbing my chest, saying, "I feel like you don't like us, Vitaly."

"Of course I do," I said. I didn't want her to feel like I didn't like her. They were popular in our class and beyond. If I showed any sign of dislike, they would tell everyone, and word would travel quickly. I would be embarrassed in front of the entire group.

"Then why don't you touch me?" she asked, reaching over to grab my hand from my lap, "You haven't even tried to kiss me."

I didn't respond. I didn't know what to say. The only girl I ever kissed was Nelya, and that was just on the cheek as her friend. I never kissed anyone else, not how she wanted me to kiss her, and I didn't know how to do it.

"Have you ever kissed anyone?" It was like she read my mind, or maybe my silence.

"No," I said, a little embarrassed.

"I'll show you how she said... if you want."

I didn't want to hurt her feelings, but I didn't want to kiss her either. I wasn't sure what to do, so I said, "Okay." It was what I had to do.

She smiled, "It's easy. I'll show you," and that's what they did. They showed me what to do.

Olena started kissing me, and she kissed Leeda on her lips, too, occasionally looking at me to see if I liked it. Step by step, from the moment her lips touched mine, I mostly just followed her lead. When she opened her mouth, I opened mine. When her tongue came out, so did mine. I didn't know where to touch her, but she showed me. I didn't know what I was doing, but I just did everything she told me to do.

I remember her soft skin, like worn cotton just before you rewash it, and she smelled like lavender. I didn't feel bad touching her, but it didn't make me feel good, either. I didn't really feel anything. I noticed the way I felt when I was with Zhenya or when Oleksiy stood next to me on the line. I didn't hate touching her, but I wasn't excited either. So, I didn't go out of my way to try.

They noticed I wasn't doing much, and my body didn't respond the way they wanted. So, Olena pushed me down on the bed and sat on top of me, rocking her hips. I think I was supposed to like what she was doing, but I didn't, not the way she expected.

She paused, trying to put together the pieces of my rejection. "What's wrong, Vitaly? Are you uncomfortable with the two of us? Are you too inexperienced? Would you like it better if just one of us stayed?"

"Ummm, actually..." I tried to think of what I could say. The more the girls wanted to excite me, the more I wanted to leave. Then, it came, "I can't stop thinking of work. Mariya said she needed me to do something I forgot to do. I need to do it, or she will be upset, and I don't want to fail school." I jumped from the bed and got dressed. I needed to get out of the room before they realized what was happening. So, I rushed away, saying, "I need to go."

    I didn't go back to the party. I was frustrated, and I didn't want them confronting me. I could only hope they weren't upset enough to say anything to the group. Everyone wanted me to enjoy what just happened, and I even tried to enjoy it. I wanted a family to love. I wanted a wife and children I could love the way my family should have loved me. I was trying so hard, but it just didn't feel as good being around girls as I did being around boys.

    I examined my feelings, trying to understand them. I tried to face my demons and fight against them, and I prayed a lot, asking God to help me. I asked Him to take away my cravings and purify my heart. I wanted to be a good person, and I hoped the Lord would help me find a way. Maybe He could help me create the family I always wished to have. I hoped it could happen one day, but I didn't know how or when.

    So, I did what I could. I still had some time before I needed to worry about marriage, and I had Nelya by my side teaching me how to be her boyfriend. I also had the goal of going to University. Then, maybe, when I had a good job and a home of my own, I could think about having a family. I still had time to be saved while working on my future and the opportunities ahead of me. Then, when I was ready, God would find a way to help me be worthy of the family I always dreamed of having.

38

New Life and Loss

I am standing toward the back and showing off my Red Culinary Arts diploma. Mariya Omelyanivna, my Master Chef, who taught me everything, is in the front just behind the beautiful flowers our group gave her to thank her for helping us succeed.

I WORKED HARD TO FINISH my culinary internship and was so excited when I completed my final exams and received my

Diploma. It read:

Magidov Vitaly Vasylyovych
*successfully completed the program for the training of Pastry Cooks
at Vocational School No 10, Chernivtsi,
September 1, 1995 – June 30, 1998.
Based on the recommendation of the State Qualifications Board of June 24,
1998,
he is awarded this Diploma to certify that he is qualified
as Pastry Cook Fourth Class.*

Because I was a valedictorian, I was the only one in class to receive a red diploma. The rest of the class received blue or green. The educational government agencies colored our credentials to recognize how successful we were in our studies. Like everything else still lingering from the time we were under Soviet rule, red indicated the highest level of achievement.

While attending vocational school, I received Certificates of Honor for active participation in the school's social activities. I also won educational Olympiads in math and physics, where we competed against twenty-seven other non-technical and technical schools. In both competitions, I took first place.

I was proud to see that my hard work paid off and grateful for the help of great teachers and instructors throughout my life. I also appreciated that our government supported higher education initiatives. It gave priority to orphans and children of less fortunate families. They wanted us to succeed, and I had proved I would follow through with every advantage they gave me. I was going to prove that my brother Roustam and Tyotya Valya were wrong about my capabilities. I would succeed, even without their support.

Because of my success, I didn't have the normal application process to attend University. Instead, I had to gather recommendation letters from various organizations and attend a single interview to prove I was prepared to handle the University courses.

I had a pretty easy time gathering my letters, but I wanted to do well in my interview. So, I did everything I could to prepare. It was my one chance, and I wanted to ensure I made no mistakes when I took it. So, I studied all I could, and even though I always did well in math, I never thought it was anyone's favorite subject. So I decided it might be helpful to get a refresher course to prepare for the meeting.

Masha, Serhij, and Nadya were a grade beneath me in school, and they had a teacher who was also a math tutor. I decided she was the perfect person to help me pass my interview. She was so helpful and offered additional tutoring hours to them for free that I hoped she could be my tutor as well.

Zoya Yakivna taught every student with such love and passion I thought I had met the best teacher in the world the first time I sat with her. But, I had no idea how much she would change my life.

I remember the first time I visited her old two-bedroom apartment near the city's center. Zoya lived in a walk-through room at the front of the apartment with her husband and in the last room lived her daughter-in-law, Tanya, with her two children, Arthur and Susanna. The apartment had high ceilings, so high I couldn't reach them, but as with many people in Ukraine, the two families shared one tiny kitchen. Still, Zoya's family welcomed everyone to share the little they had.

I met with Zoya several days a week as I prepared for my meeting. I loved being with her. Besides her excellent math knowledge and years of experience knowing how to study, she was also kind and would invite me to eat with the family when I was there. I was so grateful for the food and the time I spent there. She knew about my family situation and did all she could to help us. She helped Serhij and Nadya get good grades and was pivotal in helping me get accepted to the

University.

I loved everyone in Zoya's family and soon became close friends with Tanya. Susanna, Tanya's youngest, loved to play around me, and Arthur kept me engaged with his smartness and talents. Arthur was young and very bright. He spoke Hebrew that he learned at school, studied violin, knew tons of useless facts from the World Encyclopedias, and could also play the piano well for his age. Though he took classes for the violin, he had learned to play piano on his own, only by listening to others. I became enthralled the very first time I saw him play. I wanted to learn to play the piano, just like him. So, I often stayed after dinner to take lessons. He was young, but he was still a good teacher.

Besides just the family, there were often young men from Tanya's church who would meet with her while I learned all I could from Zoya and Arthur. Many of the young men were very cute and spoke with an accent. So I spent as much time at their house as possible, but I didn't get to know anyone but the family until Tanya began inviting me to attend Church Sacrament Meetings with her.

Though I began following atheism early in life, from the communistic laws, I became more involved in the Russian Orthodox Church, now known as Ukrainian Orthodox, when I lived with Tyotya Valya. Though I continued to live as before, guided only by my desires, I always wanted to understand why it is necessary to do some things and not others. If something is forbidden, why is it that way? Who decided what we should do? I received only vague answers saying, "It is bad, or that society will not accept it." Still, none of the explanations satisfied me. So I continued to wander in the dark and did not understand how I had to live to please God.

The information I absorbed from television, radio, books, and magazines said it is necessary to take everything from life. I learned we should seek fortune and achieve success in society. Still, behind all the hustle of society, we live, and we could die at any moment. So, I wondered, "What is the purpose of human life?" Was I to follow the rules to achieve success in my next life, or should I pursue everything to have success now? This issue became acute, standing before everything else in my mind.

I was going to Baptist School family gatherings for Bible study. I also studied with the Seventh Day Adventists at the time. I loved reading my Bible and committed to reading it every day for an entire year until I knew most of the Old Testament stories by heart. I met with Pentecostals, Jehovah's Witnesses, and others. I also talked to all sorts of Evangelicals. Chernivtsi had over a hundred different Christian organizations I could research. It seemed that maybe other people were like me and looking for answers and eager to adopt beliefs after the USSR's fall allowed them to do so, and I was ready to keep the discussion with anyone who would have it.

Zoya and her family came to me with some interesting answers to my questions. When I met the family, I was studying the New Testament, and I could remember most of the scriptures I was reading by heart, but I was always hungry for more. One day, Tanya asked me if I was interested in attending The Church of Jesus Christ of Latter-day Saints (LDS Church). She gave me a missionary pamphlet that summarized the plan of happiness and details about The Church. It also provided the address where the Sunday meeting would be.

I agreed quickly. I was excited to try it, even though my Babushka Halina, Tyotya Valya's mother, always said, "Orthodox means 'to praise God correctly.' The Orthodox Church has passed the keys to praise God correctly through generations of tradition from the early apostles. We must follow those keys. Whoever is not an Orthodox Christian is dangerous and evil."

I was not like most Orthodox Christians, so I decided to go to Tanya's church. The LDS Church was still establishing itself in Chernivtsi, so it didn't have many people yet or a building. So we took a trolleybus to the space The Church rented for Sunday Meetings.

Three people met us at the entrance door as we arrived. Two of them spoke English and a little broken Ukrainian. They were so accepting. It seemed that I had come to visit old friends who were very happy to see me. Inside, everything was simple. There were no icons, decorations, candles, or crucifixes for me to kiss.

It felt so foreign to me. I didn't know how to act, but Zoya's family was there to help me. After the Church Meeting, Tanya invited me to their home for lunch. I was happy to join, but first, I told her to go ahead of me because I had something I needed to do.

Every time I went to the LDS Church, I ran to the Cathedral I passed after to place a candle at one of the altars. Then, I said a quick prayer asking God to forgive me for changing the way I worshiped him. After my penance, I always felt relieved and at ease, knowing I had made peace with Him before heading to Tanya's home for a nice lunch.

After lunch, we read scriptures, discussed more questions, and Arthur and Tanya performed a musical number for all of us to enjoy. Arthur played the violin while Tanya and Susanna sang together a spiritual song they learned in another church when they were members there. I was so grateful for all the new people in my life. I felt blessed to have everything I needed, and I gave credit to God. I must have made the right decision to have all this love in my life. Among all the difficulties I still faced, I also had many blessings, and I gratefully recognized each one.

As it came time to celebrate the New Year, I decided to spend it with Tanya and her family. We spent the night joined by a couple of the young men from Tanya's church. We played American games like Uno and Skip-Bo. After our fun, when the young men left, I stayed to help them prepare dinner.

After dinner, Tanya read from the Book of Mormon and the Bible until midnight, when we joined the celebration. We began our celebration with a prayer and then followed some of the New Year's traditions until two or three in the morning. That is when Zoya shared with me the story of her son, who had died. We didn't drink that night. I wasn't used to having parties that didn't include alcohol. Still, I felt grateful I had spent the time with them. I preferred reading the Bible and feeling uplifted.

The following day, more church members came to Tanya's house, and we continued our festivities. The best thing was, we woke up feeling good with no headache or stomach upset to bother us, and we continued to praise God for our blessings.

Zoya's family included God in everything they did, every day, the way I always thought it should be. We started and finished almost everything we did with a prayer. I loved spending time with Tanya and Zoya. They always made me feel like family, but I still had a family of my own, as well. So, my holidays were busy, going from one family to the next, enjoying the many people I had in my life to love and be loved.

I spent Christmas with my sisters. Then, I returned to visit Tanya that night. Again, she invited several church members to dinner and caroling at the homes of other brothers and sisters from The Church. However, this time, instead of asking for donations, we brought candy we had made to lift the spirits of those who needed our visit the most.

After caroling, we returned to share a dinner of kutya. Next, we shared a traditional meal of potato dumplings with our porridge and cabbage rolls, filled with rice, meat, fried carrots, and onions, wrapped in cabbage leaves, and boiled until the leaves became soft. We also had a regular salad de-beff, a meat salad made with cubes of cooked sausage, potatoes, carrots, green peas, and onions mixed in mayo. Finally, Zoya prepared her favorite apple pie and rose herbal tea, made of rose flowers, dried tulips, and mint leaves to finish the meal.

Tanya said she couldn't have the tea. She would let us do what we wanted, but she never strayed from her commitments to The Church. The LDS Church had a doctrine called the Word of Wisdom that inspired its members to live healthy by choosing not to drink black tea or coffee and avoid unhealthy food. Tanya went far beyond what The Church taught her. She decided that it was not just any black tea that she was not supposed to drink, but it included every beverage with any caffeine. Even though the tea we drank was herbal, she knew that giving anyone the impression that she drank black tea would lead others to think that drinking tea was okay. She said it would be contradictory to what The Church taught.

I saw Tanya as a saint and wanted to learn all she knew about The Church and its scriptures.

With my many New Year's blessings, there were also significant losses. After graduating from the vocational school, I went to see Tyotya Valya and wished her well for the holidays. Unfortunately, Tyotya Valya told me that Babushka Halina had passed away when I arrived. I was sad, and I knew I would miss her. I was always so inspired by how hard-working my Babushka was. I would often walk the six miles to her village to see her. Even though she was well over eighty years old, she would still take the time to teach me how to make bread, chop wood, and gather water from the well.

Babushka was the one who invited us to go to church and pray for the Christian holidays. She wanted me to be an altar singer, but Tyotya Valya made it impossible. However, I did still love to go to the services with Babushka. She was strict, but she was also the one who inspired me to keep learning about every Orthodox saint and memorize many prayers for specific occasions. Whether it was for Christmas, Labor Day, or someone I loved, she taught me that every prayer had its purpose. She also said that praying the prayers in the original Slavic language had more power than translating them. So, she inspired me to learn them and the Bible in the old language, helping me pray in the most powerful way I could

As I left Tyotya Valya's apartment, I thought of Babushka Halina's visits and how Tyotya Valya would make our favorite delicious cake baked with condensed milk and honey dough. I knew I would never have cake with my Babushka again. No matter how much my life moved forward, I lost the things I loved as well. I guess the answer to finding joy in life is to enjoy the things that make you happy while you can. You don't know if they will be there to make you happy again tomorrow.

39

The One Who Loved

As children we all have dreams and as adults, we can't help but wonder what life would have been like if those dreams had come true.

I LOVED HAVING SPECIAL PEOPLE IN MY LIFE, people like Slavik, who were part of my every day. When I was at the orphanage, I felt that way about Martha. I couldn't remember a day in my life where she wasn't there until the day came that she was gone. Nobody knew why, but one day, there was suddenly an empty place where Martha once stood. I didn't know how I processed it. I knew other orphans might leave. Families adopted them, or they became adults and left, but as far as I knew, Martha had always been there, and in my young mind, I assumed she always would be as well.

Her absence left a massive gap in my chest. I missed her terribly. I missed her warning glances and how she called out my name whenever I did something wrong. She knew I couldn't resist pushing the limits of my educators' patience, and Martha was severe sometimes, punishing me when I went too far. Still, I never doubted her compassion. She truly loved and cared for us.

I remember one day, as I was testing my courage, I decided to climb onto a window ledge and try balancing with only my feet. I was barely stable, teetering on the windowsill with my arms outstretched. Martha entered the room right as I decided it was a good idea to see if I could stand on just one foot. She froze for a moment, looking at me as though she might be having a heart attack.

I froze as well, knowing that she would punish me, but she didn't. We stood there for a moment, just staring at one another. Then, Martha rushed forward to pull me down from the window ledge. She didn't say anything. Once I was on firm ground, she let go, and then she left without a word. I stood stunned, hearing her call for another teacher to take care of me as she continued down the hall.

A few weeks later, she was gone for good. It was as though the earth opened and swallowed her, taking her away to where no one could find her. I wondered if she died or just another person who disappeared, like my mother. Then, one of the other teachers told us she quit and started teaching in another school. They said she missed us but was happy there. I don't know if I ever reconciled her leaving. After that, everyone seemed to be going places they weren't taking me.

Though I didn't particularly appreciatate living under a communist regime, there were many generous benefits to it. Communism was about people sharing their homes and everyone taking care of each other. The tradition of sharing carried over even after the fall of the Soviet Union. Even years after graduating, teachers and students kept personal relationships alive, as I did with the orphanage and some of my teachers there.

Shortly before I started at the University, we visited Martha at her new job. Her eyes filled with tears when she saw us. She told us she often checked on us as if she was still our teacher. My chest filled with an overwhelming sense of peace, and my mind flooded with memories of Martha. I don't think it was until that moment that I realized how much I had lost. She was always proud of us and happy to see us doing well.

As our visit neared its end, Martha took me aside and put an arm around my shoulder, leaning her head against mine. "Vitaly," she spoke my name with a warmth that confirmed everything I knew about her. "I want you to know something," she said, "I want you to know that I always wanted to adopt you." Her eyes glistened with tears she tried to hold. "I wanted to be your mother, but circumstances were different than I hoped they would be. I didn't have the means to support you. The only thing I had to give you was my love and attention, but children cannot live solely on their mother's love. They must be fed and clothed as well."

I didn't know if Martha was correct or not. I would have traded all the clothes and food I didn't have for just a parcel of that motherly love—images of how my life could have been with Martha as my mother flashed before my eyes. Growing up at the orphanage, surrounded by so many parentless children, the only thing I ever wanted was to be loved and have a family of my own. Martha was probably the closest thing to a mother I knew.

Martha continued speaking, and my dreams of what might have

been evaporated into the thick air of a sunny afternoon, "At least I can say, my dear boy, that I was the one that found the family you deserve."

I always wondered why Tyotya Valya and Dyadya Grisha chose Slavik and me to live with them. Had Martha done that?

She was smiling, "You see, I knew how much you wanted to have a family of your own. So, when I couldn't give you one, I found one for you. When one of the foster families we work with came to us looking for children to take home, you were the one I recommended."

I couldn't speak. I just looked at her, speechless, my eyes wide.

"And, my dear Vitaly, when I saw they were considering you, which meant that you would be leaving the orphanage soon to join your new family, I knew your dreams came true. So, you didn't need me anymore."

Martha gave me a family. Even when she wanted to be my family but couldn't, she ensured I had one anyway. I could not move or blink for a few moments, as I couldn't believe how much love Martha kept for me behind her wrinkled, often angry face.

"You did that for me?" Her gesture impacted me. I can't imagine how much worry I gave her.

"I would do even more if I could. You know you were always finding some way to get detention or worse. But when I saw you climbing on the window ledge that day, I knew I couldn't bear it if something happened to you. So, I had to leave, and I knew I could go with some peace of mind if I helped you find the family you wanted. You deserved to have a family of your own. I knew how much it meant to you."

"I don't know what to say…" to merely thank her seemed like not enough. Forgetting the distance between us, the manners we used at the orphanage, forgetting everything, I hugged her, and she hugged me back.

"Vitaly, please, don't share this with anyone. I could…"

I nodded, stopping her words. My heart beat madly in my chest, spreading warmth throughout my body. I blinked hard, trying to prevent my tears from falling. Again, I wished I had my mother's lap to cry on, but that wasn't the case, so I swallowed the bitter lump stuck in my throat and remembered Martha's kind words instead.

We said "Goodbye," and I left, thinking about what she did for me, eternally grateful that I had a chance to be nurtured by such an exceptional woman. If someone like Martha was in the world so willing to give such unconditional love, maybe I could believe again in possibility. Perhaps it didn't need to be me on my own. It could be that the family I deserved was still out there waiting for me.

40

University

The main entrance to Chernivtsi National University, founded in 1875.

THE PROCESS OF GETTING INTO The University was complex. Our typical admission process involved taking entry exams related to the subject you were studying. Typically, the application process for an Engineering Degree required all applicants to take math and physics exams. However, because I placed first during the Math and Physics Olympiads and graduated from Vocational School as a valedictorian, they offered me a place in the program by merely speaking with the Dean of the Physics faculty.

The Dean, Mykhaylo Stepanovych, was eager to learn about my background. He checked the letters I brought with me and asked why I was applying to the Engineering Program. He reviewed documents from the various government agencies stating that I came from an orphanage and foster care. He also read teachers' recommendations and my valedictorian diploma. The Dean was happy with our conversation, and at the end of our interview, he asked me if I could start in the fall.

On September first, 1998, I was accepted to The University of Chernivtsi to pursue my microelectronics and semiconductors degree. Finally, my dream to learn at a well-established school came true. I was almost crying when I discovered I was accepted because Tyotya Valya's words did not come true. They fueled the desires of my heart instead. To be admitted to The University without growing up in a wealthy family or paying money to anyone was a success I created myself.

When I first began preparing for University, there was a lot of competition to get accepted into the Computer Science field I first considered—four people applying for one seat. So, I decided to pursue electronics and engineering because it was more readily available, and I was still interested in doing it. As a child, I was amazed by electronics, always trying to create something that had a life of its own. I was innovative and passionate about technology and entrepreneurship at a very young age. I knew I could be successful at anything by taking the opportunity to use my technical abilities.

While at the Vocational School, I had a great Computer Science teacher who taught me a lot about electronics and fixing televisions. With his help, I used the computer to program in BASIC language, assemble computers, and convert a regular black and white monitor into a television. Though Tyotya Valya didn't like it when I brought equipment home, I tried to learn everything I could, quietly hiding it from her eyes.

Going to University was very different from attending a vocational school. We had nineteen girls and only six boys during vocational training, and now, at The University, we had nineteen boys and only two girls. Another thing that changed is the number of classes we were taking, and a lot of them seem to be more challenging, taught to us at a faster pace. I barely had enough time to digest new things.

The subjects that I found interesting were much easier for me to study. Ukrainian universities offer diverse educational opportunities, so we didn't study specialized subjects for very long. Besides math and physics, I could also learn art and other topics unrelated to my preferred profession, such as economics, history, and philosophy. The main reason for that is because the educators believed it was essential to have a well-rounded education. So, if someone wanted to switch from physics or math to an economics degree, they could easily do so.

I never had problems deciding what I wanted. We had a lot of subjects, and I knew how to use them. Still, it was hard for me to manage all of them. For exams, they required us to write the answers and then stand up and explain to the teacher what we wrote and why we answered the way we did. The teachers had the right to ask additional questions.

I heard that Ukraine became independent In 1991. But, I did not completely understand what it meant. So, I continued to live without fully understanding how much that moment had impacted my life. When we discussed Independence during one of my college courses, I learned the full impact of what the people accomplished that day, simply wanting to make a difference. In one of my history classes at The University, I volunteered to write an essay and present it in front of the class about the vital subject "Independence Day."

"There are two different perspectives on what Independence means in our country. Some people believe that Independence is good because it helps us advance as other independent countries have advanced. Others believe that Independence is not offering the same opportunities as communism did.

With communism, the government provided housing and jobs to anyone graduating from college. Every person had something, but the problem with communism was that the people were not truly free. The government had a path for them to follow.

People were also close-minded and did not see what was happening outside their own country. Because of Independence, I can travel wherever I want. Independence has opened doors to the "outside" world. There is not one individual in charge of the country but the people. People control the government and have the freedom to do what they want.

Because of Independence, I can build my own life the way I want it and not as someone wants it for me. Because of Independence, I know that there are better things in life to live for me than staying at home and not progressing because someone has already made my decisions for me. Because of Independence, no one is there to tell me what to do anymore.

It is up to me to decide because I am free."

My words inspired everyone in the room, and even the teacher was inspired enough to give me an A.

I did well with my studies, but I didn't have money to pay teachers for private lessons or anything else. So, I had to do everything by my efforts. I did everything I could to take advantage of the opportunities they presented. I made sure I didn't miss a laboratory assignment because that accounted for the overall grade. If I made sure I finished my labs, it meant I passed many of the tests by default. It was the easiest way to succeed, but I didn't do it alone.

Even though I graduated in 1998, I often returned to the vocational school. I used the Internet at my Computer Science teacher's class and visited some of my old teachers and the principal. I liked keeping in touch with Nina Victorivna, the librarian, more than any teacher. She was a short lady and probably not seen by everyone, but she was all-knowing and very kind. She often helped me find what I needed for my studies or invited me to her house for dinner. While other students rented books under strict regulations, I was lucky and got to borrow books I needed for studies and return them based on the trust that we built with each other. Without her help, I don't know if I would have been as successful at school.

So many of my old instructors helped me with questions about my studies, and I could never forget the medic nurse and how she helped me with the documents I needed for my summer internship at the resort. I was so grateful for all the help they gave me as I continued to work hard toward my dreams, and I wanted them to be proud of me.

Tyotya Valya was right about The University costing money, not for the education itself, but to bribe officials into passing your tests. It wasn't that I didn't get good grades on my tests. On the contrary, I worked hard to do well, but they rewarded some people better than others, giving answers to pass the tests to students who paid for private lessons.

The Quantum Mechanics class was the most challenging of all courses. To remember all those long-winded calculus formulas was almost impossible, and only a couple of students could master it. One of those A students always impressed me with how they could derive formulas and apply them on board in front of the entire class while everyone watched him, trying to understand what he had written. I was one of those students making detailed notes, hoping they might help me with the exam preparations.

One critical exam I remember began at nine a.m. I needed to be up early because the physics and math classes were not at The University. They were across town, and it took me about two hours to get there. I remember being so worried about waking up early I didn't even sleep that night. I was also concerned about two of the girls in the class and whether or not they would pass. They helped me a lot by taking detailed notes of any lessons I missed to help me prepare for my upcoming tests. I was grateful for their help. I helped them in return by solving complicated calculus and physics-related problems. We worked together and were looking after each other. So, I was worried about them.

I spent a lot of time preparing, but I always worried when taking a test. When I started the class, the teacher wanted me to schedule private lessons, to prepare for the tests. The instructor would tell the students the test questions and their answers in the private lessons. I didn't have the one hundred hryven—almost all of my monthly government stipend—he wanted me to pay. So, for me, I knew he would make up questions I couldn't answer because I didn't give him the money he wanted.

I think that I answered the questions I knew very well. However, there were additional unexpected questions. I didn't study for those questions and could not answer them accurately. As I left the exam, the teacher said to me, "I wanted to give you a B. However, because you didn't know the answer to the last question, I will give you C."

I felt sad and happy at the same time. I didn't have anything less than a B in any other class during that semester, and I didn't think giving good grades for bribing our teachers was the right way to educate students. I passed with a C, but the girl before me, who knew less than I knew, got a B. I asked her how she did it, and she explained that she took his private lessons to help prepare for the exam. She didn't know I faced additional questions he taught her in their sessions.

I was still happy to get a passing grade, but I never forgot the experience. I did try to be positive. Still, I never felt good about getting a C, especially knowing I was more capable than some other students. Some of those students had to retake the exam instead of having a summer vacation. I was grateful for not being one of them and for knowing, I always strived to get the best grades possible. The feeling that I had passed the class honestly, and received that grade with my efforts, left me proud of my work and accomplishments.

I often felt I only passed my exams because God was helping me through them. He gave me teachers from the vocational school to help me, and he gave me the heart to study, but I wanted the world to be different. I wanted to live where teachers didn't manipulate their students and where students didn't bribe their teachers. I wanted to live somewhere where honesty was more important than greed.

41

Searching for Jesus

Susana, Tanya, Arthur, me, and Zoya with two American missionaries behind us.

THOUGH I SOMETIMES WENT TO CHURCH with Tanya and her family, I still met with the Jehovah's Witnesses and stayed loyal to Orthodox teachings. I wanted to understand life after death and what eternal punishment meant. I did not know at the time that the answer would come when two good-looking young men with badges on their chests knocked on my door.

I was running late for school and didn't have time to talk to anyone. So, I didn't answer until the third knock. As I opened the door, I was surprised to find the well-dressed men standing side by side and smiling at me, almost as if they knew I would be glad to see them. I recognized one of them from Babushka Zoya's house. If it weren't for seeing him there, I would not have known how they knew me.

I was excited to see them. They weren't like anyone I knew in Ukraine. They wore neat black suits and white-collar dress shirts with ties. I thought they must have a lot more money than I did or anyone I knew to dress so well at their age. Still, the things that made them obvious foreigners were their neatly cut hairstyles and beautiful white smiles. People from Ukraine seldom had such white teeth because personal hygiene was not the same. Most of the people I knew took baths once a week and didn't brush their teeth every day. They established habits living during communist times when paying attention to personal needs over the Party was not expected. When you share a bathroom with other families down the hall, you don't always have the luxuries people in other countries take for granted.

"Hello, My name is Elder Bradley, and this is Elder Wilson. We are missionaries from The Church of Jesus Christ of Latter-day Saints." The taller one spoke confidently while the other stood back. I couldn't help but admire his accent, knowing that he must be learning to speak my language so he could visit me. Most of the visitors I met from Canada and the United States spoke Russian, but these two young men caught my attention when they introduced themselves in my native tongue.

I remembered hearing the same young man speak English to Arthur. Arthur was fluent in English and understood everything they said. Although Tanya was also learning English, she encouraged Arthur's development and allowed him to speak English with them whenever she could. She always told me that even though she didn't know the language well, the Holy Ghost and her heart helped her understand what they said.

Like Arthur, I wanted to practice and perfect my English. I was learning the rules of English in school, and I thought maybe they would teach me too. Also, I knew they must be Americans because of their American accent and their names. So I wanted to learn about America. I wanted to know everything I could about them, but I did not know what to say.

I didn't need to. Elder Bradley continued, "We are here to speak to you about the Gospel of Jesus Christ. Do you have a few minutes where we can talk to you?"

I wished I could stay. They were so intriguing to me. I was curious about what Elder meant, but I knew I had to go. "I am so sorry," I said. "I am excited to meet you and talk to you, but I must go to take a test."

"Would it be okay if we came back some other time to talk to you?"

I was so happy they were willing to return. So, we set a time for them to visit.

I thought about them on my way to school and every day after. I spent every moment I could planning for our visit, but my classes stood in the way once again. I had a class that ran late on the day our scheduled appointment arrived. I was heartbroken. At that time, I still lived with my brothers in the very last building at the city's edge, on the road to Romania. To get to and from school took me two hours each way by Marshrutka. I worried the whole way home, thinking of how I had missed my second chance to talk to them. I hoped they would not be too upset and believe that I was ready to listen to what they had to say.

As I came to my front door, I saw a little note saying, "We returned, but no one was at home. We're sorry we missed you. We will return next Thursday at the same time."

I was so happy when I saw the note that said they would come back. So, I made sure that I was ready for them the following Thursday. I had everything in the apartment set an hour before they promised to arrive, just in case, and I did everything I could to help them feel at home. First, I cleaned. After that, remembering that Tanya's family always fed the young men when they visited, I made tea and perogies to eat if they were hungry. Then, I sat waiting, counting the minutes until they arrived.

Finally, there was a knock on my door. I rushed to answer it. When I saw them standing there, I was so impressed by them. They wore the suits as before with perfectly placed badges on the lapels. "The Church of Jesus Christ of Latter-day Saints" was written in bold lettering, right below their names, "Elder Bradley" and "Elder Wilson."

I was nervous but very excited to meet them, "Hi. My name is Vitaly. You said your names are Bradley and Wilson? Are those American names?"

Elder Bradley smiled, "Yes, but they are not our first names, Vitaly. When we do our work, we don't use our first names. We only use our first names with the people in our community back home. Then, when we visit new people on our mission, we use a professional title, followed by our last names."

His answer was so honest. "So, the name Elder is like a greeting? We also use different words for the people we know here, like my Tyotya Valya. I always called her Tyotya Valya because she took care of me as an aunt would. I only use that name because she is close to me, not because she is my real aunt."

"Well, it's kind of like that, but not exactly. Elder is more like a professional title. It means someone who is appointed to do the work of The Church."

"Oh, I see. It's like the Orthodox Church when we call someone a

Bishop."

"Yes. We have Bishops in our church too. Is that your church Vitaly? The Orthodox Church?"

I looked at Elder Wilson. He hadn't said anything yet. I think he was shy to speak. Elder Bradley did most of the talking, but that was okay. I thought they would both have things to say as we came to know each other.

"I'm not a practicing member. I grew up in Communism, in an orphanage, but when I went into foster care, my foster mother taught me about the Orthodox Religion and baptized me in the church. So, it is what I practice. Please come in. I will get chairs from the kitchen."

We lived in the tiny two-room apartment we received when we left Tyotya Valya. Our separation was a joyous moment since we no longer had anyone telling us what to do. We were free to do what we wanted, but we didn't get a perfect place to stay. Tyotya Valya always won her prizes, but we won our freedom at least.

When we moved in, we decided to share one bedroom, putting beds against each of the three walls to leave the second room as a living room. We also had a small kitchen and a bathroom that Slavik, Serhji, and I shared between the three of us. Unfortunately, the bedroom was so small, the beds overlapped each other, reminding me of the small rooms of the orphanage. But it gave us a living room, so we lived with it.

I wished I had a better place for these polite men, but I did what I could. We sat on the few chairs I had in the center of what should have been a bedroom for our first discussion about God and the eternal family.

Elder Bradly was understanding, responding to my apologies with kindness in his eyes. "It's not always easy, Vitaly," he said. "Like with us. We live our lives in service to The Church. We go out every day to help people like you find the true meaning of Christ, but we struggle too. It is hard to find a good place to live or to have time to do all the things we need to do, but we do it to serve the Lord and His calling."

I was surprised to see they sometimes struggled like me. Still, we were all happy and talked about everything we could imagine. They told me about some of The Church's doctrines and were willing to answer all my questions, no matter how many I had and how hard they were.

I asked them why they didn't worship the saints, asking for their prayers or wearing crosses to remember Jesus' sacrifice. I wore a silver cross that an Orthodox priest sanctified for my protection, and I often wondered why they didn't have any cross emblems on their scriptures or in their churches. I believed that the main reason I was wearing the cross and making a cross sign on my body before entering The Church and before and after my prayers was to remember Christ's sacrifice for us and that I had to remain pure. However, they told me something that I found very interesting and convincing. "Vitaly, we believe in Jesus Christ and His sacrifice. We remember Him in our hearts and don't place any icons outside on buildings, on scriptures, or wear them. If wearing the cross on your neck is something that you like to wear to help you remind you of Him, then you can continue to do that. There is nothing that prohibits you from continuing to follow the traditions you've learned. We believe that every religion has something good in it. And whatever is good comes from God," I smiled and thanked them for this explanation.

"Why do you fast for only one day? After being baptized, Jesus fasted for forty days, being tempted by Satan the whole time. As He prevailed through all those temptations, we fast from eggs, dairy, and meat for forty days in the Greek Orthodox Church. Why do you starve yourself from everything and only for one day? "

"God gave us one day to fast so that we could feed the poor, Vitaly. So we fast and save the money we would have spent on food to give to someone who needs it. It's another way to be of service."

I never thought of fasting for that reason. I liked helping people, so I followed up with another question, "What is a Sacrament? I've been to your Church with Tanya. Why do you call it a Sacrament Meeting?"

"Sacrament is a ceremony where members partake of bread and water in remembrance of Jesus Christ's sacrifice. It allows us a moment to remember the ministry of Jesus and his Atonement as the Son of God."

"Why do you use water and not wine? Wasn't wine on the table at the last supper?"

"A revelation was given to the Prophet Joseph Smith said that what we eat or drink when we partake of the sacrament is not important as long as we do it with an eye single to His glory. The revelation also advised that we should not purchase our enemies' wine or strong drink. We choose to honor Jesus through both of these teachings. We take the sacrament as a symbol of his sacrifice, and we do not consume alcohol to keep pure the intention in our hearts."

They taught me about the Word of Wisdom I first learned from Tanya, explaining that it is a healthy way of living given to them through their prophet Joseph Smith. Next, they explained the Book for Mormon and told me about the teachings of Joseph Smith. It all made sense, but what surprised me most was learning that The Church is still led by a modern-day prophet, along with his chosen apostles and seventy disciples.

They also taught me that the prophet of the LDS Church emphasized the importance of tithing ten percent of our income to The Church. This subject did not fit in my head, but they showed me that this law goes way back to the Old Testament. Elder Bradley said, "God gives us all we have, and therefore it is fair to give a tenth back to Him. Therefore, I have agreed to give my share."

I asked many questions, and they answered every one with a smile. I was happy so many of their answers made sense to me. I searched for a long time to understand God and why things happened the way they did. The Greek Orthodox Church didn't always explain everything, and the Jehovah's Witnesses didn't listen. They just waited to argue with everything I said. Now, the missionaries were talking to me about the things I believed. They committed to living their lives in the best way they could. It sounded like the way I wanted to live.

As we finished our discussion, Elder Bradley pulled a book from his backpack and said, "Vitaly, we have something for you."

I wasn't sure what was happening. It wasn't my birthday or any holiday I knew. Elder Bradley barely knew me, and he was giving me a gift. I was very grateful and excited to see what it was.

Gold lettering shone against a blue background on the book he handed me. I caressed the letters as I read, "The Book of Mormon - Another Testament of Jesus Christ." Looking at the book's title written so beautifully in my native language, I realized why some people in the community called them Mormons. I was surprised by such an elegant gift and so full of appreciation.

Elder Bradley smiled as he watched me. "We know you love to read and study the Bible," he said, "and you know it so well. This book is a supplement to the Bible. A verse from the Gospel of John twenty-one verse twenty-five taught us the need for additions like these. This book is a record of those teachings. We want you to have it."

I was blessed to have these men in my life, and now they gave me such a wonderful gift. They asked me to read two chapters from the first book of Nephi and pray about it to receive my testimony about the scriptures from the Holy Spirit. I committed to reading The Book of Mormon every day as I had committed to reading the Bible. I wanted to be worthy of the new friends I had found.

At the end of our discussion, the missionaries asked me to pray with them. In the Orthodox Church, I memorized prayers for various purposes. So I thought he would recite The Lord's Prayer or maybe one of the other sacred prayers I had learned from my Babushka, but Elder Wilson closed his eyes and prayed a prayer I didn't know instead. He thanked God for our discussion and asked Him to bless each of us and my home, ending with the words, "In the name of Jesus Christ, Amen!"

I was sad when it was time for them to leave, but they scheduled an appointment to return. So I knew I would speak to them again soon. After they went, I knelt and thanked God in my own words for those two incredible men.

Over the next several weeks, I looked forward to their visits. They were friends with my friend Tanya, so I knew they were my friends too. The three of us shared conversations about The Church, but it wasn't all about The Church. They shared their family pictures with me and talked about what they did before their missions. We talked for hours about their lives or the things they did for fun.

I did everything I could to get to know Elder Bradley and Elder Wilson better. I loved being around them. Elder Bradley had bright eyes and spoke Ukrainian. It was easy to talk to him, making him feel like a good friend, but I loved seeing Elder Wilson most. He was handsome, with bright white teeth and shining blue eyes. He was a little shy, but I knew he would open up over time and want to be my friend.

The missionaries were so supportive and generous that I spent more and more time with them and Tanya's family. As I did, I started to feel like maybe they were my family, giving me the love and support I always wanted. It was interesting that when I finally decided I could do things on my own, I met such amazing people. I was grateful and realized that God had once again given me all I needed to support my journey through my new life, just like He had with my education. I now understood that my commitment above all things must be to Him.

42

The Evils of Alcohol

*Preparing for my birthday party at Uncle Lonya's. I prepared the beautiful three-layer cake
for everyone to enjoy.*

IN 1993 A GROUP OF MEDICAL PEOPLE traveled from America to the Chernivtsi X-ray Ecological Department to assist children with complex diseases. Roman Plachinta studied at the Medical

Academy and got closer to the family of these children. Their kind and supportive relationships with the people around them impressed Roman.

As he asked them about their generosity, they shared their testimonies for The LDS Church and gave him a copy of the Book of Mormon. Over the years, they continued to keep a relationship with him through letters.

In 1996, Roman was one of the Medical Academy's best students and went for an internship in Salt Lake City, Utah. While in Salt Lake, Roman lived with a family who were members of The Church. Living with them, he understood that only high ideals and moral principles could make people so kind-hearted. The ideology inspired him, so he decided to be baptized and return to Chernivtsi to establish The Church in our city.

After spending ten months establishing The Church, the first missionaries came to Chernivtsi in 1997. They rented a room in the Kvarts Plant for the first Church Meetings. At the time, it was one of the biggest electronics manufacturers in the USSR. Every Sunday, the members would gather for three hours of spiritual services, one hour for the sacrament, an hour for women's Relief Society and men's Priesthood meetings, and the last hour for Principles of the Gospel, a study of the scriptures.

The official registration of The Church with the local government happened on September 11, 1997. The LDS Church divides itself into three levels; wards, branches, and stakes. As The Church was still small in Chernivtsi, it didn't have all the levels of larger congregations, boasting only one branch. Roman became the first president of the Chernivtsi branch of The Church of Jesus Christ of Latter-Day Saints. During his two years of presiding over the Chernivtsi branch, The Church grew to sixty-three members. After a few months, they changed the place for Sunday meetings to Grebinki street, where they had multiple white rooms with one big room where all members could sit for testimonials, prayers, singing hymns, and taking the sacrament.

The thing I remembered most when first walking into the meeting room was a thing they called a whiteboard. It had colored markers, and you could write with markers and then erase what you wrote. It was the first time I saw anything like it. The brilliant ideas and success this Church must have to afford such a fantastic tool inspired me.

With each room I entered, my inspiration grew. The white rooms had desks, chairs, a bookcase with religious books, a piano, and images of Jesus Christ everywhere. If it were not for those images and the words spoken there, one would think they meant to use the room for corporate coaching meetings.

I began going to meetings towards the end of my first year at University. It was strange at first. Women covered their heads before entering the Orthodox Church, and men took off their hats. Also, people wouldn't talk to each other. So I was surprised to see the warmth and love of strangers sharing hugs and updates of what was happening in their lives and not worrying about what was on their heads.

The meeting began with President Roman's notes. Then, we sang hymns and prayed before the sacrament. One of the young men offering sacrament, a deacon in The Church, recited words that weighed heavy on my heart. "O God, the Eternal Father, we ask thee in the name of thy Son, Jesus Christ, to bless and sanctify this bread to the souls of all those who partake of it; that they may eat in remembrance of the body of thy Son, and witness unto thee, O God, the Eternal Father, that they are willing to take upon them the name of thy Son, and always remember him, and keep his commandments which he has given them, that they may always have his Spirit to be with them. Amen."

The young man made a mistake while reading the prayer from his sheet. So he had to reread the prayer four times until he got it right. I felt terrible that he had to keep trying in front of the entire congregation when he made such a small mistake. So I asked Tanya to explain why. She said, "Those words were given to us by the Prophet, and no mistake can be made when they are spoken. They are sacred words, a blessing for the sacrament and our souls."

The sacrament wasn't much different than my experiences in the Orthodox Church. We had water from paper cups instead of wine, but I was glad we used cups. When the Priest at the Orthodox Church dipped the bread into the wine, he gave it to us on a spoon. I always wondered how many before me ate from that spoon, but I didn't say anything. I knew it was a sacred ritual. Everything about it spoke to how consecrated it was, but as I listened to the words spoken time and again by the deacon, I did so with a heavy heart.

When it came to the LDS Sacrament, I didn't partake. Some people felt only church members should be allowed the sacrament ritual, but that's not why I didn't participate. The missionaries told me, "Vitaly, if your heart is pure and you want to remember the atonement, you can participate in the sacrament. Still, it is important to find yourself worthy. If you do not keep your commitments, you should not participate. However, if you have been pure and are ready to renew your commitment, the sacrament is a time to do that."

I knew I was not worthy of the sacrament. I had impure thoughts during the week when I went to the internet club to do homework. I could have closed the pop-up windows that interrupted my work offering pornography, but I didn't. After repenting and accepting Jesus Christ as my savior, I knew I should not have watched sexually explicit content. I betrayed my commitment to the prophets, God, and Jesus Christ. Now, I worried they would not want me as a member. I couldn't make any more mistakes.

After sacrament, President Roman shared a teaching from Elder M. Russell Ballard of the Quorum of the Twelve Apostles called "Oh, That Cunning Plan of the Evil One."

He said, "The battle over man's God-given agency continues today. Satan and his minions have their lures all around us, hoping that we will falter and take his flies so he can reel us in with counterfeit means. He uses addiction to steal away agency. According to the dictionary, addiction of any kind means to surrender to something, thus relinquishing agency and becoming dependent on some life-destroying substance or behavior.

"Researchers tell us there is a mechanism in our brain called the pleasure center. When activated by certain drugs or behaviors, it overpowers the part of our brain that governs our willpower, judgment, logic, and morality. This leads the addict to abandon what he or she knows is right. And when that happens, the hook is set, and Lucifer takes control.

"Satan knows how to exploit and ensnare us with artificial substances and behaviors of temporary pleasure. I have observed the impact when one struggles to win back control, to become free from destructive abuse and addiction, and to regain self-esteem and independence."

Roman helped many people come to Christ and, as a medical student, who was at the top of the class soon to be a doctor, he also knew how to help people struggling with addiction or mental problems.

I went home and asked the Lord for forgiveness and remittance of my sins. He gave me the wisdom to be strong. I'm glad God gave us the Holy Sacrament and taught us to be pure and repent of our sins. I had been drinking since I was seventeen years old. My whole family drank and my friends. Most people in Ukraine drank, but they could not know the right thing to do if they had not 'regained self-esteem and independence.' Independence was freedom. I knew I would never be free if I were not also free of sin.

As I deepened my religious practices, it dawned on me that maybe drinking was the sin that caused Tyotya Valya's greed and my birth family to abandon me. I forgave them, and I forgave myself for the ignorance I once had. I committed to stop everything. I quit drinking, and I worked to purify myself of the evil thoughts I had about men. I wanted to have a successful and happy life, and sin did not give me real happiness. Tanya, Arthur, and Zoya were delighted. I wanted to live in joy like theirs, and I wanted to share it with the world.

One night, I prayed and read chapter two of The New Testament Ephesians, verse twenty. It said, "the true Church is built upon the foundation of the apostles and prophets, Jesus Christ himself being the chief cornerstone." I felt good reading the words I heard them using at The Church, and I thought to myself, 'If Jesus did call the prophets in the past and establish The Church, then The Church should be called by His name–Jesus Christ.' That truly opened my eyes. After that, I did not have any other reason not to believe that the LDS Church was The Church of Jesus Christ with His modern Prophets and Apostles.

The following Sunday, I returned to Church with a new commitment. I was ready to be a member.

43

Disappointment

*In one of the classes, I'm sitting with two of my favorite and the only girlfriends,
who I loved spending time with after University studies. They are the ones who invited me to dinners and to visit their families.*

I KEPT IN CONTACT WITH MANY Of my friends from the orphanage. Slavik and I often went back to play volleyball and other sports. It was nice to spend time with them and learn how their lives had turned out. I saw Igor there too. He had a girlfriend with him and told me that he had joined some evangelical church. He planned to go to another city with her to spread the gospel. I was happy that he didn't turn out like some of the other people we knew from the orphanage, ending up in jail for one reason or another. I was also glad to see he had a girlfriend. Remembering the time we spent together gave me hope that I could live my life like him. I could be happy with a girl like he was. I could get married one day, and we could have children together. Seeing him made me believe.

I didn't have much time to visit our old friends between school and work, but Slavik kept in touch with everyone he could, and I was glad he did. The children from the orphanage were my family, the only family I knew before living with Tyotya Valya and Dyadya Grisha. So when I watched my friends Nadija and Rostik walk out the door after being adopted, it wasn't to say goodbye forever, even though it felt like it at the time.

Chernivtsi was not a big city, and many people who grew up in our orphanage stayed in touch, remaining friends for life. One year, as Eastertime approached, I decided to spend the sacred holiday visiting Nadija and Rostik in their village. I remembered how wonderful the family who adopted them was, and I couldn't wait to see everyone together.

It had been months since I spent time with anyone but the members of my church. I loved spending time with Tanya, Arthur, and Zoya, who I now called my Babushka, my grandmother, but I also missed my traditions. So, I decided to spend the Easter weekend with the family in the village and connect with my Orthodox roots.

We had a short break from school for the holiday, which was good. I was ready for some relaxation. So I woke up that morning at 4:30 to catch the train. People lined up waiting for the bus, some waiting for an hour or two before the bus finally arrived. As many people traveled to see family for the Easter Holiday, the buses were cramped and slow getting to their destinations. It was a long day traveling, but eventually, we all got to where we wanted to go.

I was surprised by the village when I arrived. Years of occupation and war left most of the small cities in Ukraine without the resources they needed to keep their towns clean. As a result, the air often stunk of garbage and cow manure. There were no paved streets, and the people in small villages weren't very welcoming. They were poor and unhappy from generations of pain and financial burdens, and they didn't care to know new people.

This village was different. It was clean. There was asphalt on the main road and a water pump for anyone to use. Having clean, accessible water was very unusual for a village. I imagined the people there must have money. Everyone was very welcoming to me like I had come home from a long journey and the scenery was as beautiful as it could be. The day was sunny, and the streets were clear of debris, surrounded only by the landscapes where the farmers grew wheat and sunflowers. Everything about the town was so different from the city I called home. This place was more than I imagined any home could be. I took a long deep breath of pure, fresh air, and I committed. This was the life I wanted and would work toward, the one where everything was clean and happy.

"Vitaly!" It was Nadija. "Vitaly! You're here!"

I turned to see both Nadija and Rostik as they approached me. They looked happy like the village. "Nadija, Rostik, it's so amazing to see you. This is where you live? I could never imagine living in a place like this."

"Wait until you see what we have planned," Rostik said, "We're going to have such a wonderful time together, celebrating every moment. Come with us. Some of the friends in the village want to meet you."

I was so happy to be with my friends again, living the life I always wanted. The Timoshenko family that adopted Nadija and Rostik from my orphanage treated them like their own children. They were so generous to have seven foster children in addition to the four children they had of their own, and they treated them all alike. Everyone loved each other, and they were happy. Even their adopted children called their foster mother Mamma instead of Tyotya Olena, as I had to do with Tyotya Valya. I couldn't wait to spend Easter here. Maybe this would be the kind of family I would like to have one day.

Everyone welcomed me with arms open wide when we returned to the house. Their mother, Olena, was so kind and treated me as well as she would treat her children. Every moment was a celebration. There was a lake nearby, and although the water was cold, Rostik, his brother, and I went swimming. Then, they took me around, showing me many of their holiday traditions. We spent the afternoon walking from one house to another, eating plates full of traditional foods and having drinks with friends. We even went to see them slaughter a pig in preparation for a feast. I loved to eat pork, but I never saw it happen before. Luckily, they stabbed in the neck to make quick, but I knew I wouldn't want ever to have to do that myself.

Spending time with them made me realize how difficult it was to live with Tyotya Valya all those years. I never felt this love. Even being there for so long, I never felt what I saw in them as their Mamma Olena accepted them as family. I noticed how there are two kinds of people in the world, those who are generous and love everyone and those who are greedy and will leave children to survive alone. They were so close, and I was jealous of them. I couldn't help it.

I decided to try and forget the life I had and enjoyed the many traditions of the village they were showing me. We went to a church liturgy that started at midnight. The church was full of people, and even more of them stood outside. We joined the service inside. As we walked, each person lit a candle for the remission of our sins and sang Christian songs that praised Jesus's resurrection and glorified God with the words, "Jesus has Risen! Indeed, He has Risen!".

After the Resurrection Mass on Easter morning, people brought baskets with food to be blessed. We carried Easter bread called Paska wrapped in cloth. We also had pysanky—Ukrainian Easter egg, ham, and sausages, and some brought cheese and butter, pork fat, salt, horseradish, and seeds. After the ceremony, the family would enjoy their blessed food as an Easter breakfast.

Being in an Orthodox Church service reminded me of my childhood. There were icons everywhere, and there was no sitting. So, we all stood listening to the priest speaking in the Slavic language. The whole experience reminded me of my Babushka. She always wanted to make me a priest, but I knew I was not worthy to stand before people and guide them to God, not yet. I could only hope to change and make her proud one day.

In the evening, Masha, my sister, and Luda, the sister of another orphan I knew from Fastivska Street, joined our adventure. We all went to visit other families in the village. I was so happy to see Masha. As I was busy with school and my new family from the church, I hadn't had much chance to see her. So I was looking forward to spending a whole weekend together, building our family bonds.

We visited a close friend of Luda's, where everyone dressed in traditional Ukrainian clothes. They were singing and celebrating at a large fire made out of vehicle tires. Everyone there was drinking vodka, which didn't surprise me. Most people in Ukraine drank vodka. Drinking was as much a part of communism as shared homes. Employers gave alcohol as gifts to workers by the caseload. So, I was used to people drinking, but when Masha and Luda started drinking too, I was very disappointed.

DISAPPOINTMENT

When I joined the church, I learned how harmful drinking is. So I committed to God that I would not drink, but I was also responsible for looking after my brothers and sisters. I did not want alcoholism to harm her or anyone else in my life. I felt my heart breaking inside and wanted to be an example of how we could celebrate without drinking. So I told her, "Everyone here is drinking a lot of alcohol. You don't need to drink so much."

She brushed me off, saying, "Vitaly, it's a celebration. Everyone is drinking, but you. It's okay for us to have a little fun, isn't it?"

Masha had always been a little wild like my mother, but she was Tyotya Valya's favorite. Tyotya Valya loved Masha more than anything. We all thought she was the best. Now, watching her, I realized that she became someone different after we left Tyotya Valya's house. She was drinking and smoking too. I always trusted her to be a good person, doing good things. I thought she'd be okay, but she wasn't. She was so different than I imagined she would be. I was not happy watching her. "Masha, I thought it would be different for you. You don't want to be like our parents, do you?"

She turned on me, "You don't know what it's like, Vitaly. You've been so busy with your friends. You haven't been around to see. We're not like you. I just want to enjoy myself. It's not that bad. You know, I could have ended up like Nadya, but I'm not. I'm just having a little something to drink."

I was shocked by her words, "Wait! What happened to Nadya?"

"Nadya had a baby," she said. "She isn't living a healthy life, Vitaly. She was smoking and drinking the whole time she was pregnant, and she was doing drugs and having sex with men she barely knew. All the things she was doing affected the baby. He was only two and a half kilograms and forty-three centimeters when he was born, and he has some physical problems.

"I wouldn't do that! I want you to know that. I wouldn't do what she did. I'm just having a drink." She went quiet for a moment like maybe she didn't want to continue. Perhaps she was sorry she began the whole story.

"What is it, Masha? Tell me." Nadya was my sister, and I loved her. I wanted to know what was happening to her.

Masha took a deep breath, "First of all, she didn't want to. I want you to know that, but she didn't know what to do. She didn't have the money to take care of him." She was quiet for a moment, but I waited. "She took the baby to the Maternity Hospital, Vitaly. He's in an incubator right now, but he'll end up in an orphanage like we did. Nadya can't take care of him."

I didn't say anything. I couldn't. I was too angry to speak, so I just got up and walked away from the fire. Nadya abandoned her child, just like my mother left me, and now Masha was going down the same road. She didn't think she was, but she would do the same thing her family had done to her. It was like a vicious circle, everyone doing the things they swore they would never do.

I didn't know what to do. Like me, Nadya's child was beginning its life in the hospital, having health problems. His mom was not taking care of herself. She didn't listen to good people who told her not to smoke or drink. What would happen to the child now, I wondered? Here we were orphans, growing up in a world with no parents. Not long ago, someone abandoned her, and now, here she was, joining a whole new generation of people leaving their children behind. Here was my sister acting just like my mother.

I was glad I made a choice not to drink. I was happy I had found the church, and I knew God was there to help me be strong against alcohol's temptation. I didn't like that everyone else was drinking, but I decided to let it be for now. I was furious, but I was also worried about Nadya. I wanted to see her and talk to her. Maybe there was something I could do. As long as the night continued to be a good night, I could speak to Masha and Nadya later.

As I returned to the fire, they were already on to another conversation, as if nothing had happened. "...what did you do?"

It was Masha. She was talking to Luda.

"My brother prevented the fight and ended the issue. He saved me from being beaten up again."

"Why didn't you leave before, Luda? If he was beating you, why didn't you leave him?"

"I tried. I separated, and I wanted to get a divorce. He beat me up all the time, but I couldn't do anything if there were no witnesses. Andrij said, 'Witnesses do not live long, Luda.' So, I was worried. If anyone said anything about what he did or how he beat me, I thought they might be hurt."

I looked across the room to where Andrij was laughing with some friends. Luda said her brother had saved her, but she was still there, at the party, with her husband.

I sat listening to her story, listening to all their many stories, and I realized this was not the place I wanted to be. I always thought they were different. I never thought Masha would do bad things. I never thought Mamma Olena would let Luda live this way. I thought they were the family I wanted. Easter was supposed to be a holy time, not a drinking time, not a fighting time.

Everyone in the church said they believed in God and the Easter Celebration, but I didn't see their faith in their actions. Everyone was still awake at four a.m., drinking and yelling, and not even thinking of the life of Christ. I thought it would be different here. I had dreamed of being with a family like this, but it seemed everyone here drank too much. Maybe I would be drinking too if it weren't for the church.

When I decided I wanted to become a member, I quit drinking. I wanted to have a different life than my mother and the other people I watched ruin their lives with alcohol. Seeing people who loved God, saying God loved them, and that they had devoted their lives to Him but still loved to drink was not honest to me. From what I had learned at the LDS Church, I didn't think they were righteous or that they truly loved God. The church inspired for me a connection between God and no drinking.

This place wasn't a place where the saints were. When I arrived, I saw a pure village with kind people in it, but in the end, I saw this village was as unclean as any other, washing away their lives with vodka and not loving each other or genuinely being there for each other. I was so happy to see everyone again, but it didn't stay in my head as the right place to spend my time.

The wisdom of our Ukrainian traditions comes through sayings. There was a saying I always remembered. "Whom you spend time with, so much you will learn from and become." I loved spending time with my family, and for much of the weekend, I enjoyed it, but they were also people who were drinking and doing bad things. It didn't make sense to me. I wanted something more.

Tanya once told me, "If someone sees you with a can of root beer, you are not following the Word of Wisdom. Instead, you present the opportunity and temptation for them to do the same. You are encouraging them to think of beer because you are drinking something that looks like beer."

Tanya was such a good person. I wanted to be a better person, like her. I thought this family was perfect. I was so happy that they adopted so many children. Their mother welcomed me like I was her child. They were better than any family I knew, and now, they were nothing more than what my mother had become. But, again, I was disappointed as I did not find the family I hoped I could find. Only the church members were living the life I wanted to live.

More than ever, after so many teachings by the church members about how families can be happy on earth and live together for eternity,

DISAPPOINTMENT

I wanted to earn my opportunity to visit the Temple and leave evil behind to find a better life.

44

Broken Families

Me, my brother, his father Alec, and Alec's son—my brother's brother from left to right.

MAKING IT ON OUR OWN WASN'T ALWAYS EASY. The state continued to give us about one hundred hryven a month as long as we went to school. It was the same as they gave Tyotya Valya for each of us. Between that and the fifty hryven we made at the restaurant, I found a way to pay for utilities, clothes, and food. I often worked for food credits, getting money only for my tips. Still, sometimes if we catered a banquet, there were tips to share, and I could buy fresh vegetables and fruits to preserve for winter.

I also received help from my Uncle Lonya sometimes. When we lived on our own, Uncle Lonya had a little garden at his house, and Aunt Lena would invite me over occasionally to help her tend it. We would plant vegetables and strawberries or pull weeds, the way I learned at the orphanage. Sometimes we gathered cherries and strawberries or vegetables that she would let me take home with me. She also taught me how to make preserves for the winter. We would spend hours together, cooking and canning the fresh fruits and vegetables we found, or we would make pickles and crush cherries and strawberries into juice. We spent all the time we could during the summer to preserve enough food to last everyone through the winter. We worked hard, but I was happy. I found a way to take care of myself and never asked Tyotya Valya for another thing. I did everything I could to earn money and be a welcome visitor at Uncle Lonya's home for dinners and holiday celebrations. They were the only family I had left.

Besides getting money from my uncle, I excelled in math and physics and was ahead of many other students at my school. So, along with avoiding tests, I was also able to tutor others who needed my help. In exchange for that help, my friends often invited me to their homes for the weekend. The village where they lived was not that far from the University, so I returned often and made great friends. I would eat and spend time with their family, and it was enjoyable. It also saved me from having to spend money on food.

I also helped Tanya's missionary friends with cooking and cleaning. They were helping me as well. Living with Tyotya Valya, I helped scrub the whole house every week. She always wanted detailed cleaning. We cleaned the windows, the window sills, floors, doors, bathroom, toilet, and carpets. So, I became good at cleaning. As I spent more time with the missionaries, I found they needed someone to help them around their rooms. I would clean their apartment for two hours a week to receive ten American dollars.

Cleaning for the missionaries was easy compared to what I did on Subotnik, and I loved getting American money. Every time I received American money, I saved it, only taking it to the bank when it was time to exchange it. When I was small, an American dollar was worth two and a half hryven. By the time I lived with Tyotya Valya, it was worth five. As I did work for the missionaries, I could get ten hryven for a single American dollar. So when I saw American dollars, I knew they could make money for themselves without any effort on my part.

Money was important to me. But it wasn't just about the money. It was the lifestyle I saw of families who had money. Money meant happy families who loved each other—never feeling hungry or cold. It meant I could travel and spend more time with the church members. The missionaries there introduced me to many amazing stories of what is possible when people aren't greedy or mean. Being poor is what makes people greedy. Though sometimes, some have little who want to help others. I couldn't wait to get enough money to help other children like me.

I also wanted to travel outside of Ukraine and see new ways to enjoy life. The American missionaries shared many amazing stories about being where anything is possible. They told me about opportunities in America, and I knew I wanted to go there one day.

Along with helping the missionaries and Uncle Lonya, I also did work for Roustam's father, Alec. They needed someone to help them with renovations at their apartment. It was a tough job. Every day for two months, I spent three to four hours painting, repairing, and cleaning. I offered to do it for free. I would have done anything to build my relationship with my brother back then, but Alec's girlfriend,

Masha, wanted to pay me, and I needed the money. So, I agreed. I had to do a lot of work, and it was hard, but I loved learning new skills by doing the renovations.

Besides the money, staying connected to Alec strengthened my relationship with Roustam. I did what I could to keep in touch with my brother. Even when I was not doing work, I would call Alec every week to see if he had any news for me. Not long after testifying that Roustam would take care of me, I turned eighteen, and my brother moved to America. I hadn't seen him for a long time, but I still wanted to be close to him. He was the only brother I had. I thought of Slavik and Serhij as my brothers because we lived our lives and grew up together, but Roustam was the only other person I spent time with that had the same blood as me pumping through his veins.

Alec's girlfriend, Masha, was the one who invited me over the most. She was so sweet and treated me very much like her own son. She loved to feed me and talk to me about the renovations. She also did beauty care on the side, cutting my hair when I needed it. She worked very hard, but Alec was lazy. He worked in real estate, but he was not very good at it. He was not good at anything.

Nevertheless, they found ways to get by, primarily by her effort. She did everything she could to ensure we all had what we needed. I always trusted Masha to be a wonderful person.

"Can you come by later? Roustam sent a surprise for you." I was so surprised by Alec's comment that I couldn't breathe at first. I was just finishing for the day and didn't know I would be getting a surprise from Roustam.

Still, I was afraid the chance would go away if I did not answer soon, so I blurted out the only promise I could make. "Of course, I can come back. I would love to have a chance to talk to my brother."

I asked uncle Alec every week if there was news from Roustam. There was never much to report. Roustam didn't reach out to me anymore.

He was happy in America with his wife and didn't seem to have room for me in his life.

Masha smiled. I could see she was happy to see me so happy, "Okay, be back by nine p.m. That's when he will call. And I will make you a nice dinner to fill your belly too."

I could hardly wait to return and see what Roustam had planned for me. This conversation would be our first since he left. I had been waiting for news for a whole year and hadn't heard anything at all from him. Now, here it was. He would be calling me, and he sent a gift as well. I was elated.

I rushed through my afternoon responsibilities and arrived back at Alec's home before nine p.m. Of course, I was a little early, but I didn't want to miss my chance to hear Roustam's voice again.

As it turned out, there was no reason for me to rush except to enjoy Masha's excellent food. We waited more than three hours before Roustam's call finally came.

"Hey, little bro. How are you doing?"

My heart smiled when I heard his voice, "I'm doing great. I'm still living with Slavik and Serhij, going to school. Sometimes it's hard to pay the bills, but I work hard and find ways to earn money."

I had so much more to say, but Roustam didn't wait for me to finish before jumping in, "Yeah. Things are hard for everyone. I don't know if you know, but my wife is a nurse. She works day and night, two shifts. I'm going to school, so she's the one who is working right now." He didn't say it, but I knew what his words meant. 'Don't tell me of your troubles,' he was saying. 'My life in America is hard. Feel sorry for me. Don't ask me for anything.'

"You know we have to feed the kids, and they have school too," he continued. "We live with Ludmila's parents in Los Angeles right now. We'll move out when I find a job, but until I'm out of school, things will be hard for us."

I wondered how much money he needed living with Ludmila's parents, but I didn't ask. I decided it was best to keep him happy, talking about his life. I also had curiosity, so I just decided to ask questions. "What are you studying? I know you finished technical school as an architect and construction engineer before leaving. Are you taking classes about construction?"

"No," he said. "Sometimes it is better to go easier ways. I wanted to continue construction studies, but it was better for me in America to study economics. I hope to go back to my specialty one day, but I will stay in business and become an accountant for now. I will get a Business Degree. So, when do you graduate, Vitaly?"

"I still have a year or two of school, but I'm doing very well. I get the highest grades, and I also help others to improve their grades." Roustam shared my excitement for school, and I wanted him to be proud of me, so I boasted about my successes. I wanted him to see I am unique and want to have a relationship with me. Sometimes, I felt he was jealous that I was doing life on my own, but I think he was happy about it, too, because I wouldn't need anyone's help.

I answered his questions about school, but I wanted to continue on the most crucial topic. Alec was Jewish, and he told me how the Jewish people in Russia or Ukraine sometimes took their families to America. It starts with one of the family members moving to America and living there for a while. Then, after they have established themselves, they can bring the entire family. So, I thought that Roustam might help me go to America, but I didn't want to just come out and ask him because I knew I must convince him that it was a good idea first. So, I decided to take it slow, "Did you receive my letters? I sent mail to you through Alec, but I didn't hear back from you. Did you read them?"

"I did. I did. I wanted to write back. I'm so happy to hear from you, but things have been so busy and sending letters back to Ukraine is expensive. The surprise I sent you cost me seventy-five American dollars and another hundred fifty for shipping. I sent you the gift for your birthday and to let you know I love you and am there for you, little brother."

He mentioned the expense like I didn't know how much even the smallest stamp cost, but I knew. I used the little money I had trying to stay connected to him, sending him letters with some pictures and greeting cards, as well.

"Great!" I wasn't as enthusiastic as I sounded. This conversation wasn't going the way I hoped it would go, but I decided to see how he would react to my wish. "Maybe someday, we could live closer together, Roustam. I am very excited to come to America. I know there are other people there who like to bring their families to live close to them."

"Well, we'll see," he said. "As I mentioned, I'm living with my wife and her parents. So I don't have time to take care of a little brother. But I sent you a gift, Vitaly. I wanted you to know I love you, so I sent you a gift. Your uncle Alec has it."

I was quiet. I didn't know what to say. I thought I could live in America with him because he was my brother. I was hoping he would help me after I graduate. I even wished we could be a family one day, like the Yakivna's. They were together, supporting each other. I hoped maybe, one day, we could be a family like them.

Roustam grabbed hold of the silence before I could respond. "Listen, little bro. We've been talking for thirty minutes, and phone calls are costly here. So, I need to go, but I'll talk to you soon. Uncle Alec has a surprise for you."

"Okay..." I didn't get a chance to say, 'Thank you.' The phone disconnected before I could speak any words.

Alec stepped forward the moment I laid down the phone. "Well, Vitaly. Here you go!"

He approached me like he was giving me an invitation to dine with royalty, but all he handed me was a box of American candy and a ten-dollar bill. Then, he walked away. So, after everything, after all the money Roustam took for the apartment, the deal he made with Tyotya Valya, and the money I knew he was making in America, all he sent me was ten dollars. I didn't know if Roustam was lying or if Uncle Alec had decided to keep some of the gifts for himself, but I was pretty sure the box of chocolates I held in my hand didn't cost him seventy-five American dollars, and I was probably to the point where I didn't care.

Masha approached me when Alec was out of the room, "I'm so sorry, Vitaly. I thought he would give you more than that. Alec said he gave eight hundred American dollars to the Born Again Christian Church last week. I was sure he would give that or more to his brother."

It was hard for me to understand why Roustam would give that much money to a church, but only ten dollars to his brother, but I knew Masha would always tell the truth. Right then, I knew the money Roustam gave me was not because he loved me. He just did what everyone else I knew growing up did. He took what he needed, not thinking of who it hurt. But then, he gave back as little as he could to make it seem even.

Everyone in Ukraine was poor, too poor to help others. So, they didn't know how to be generous. I left the house knowing things had changed. I worked so hard to try and stay connected, but Roustam wasn't there for me. He hadn't acted like my brother in a long time, but maybe I didn't need him to be my big brother anymore. Maybe, I found something better. I found a whole family, and we weren't going to take what we needed to leave nothing for others. We would help others find happiness too. We would show them the true church and how to create happy families for eternity.

I knew I couldn't count on Roustam anymore, but I was grateful anyway. I didn't need him. I was the one now who would do what he couldn't. I wasn't an orphan anymore, needing someone to save me. I wanted to be like the people in Germany, who sent us gifts for Christmas. I wouldn't be the one who took. I wanted to be the one who had enough to give. I would be there for the people who needed me. Ten dollars wasn't a lot, but I knew it could get me one step closer to my dreams. I would add the money to what I was saving to visit the Temple in Frankfurt. From there, I would serve God, and He would give me what I needed to serve the world.

45

Choices

In my tiny apartment where Serhij, Slavik, and I lived after we left Tyotya Valya.
I made a nice dinner for everyone and invited friends to come.

I WAS STILL THINKING A LITTLE about Roustam after leaving uncle Alec. I was sad, but mostly I was grateful. Even though the person who was supposed to be my brother was not there to help me, I still had my brothers waiting at home, and I knew they were there for me. My friends at the church were there for me as well. I was not alone.

I had been praying for weeks to find a way to get to the Mormon Temple in Frankfurt, Germany. The Mormon Church was not like most churches in Ukraine. All the churches I had visited were called holy temples, and anyone could enter. But the Mormon Temple was not like their churches. It was secretive and memorable, and no one could enter unless they were baptized and following their commitments. To go, I had to be more than just a member. I had to be worthy.

Other church members were preparing with me, and we were all excited to feel the blessings of the church, but I think I was more inspired to go than anyone. I listened to the testimonies of church members who had visited there. I knew, if I could go to the Temple one day, I might be exalted in the Heavenly Kingdom of God. I needed this trip to purify my sins.

I was poor and barely had enough food, but I knew I needed to save to go to the Temple. With the money from Roustam and the money I had saved from the social worker after buying a new coat, I now had sixteen dollars. Imagine that. I was so happy. I had sixteen American dollars. It felt like God was there for me and was answering my prayers.

As the days passed, I decided to distance myself from my brother. Instead of calling Alec to check on Roustam, I spent as much time as I could around the people who inspired me. I loved spending time with Tanya and her family, and I especially loved being with the missionaries. But more than anyone, my favorite person to be with was always Slavik. We had so many adventures together.

One day we were up hours before the sun to catch the train and go to the Kalynivskiy Rynok Market. Tyotya Valya used to go to the market with her son and daughter-in-law. They bought containers of imported clothes from Germany to sell. It was the most prominent street fair in Ukraine, maybe in all of eastern Europe. It was so big. It had its own police force, bank, and bus station. Vendors came from all over the world to sell goods there, people from Italy, Germany, Spain, and many other nations. You could buy anything you wanted or could even imagine.

The market was open all year long, and we knew if we needed something, we could find it there. So, one day, we took one of the Marshrutka across Chernivtsi to three kilometers north of the city center, where the market was located. Because we first had to travel an hour on the bus to the city center, it took the better part of a day, but we needed to go once in a while, so we took the trip. For some things, this was the only place you could find them.

Today, I needed pants, and Slavik was going along with me as an adventure, and maybe he would decide to get something too after I found what I needed. So we searched a sea of vendors for what we needed. Each was eager to convince us to buy what they were selling. I had earned twenty-two hryven working a long banquet. At that time, it was equal to less than five American dollars, but I found a nice pair of pants for twelve hryven, and Slavik found shoes he needed for one of the modeling classes he took.

I was always excited to get new clothes with no holes or places too thin to keep the cold air out. Now I had new pants, but we still had a lot of looking around to do. So we traveled through the shop looking for what else we could buy.

Just as we were ready to leave the market, I realized my pants weren't where I thought I had put them. "Slavik. My pants. They are gone." I was devastated. I didn't know what had happened. "I think I must have set them somewhere. I think I lost them."

Slavik said, "Don't worry about it, Vitaly. We will just go and get you another pair."

"But the pants were twelve hryven. I only have ten left. I can't get another pair of pants."

"Do you know what, Vitaly? You are my best and oldest friend. Here are two hryven so you can get another pair of pants."

When we left with my new pants, I was so excited. Whenever I got money, I spent it on more than just myself. I would always buy ice cream and take it to Slavik and Serhij to share. I always thought of others, and I was so grateful when Slavik did nice things for me, but his gift was better than anything else I could imagine this time.

Slavik was always showing kindness to others by helping them in any way he could. I often came home from school to find Slavik with new friends helping them somehow. One time, he invited two friends, Roman and Vassily, and allowed them to stay with us. I didn't mind. I was always happy to help people who needed it, and I was glad to have a brother like Slavik, who also liked to do kind things. Still, my mind changed a little about helping them only a few days later.

I returned home one evening from discussions with the missionaries. I felt very positive, inspired, and close to God, like he was there with me. However, as I walked into the apartment, I saw it was a mess, and it was warm as well, after being a hot day.

We lived on the eighth floor of a concrete building. They heated the entire building with a water heater located in the basement. It was cold for us in the winter because the hot water often didn't make it to our floor. Sadly, we suffered the opposite extremity every summer due to the concrete walls and being so high off the ground.

When I first arrived, I wasn't too worried because I saw Slavik was cleaning up the mess, "What happened?" I asked.

"Roman," he said quietly.

I wasn't surprised, and I wasn't worried at first. Roman often left a mess, and I knew I could do something about the heat. Every time the missionaries left an apartment or moved somewhere, they would leave behind valuable items. I often took the things they didn't want.

Not long before Roman came, one of my missionary friends had given me an air conditioner he no longer needed, along with a voice audio recorder.

I felt the gifts were exceptional because Elder Wilson told me they bought the recorder as an early birthday present. They didn't want to just give me leftovers for my birthday, and they didn't have a lot of money, so the missionaries gathered money to provide me with something they knew I would love.

Thanks to their gifts, it seemed everything would be fine again until I found the air conditioner wasn't where I left it, and neither was the voice recorder. I looked for several minutes before returning to the living room, where I found Slavik was still cleaning. Finally, I asked him, "What happened to my air conditioner and my media player? I looked everywhere, but they are gone."

Slavik sighed, "My friend Roman said someone wrote a complaint about him to the police, saying he beat them up and stole one hundred and twenty dollars. He thinks you wrote the complaint, Vitaly. He is furious. He made this mess in the house and took the media player and air conditioner, saying he wouldn't give them back until you made it right."

"I didn't make a complaint to anyone," I said. "I want my stuff back." Now, I was angry.

"I told him you wouldn't do that, but he wonders who it is if it's not you and not me."

"Why would he think I said those things? I don't take anything from anyone!" I was so upset. I couldn't understand why he took the items given to me by the missionaries. Those items were special to me because they were gifts.

"Well, the guy who talked to the police said his name is Vitaly. So, Roman asked me, 'Who was it if it wasn't your friend, Vitaly?' I told him I didn't know, but I knew you wouldn't be the one to do something like that. I don't know. Maybe they made it up, so they could steal your stuff. He's the one that made a mess of the house. He said he would return your things to you, but we need to meet together tomorrow to go to the police."

After helping Slavik clean a little, I walked out of the room. I felt punished for doing something nice and helping Slavik's friends and didn't want to be angry for being helpful. I knew I could do anything with the help of the Lord. So, I kneeled by my bed and prayed for God to give me the wisdom to handle the situation. I prayed for understanding, and I also prayed for Slavik. I felt terrible for him to be in this mess with me. I counted him as my closest brother, but sometimes he hung around the wrong people. I prayed to God that He would protect Slavik and help him through his life. I gave Slavik everything I had and could provide at that time, but now I wondered if he needed more than just my help.

I knew what it was like to live the way Roman lived. I remembered being younger. I was always looking for ways for people to help me. When I was very young, I asked, but everyone said, "No," so I discovered that the easiest way to get what I needed would be not by asking people but by borrowing from my teachers.

One day, when I was at the orphanage, while everyone was changing to go to class, I hid in the wardrobe of the changing room. We had the same routine every day, so I knew my teacher's bag was on the table by the door. I also knew, when everyone finished getting ready, the teacher would lead them out and lock the door. Once it became quiet, I came out and went straight to her purse and found ten rubles inside her wallet. I took it. I was shaking the whole time, even as I ran from the room.

I couldn't lock the door after me, so it remained open and available for anyone else to see. I didn't care. I went to hide in a classroom located in a different building, away from the scene of my crime.

I sat panting, feeling breathless. I couldn't believe what I had done. I remember there being some change left in the bottom of the bag, but other than that, the money I took was all she had. Ten rubles was a lot of money at that time. I didn't know what to do with that kind of money, and I began to panic. I couldn't take it, so I decided to tear the cash into pieces and throw it away.

When I returned to class, I saw my teacher's purse again, sitting on the desk. The teacher knew I was the only one missing from class. So, she called me to the front of the room and asked me, "Where were you?"

"I was in the changing room, hiding."

She asked me, "Did you take the money from my bag?"

"Yes." I knew she knew I was the one who took the money. There was no point in denying it.

"Where is it?"

"I was so afraid I tore it into small pieces and threw it away."

She stared at me for a minute. I couldn't tell if she believed me, but it didn't matter. I knew there was no escape from punishment. "Put your hands on the desk, Vitaly."

The room was silent. Everyone knew what happened when we stole. The teacher grabbed the pointer stick hanging next to the chalkboard and struck my knuckles several times, saying, "You will learn not to take things without permission."

After leaving her class with sore knuckles, I had more punishments, but they did not teach me not to steal. Instead, I learned that day that somebody was always watching me and that even if I thought I could hide my worst actions, in reality, I wouldn't be able to do that.

Maybe, it also taught me not to get caught, but I was poor and hungry, so I still took things. I stole pastries and bread from the shops when they left them by the doors to cool. We would hide behind the security guard and take our treats, running into the bakery to hide, or we would wait for pallets to be set on the curb and take our chance before they could load the food into the delivery trucks.

We took our treasures back to the orphanage and hid them in our wardrobe to have food when we were hungry. Slavik was always so generous, sharing his treats with everyone, but I was not as helpful. I only shared my treasures with my botsya Slavik. He was the only one in the whole orphanage who ate with me.

The greatest lesson I learned in my life was, to be honest with others and grateful for anything they gave me. Over time, I also learned to steal less. I realized I could make more money by collecting bottles and selling them. There were a lot of empty bottles in Ukraine. I knew I could find a whole bunch of them all around our school. So, I learned to work a little gathering bags of bottles to make money instead of stealing it.

I also learned to make money other ways and accept gifts. Whether it was benefiting from the missionaries, new pants from Slavik, or a free meal with Tanya's family, I learned that some people would help, but I had to ask for it. I wasn't afraid of asking for things because I knew that I would receive almost everything I needed. I just had to ask the right people.

After Roman took my things, I imagined the pain those people felt when I took their items, but I didn't judge who I was. There were plenty of reasons for me not to succeed in life. Living in poverty, feeling disrespect from the outside world, and not having the opportunities inherent to living in 'normal society' all have their effect. As a result, many people coming out of the orphanages were drug addicts, alcoholics, or thieves. Unfortunately, I've met many peers from the orphanage who have been in prison and lost everything through drinking and crimes.

I felt sorry for them because I knew there were not many good people willing to help them. Still, some orphans had done well in their lives after graduating from the orphanage school. Forty percent of teens did end up graduating. Unfortunately, for many, there was nowhere else to go from there. A few like me were lucky. I had opportunities, and I was determined to make life successful. I wished that was true for more orphans, but I was beginning to see that maybe I was the exception and not the rule.

Slavik seemed to land somewhere in the middle of it all. I wanted the world to be different. I wanted to live in a place where people weren't scamming each other. I wanted to live in an area where love was more important than greed. But, we all begin as children, greedily suckling at our mother's breast if we have one, and eventually, we must grow and learn to think of others. Orphans need people to guide them through their lives, just as if they were parents. We all need parents, in the beginning, to help us understand what having enough to share means. Slavik seemed to be born to help those people who didn't know how to help themselves.

Being Slaviks' friend taught me that there are people in the world who do good things and people who do wrong. Of course, this didn't make the people good or bad. It just meant there were people you could trust and people you couldn't, but I was starting to feel like almost everyone in Ukraine was the kind I couldn't trust.

The day after Slavik and I cleaned up the mess in our apartment, Slavik told me that Roman wanted to meet with me alone, but I didn't trust the situation to be safe. So Slavik went with me. We met Roman in the park, and all went to the police station together to correct the issue. The police told Roman it was a different Vitaly who had filed the report against him. He still had the charge against him, but the police released him, telling him that he must return the items to me right away.

It all worked out in the end. Roman returned my things, but I still didn't trust him. I didn't like having him around. I felt God had protected me and helped Roman see what he needed to do, but I didn't know what he would do next.

I felt sorry for Roman and Masha and Nadya and all the orphans who grew up to suffer because they didn't have any real-world lessons. Maybe if people didn't stereotype them and realized that they are the ones that need help and guidance, perhaps their lives could have been different. I wished Roman's life could have been different, just as many lives of other abandoned children. I still wonder who he might have been if he had been given a good life with a good family. Would he have learned respect, hard work, and not to take things for granted? I wondered what could happen if all orphans had a chance to live with loving, supportive families. How different would their opportunities be if they had an opportunity to look, dress, speak, and behave differently than society expected?

All of these thoughts left me with a big decision to make. What life was mine to live? Was it here in Ukraine, surrounded by the small community of my peers who still suffered their social injustice, or was it somewhere bigger I needed to be, somewhere where I could make a difference in the world? Was it maybe with the people who wanted to make the world better with me?

46

Beginnings Start with Endings

At Tyotya Lena and Uncle Lonya's house. Tyotya Lena and I prepared the table filled with food for our birthday celebration. We invited friends from the church to join us.

WHEN MY TWENTIETH BIRTHDAY CAME, I decided this was a good time to forget all my worries and enjoy my family and our love for one another. Today was my day, a day where everything could be about me, and I knew we could have a wonderful celebration, the kind I always dreamed of having when I was a little boy feeling so alone.

I spent my life never having a day of my own. We didn't do big celebrations for birthdays at the orphanage because there were too many children. Then, when we lived with Tyotya Valya, she never believed we should make a huge deal for our birthday. So today, I wanted to make up for all the years and enjoy everyone celebrating my day the way I always wanted. I invited my whole family to celebrate it with me.

Tyotya Valya came with Dyadya Grisha. She and Masha helped me prepare food for my party, and it seemed Tyotya Valya was much happier when I supplied the food for our dinner. So we all cooked together and enjoyed having our time as a family. I was so grateful. I also invited some friends from university, and Slavik also asked a couple of people. So, Masha, Nadya, Slavik, and Serhij, plus a few friends, were all there for my birthday celebration. There were around ten people altogether, so I made a big meal that overflowed, leaving barely any room on the table for us to eat. After the celebration was over, Nadya stayed to help me clean, and I gave her food to take home with her. It felt good that I had enough to share.

After having a party at home with my family, my Uncle Lonya also hosted a second birthday party for me the next day. I was so grateful to have Uncle Lonya in my life. He was always so kind to us as we were growing up. He gave me money when I needed it, and since I no longer had Roustam in my life, he felt more and more like the father I never had. So I wanted to be close and build a relationship of trust between us.

To celebrate my birthday, I made two cakes that I decorated myself. I felt inspired to use the talents I learned in culinary school and was proud of my creations. One cake was for my friends and family to enjoy at my first birthday celebration, and the other I took to my Uncle Lonya's the following day. I was so excited to share what I had created with him.

He made the day special for me. Tyotya Valya always thought that family should be the only ones to celebrate our birthdays, but when Uncle Lonya offered to have a party for me, he said, "It's up to you who comes to your birthday. We'll cook what you want. We'll invite whoever you want." So, I invited Tanya, Arthur, the missionaries, and a few other church friends to celebrate with us.

Aunt Lena helped me prepare food. We had fresh juice, cabbage rolls with meat and rice, a salad made with boiled veggies and sausage, black and red caviar, and Ukrainian sausage. We ate beaten meat, fried pork chops with onions, and torte, candies, with ice cream for dessert. There was so much food, my belly finally felt as full as my heart. I was so grateful that everyone came to my party. Having family made me feel more prosperous than all the presents I received. I did not feel poor today.

My birthday celebrations left me feeling so blessed for my life and everything I had. I wanted to share it with everyone. I saw people being generous and giving to me. Now I could be the generous one. I could help others as much as they helped me.

Being part of the church also meant helping in the local communities. As a curious twist of fate, it turned out that one of the church members, Vasyl Ivanovych, was also the headmaster of the orphanage where Slavik and I began our lives. When we moved out of this orphanage and into foster care, he often checked on us to ensure our family cared for us. He also gave us the culinary school recommendation.

I spent a lot of time catering and working in bars in addition to the restaurant where I worked. I also went back to the orphanage with Vasyl to help when I could. It felt strange donating my services at the place where I needed someone to take care of me so many years ago, but I was so grateful when people would visit or bring donations, as we often felt as though the world had abandoned us. Now, I was able to give the same to the children there. I wondered if the children felt grateful and inspired when they saw me and what I had become. I hope I motivated them.

I was so happy to have Vasyl there as a mentor and friend in my church. The Mormon Church was still small in Ukraine. Because we were small, we often faced the challenge of finding a building where we could worship. Vasyl was very generous, allowing us to meet at the orphanage. It didn't surprise me. We all knew one another, calling our fellow church members brother and sister. Feeling so close to everyone there, I knew Brother Vasyl had the same values as me and the same generous heart.

After one of our Saturday meetings, I decided to see Masha and Nadya. After seeing Masha, I was concerned about them and wanted to talk to them. When I gave Nadya the food I had left from my party, they were so happy. So, when the church moved to be not far from them, I decided to visit them and take some of the Napoleon cake I made. It was my favorite cake to make with boiled cream inside, like an eclair. I loved sharing my creations with them. I knew they were hungry, so I always tried to bring them something.

I spent the whole day visiting them and talking to them about their lives, but I knew I needed to do more to help. I always tried to be a faithful person. I learned a lot from the missionaries, and I wanted to live my life the way they lived, helping others find the truth of the gospel. So I often invited Slavik to different church events. After a few visits, he said our church events were boring, and he didn't enjoy them. I couldn't see how they were more boring than standing the whole time, listening to a liturgy in a language we didn't even know, but he said the only thing he liked there were the sweets after.

Slavik didn't react to the church the way I hoped he would. I could see he didn't feel the same inspiration I felt when I was there, but I still encouraged him to join me when I could. Maybe one day, he would find the happiness I had found, and we could join this new church family together.

I could only hope that Masha and Nadya would see what Slavik didn't, but I knew I needed to take the chance. So, as it was getting later in the day, I said to them, "I'm tired today. Maybe, I could sleep here tonight, and we could all go tomorrow for an event we're having with my friends tomorrow. There will be a lot of food there, and I think you will like many of the people."

Masha was Orthodox, so I didn't invite her to our sacrament meetings. As I had done with Slavik, I knew I needed to start slow and ask her to church activities instead. Happily, they agreed, and so I stayed the night. I made a delicious dinner for them, and we enjoyed spending time together as a family.

"How is Dima, Nadya? Did you go to see him this week?"

I thought my question was one a brother should ask his sister, but Nadya was quiet. I think I knew why, but I just kept looking at her, waiting for her to answer me.

Masha finally broke the silence, "I went to see him, Vitaly. He was very small initially, but he's growing so fast. I know he will grow to be such a strong and healthy child like you did."

"Have you not seen him, Nadya?" Masha was trying to make up for Nadya. I couldn't pretend I wasn't upset. I couldn't believe she would do this to her child. I spent my whole life waiting for my mother to come and see me. I felt abandoned, and now, Nadya's child would feel the same way. "Nadya, how can you do this to your child," I said. "Have you never visited him?"

"You don't understand, Vitaly. I can't. I don't have money to see him." Nadya wouldn't look at me as she spoke.

"It's true, Vitaly." I saw Masha wanted to protect Nadya again.

"Uncle Lonya has been buying medication for Dima, and he comes by to give us food and money, but it's not enough to include a visit. It is challenging. We don't have much."

I remember all of the times Uncle Lonya did the same for me. I was grateful that he was worried for us as if we were his children and continued to care for us even after Tyotya Valya ended her relationship with us. Uncle Lonya was the only family we had left at this point. Tyotya Valya attended my party, but that was the only time I had seen her after moving out. I knew she would never contact me if it were up to her. Uncle Lonya, on the other hand, was there for us, and I thanked God that he existed.

Nadya didn't say anything else. She just began cleaning from dinner. She was distraught, and I could tell she had regret for her actions. Watching her made me think of my mother. I wondered how much trouble she had trying to come and see me. Perhaps she also had problems with money and regretted not visiting more.

I spent much of the night sleepless, thinking of my mother. I remember little of the church event we attended the next day. Even though I was grateful to have my sisters there, I could only think of getting home and seeing if I couldn't find some solace in my prayers.

When I arrived home, my mood got worse. Slavik and Serhij had friends over, and everyone was drinking when all I wanted was to be alone.

I walked past the group, closing myself in the bedroom. I spent the whole night thinking of my mother. Maybe she was struggling like Nadya. Perhaps that was why she didn't visit me. What if she needed my help? If she was still having a difficult time, I could be there for her."

I remembered visiting my mother's small apartment before Roustam sold it. Slavik and I also went to check on her.

I was quiet as Slavik and I approached her door. I stopped a few feet before Slavik did. I couldn't go in. I wasn't ready to face her yet. I just wanted to know if she needed help. So, I stood to the side of the door as Slavik knocked.

She answered quickly and cautiously, opening the door just a crack and not saying any words.

"Hi. Are you Yevgheniya Nikitichna?"

"Yes? Who are you?" She was short with her answer and seemed suspicious right away. I wondered how anyone could be doubtful of Slavik, with his cherub cheeks and pure kindness radiating from his eyes.

"My name is Slavik. I'm a friend of your son. He just wanted me to check in on you?"

"My son? You're a liar. You don't know Roustam. Why would he care about me?"

"Not Roustam. Vitaly. I'm a friend of Vitaly."

"Vitaly?" Did she hesitate when she heard my name? I couldn't tell without seeing her. I wondered if there was longing in her eyes, but her answer came too quickly, stopping my thoughts in their tracks. "I don't know any Vitaly!" she yelled.

I don't know what happened next. Tears burst from my eyes before I could stop them, and I left, running down the street and away from mothers who forget their children.

I remembered that day, but I also thought of the pain I saw on Nadya's face. I wasn't sure what to do. I couldn't help but wonder if the first person I needed to save wasn't my mother.

A knock at the door startled me back to the moment. It was Serhij, "Vitaly, you can't stay in this room forever. You must celebrate with me."

I looked at him for a moment. "What are we celebrating tonight?" My tone was sharp. There was a party in our apartment every night, and I was tired of celebrations and everyone drinking.

"I'm going to live with Vera."

I just looked at him. Serhij was the most progressive of all of us. People in Ukraine didn't live together without being married, but Serhij didn't care. He was moving out to live with his future wife, and now we needed to decide what to do with our home. What would happen to our friendship and our lives? I didn't know.

The one thing I did know was that everything was about to change. Serhij would want his share of the apartment, and I wasn't sure how we would give it to him without moving. For the first time in my life, I wasn't sure where to go or what to do next. I always had a goal, but I couldn't imagine any place that would give us what we had here. I didn't want to live without Slavik in my life, but I wasn't sure where we would go together. There wasn't a plan I could make for how we would get through this.

The only sure thing I had in my life that day was the church. Maybe it was time for me to move out and move on with my life the way I wanted to live it. But, it was a big step, and I didn't feel ready. I could only hope my new church family would be there for me in a way my birth family never was.

Epilogue

Serhij's wedding with Slavik, Serhij's wife, Serhij, Masha, and I, but no Nadya.

I HAD LIVED WITH SLAVIK AND SERHIJ in our apartment for about two years when Serhij decided to move in with Vera. We could do nothing to give Serhij his share but to sell our wonderful home.

We scheduled to meet with a woman who was supposed to buy the apartment. Still, before we finished the paperwork with her, we asked Uncle Lonya to help us because he knew a lot about business and understood property sales.

"She's trying to cheat you." We all looked at Uncle Lonya as he shuffled through the documents. "There is not adequate documentation for selling the apartment properly. If you go forward with this, she will leave you in the streets."

It didn't surprise me. Everyone was trying to take advantage of us.

"Don't worry, though," he said. "I'll help you to sell your apartment in the right way."

Uncle Lonya negotiated a new contract, and just a few weeks later, Slavik, Serhij, and I went with him to the notary to sign the agreement. Uncle Lonya asked me to count the money as she finalized the paperwork. For the first time in my life, I held four thousand five hundred American dollars in my hands. It felt great. I had worked hard so my brothers and I could have a place to live. This money was the result of my effort.'

Uncle Lonya smiled as we all took our turns holding the money. As the notary left the room to gather the last of our documents, he spoke to us as a father would. "You boys are growing up, but you are still young. I am worried that if you take all this money now, you might drink it all away." He looked at Serhij with his last comment. I had to agree with him. Serhij drank a lot, but Uncle Lonya continued optimistically, "Serhij, you are moving in with Vera. What if I gave you three hundred dollars of this money so you could get everything you need for the wedding."

"Three hundred dollars is not enough," Serhij said, staring at the pile of money that now sat in our Uncle Lonya's hands. "I need five hundred, at least."

"If I give you five hundred now, you will regret that amount in the end," he said, handing Serhij three hundred dollars.

'That leaves nearly four thousand dollars,' I thought, but I didn't say it out loud. Instead, I wanted to wait and see what Uncle Lonya was planning to do with the rest of the money.

"Vitaly, you and Slavik could stay with me for a while until you can get another place of your own. I need some renovations in one of the apartments I own. I could give you two hundred dollars each to help you with school and other expenses. Then, I will take the rest, and I will invest it for you. I am working on many projects, like the house and the salon. I will use the money and pay you back with fifteen percent interest over the next three years."

It sounded like a great opportunity to me. The best part was, I would still get to live with Slavik, and we would have a place to stay where I wouldn't need to pay the bills for a while. Slavik agreed it was a good idea, as well.

In the end, I took only one hundred dollars. I didn't need more than that, and I was excited to make interest through the money Uncle Lonya kept. Slavik decided to take two hundred. That meant we each had over a thousand dollars invested and earning interest.

We were still with the notary signing the last of the documents when uncle Lonya shared his plan. "That is quite a special deal your uncle is offering you," she said smiling. "Would you like me to create a document to show your investment and when you plan to make payments?"

Uncle Lonya jumped in right away, "It is expensive to have all of those documents. We are family, and our word is enough."

I was excited by the idea of having a document to show how I was a man now making investments, and I had seen the way banks were able to recover their money by having loan agreements when the borrowers didn't want to pay. So, I suggested, "Maybe we could create just a note, Uncle Lonya, and not add all of the other documents."

"We could make a promissory note," the notary added.

Uncle Lonya became quiet for a moment, and then he asked, "Why do you need a document, Vitaly? Do you not trust me to pay you?"

Everyone looked around nervously, including me. I trusted my Uncle Lonya more than anyone, "No. I was just so excited by my first real business transaction. This is my first investment. I wanted something to show for it."

The room became thick with silence as I glanced at the money in his hand.

"What if we just did a simple IOU?" The notary asked, breaking the awkward emptiness before anyone else even moved.

"Of course, if that would help." Uncle Lonya's tone was terse. I hoped I didn't offend him too much, but that apartment was the only thing I had in my life that had any value, and it suddenly seemed that the money I had earned from it was passing through my grasp too quickly.

We all signed beneath the short paragraph summarizing the terms of our agreement. We then left the notary's office without even a stamp or any words from Uncle Lonya. I took my money, along with some cash Slavik owed me, and I bought dress shoes and sneakers. I lent the rest to the branch president because he said he needed renovations. It felt good to be independent enough to invest my money in worthwhile things. Finally, I was ready to live the life successful people lived.

Serhij's wedding wasn't far behind the sale of our apartment. I was excited about the event. Traditional Ukrainian weddings are big celebrations with music and dancing that sometimes last weeks and include the entire community.

In the traditional pagan ritual, the celebration begins with young unmarried girls donning wreaths and entering the forests to search for the 'paporot' flower. Legend said they would receive good fortune and a handsome mate if they found the flower. Many Ukrainian girls had run into the woods over the centuries, more playing than searching, excited to be part of the traditions they had watched growing up. I think they were also excited because they knew the unmarried young men of the village would soon be joining them, as they followed behind the women, looking for their mate.

Once they found a mate, the young suitor would then emerge from

EPILOGUE

the forest wearing the wreath the young maiden wore when she went in. The villagers would be waiting to celebrate, knowing they desired to be married, but the game wasn't over. The potential groom still needed to ask permission of the parents. So, the young woman's friends would hide her in the back room of her home to prevent her from being stolen by any man. The suitor's job was to offer her parents ransom to take her as his bride. The parents would then bring him an imposter; someone dressed to look like the maiden.

The best part of the tradition was when the suitor demanded they bring him his true love. The most traditional men made a grand show of realizing they tried to trick him and claim his bride as the only woman he could love. The families then responded to his outrage, saying, "We will bring her, but she is valuable to us. So, we demand more ransom."

After negotiating a fair amount, they sent the suitor to gather his promised money. As everyone in the town was involved in the courtship, they would contribute what they could, but that still wasn't a guarantee. After the suitor gathered the dowry, he returned to the home, and they would either give him his bride or her parents would meet him at the door, carrying only a pumpkin.

If the girl's parents came to the door with a pumpkin, it meant the family rejected his offer to marry their daughter but offered the pumpkin instead, as a gift, so he would not leave with his hands empty.

All of this happened days before the wedding. So it was an exciting celebration of tradition for the entire community, but Serhij liked to be progressive and didn't follow the conventions. He proposed to Vera without ever stepping foot into the trees and lived with her before they were married. He also skipped the ransom he would pay to Vera's parents, probably because he didn't want to give up any of his money.

I wished he had followed some of these traditions. With everything Chernivtsi had been through, our ceremonies were important. There were times when they were the only thing we had.

Luckily, there were some traditions even Serhij could not avoid, as wedding ceremonies were all the same. On the wedding day, Vera's parents offered a ritual blessing for the couple called 'Blahoslovennia.'

To begin the blessing, the 'starosta' or elder from the church turned to Vera's parents, saying, "Please, sit on the bench." He then placed a long embroidered cloth called a rushnyk on their lap.

The starosta continued with words that were centuries old, "As these two children stand before their own mother, before their own father, before their uncles, before their godparents; maybe they did not listen to one of you, I ask you to forgive them and bless them."

The family members responded with equally ancient words, "Bih sviatyi," meaning, "May Holy God forgive and bless you."

After reciting the blessing three times, Serhij and Vera bowed and kissed their parents' faces. They then kissed their hands and feet, as well. Finally, they repeated the kissing three times to forgive any sins and thank their parents for blessing the wedding.

Traditionally, they would have had the ceremony at the bride and the groom's houses, but Serhij was an orphan. So, they would not have a chance to do the ritual a second time, but I don't believe they cared. What happened after the blessing was my favorite part.

The moment after they gave the final kiss, Serhij and Vera ran laughing, forgetting the sadness of only one ceremony. They raced, trying to beat each other to a rushnyk of their own, as whoever's foot landed on the rushnyk first would be the one to have the final say throughout the rest of their marriage.

As the ceremony ended, the elder covered Vera's hair with a traditional crown, showing she was now a married woman. He then donned Serhij with a hat to represent his responsibilities as a man. Then, we all traveled together to the city clerk's office to witness the city official registering them as a married couple.

Everything was official now. So we all left the office to stand on the street and watch Vera's parents open a bottle of champagne, giving glasses to Serhij and Vera. They drank together, and then, as they both swallowed the last of their champagne, they ceremoniously threw their glasses to the ground, shattering them to bring luck and happiness to their union. And with that, the ceremonies were over. Serhij and Vera were married, and now it was time to party.

The wedding party gave everyone a loaf of wedding bread to begin the celebration. I was pleased about this because I loved wedding bread. I couldn't wait to enjoy it and all the food and drinks we would have after finishing the ceremony.

I was even more excited to celebrate with my friends. I had been so busy with school and the church I hadn't had many opportunities to spend time with them, but I knew I would now. We would be awake all night and maybe even the next day, singing and dancing and, even better, having delicious food and drinks.

We were all very happy for Serhij and caught up in the ceremony, so I didn't realize Masha was there alone until I saw her standing near the food, and Nadya was not with her.

"Where is Nadya?" I asked as I approached her.

Masha responded, speaking to the floor and not to me, "Serhij didn't invite her."

"What? Didn't invite her?" Serhij had invited over one hundred and twenty people to his wedding. Everyone I knew was there, except Nadya. "How could he not invite his own sister?"

"She didn't have any money," Masha's face was still facing the floor. She knew how I would feel.

Of course, one of the traditions Serhij still wanted to honor was asking each guest to bring no less than twenty dollars to his wedding. Of course, twenty dollars was a lot of money to many of us, but it was traditional to give a gift, and we honored his request. Still, I couldn't understand his decision to leave his sister out of his wedding just because she didn't have money.

I often thought Serhij was as greedy as Tyotya Valya, and today he proved it was true. His only concern on his wedding day seemed to be making a profit. "I guess I know now how we will pay for this wedding," I said with my blood boiling.

Masha sighed.

"What now?!" I knew Masha. She had something more to say, and she didn't want to say it.

"Uncle Lonya gave him the money for the wedding." She looked away, nearly weeping.

I felt terrible for Masha to watch Nadya go through all her suffering and try to be strong, but I couldn't stop to comfort her. I was so upset.

Uncle Lonya was still upset with me, not speaking to me since the day I asked for a promissory note, except to give me chores to do around his house. He hadn't paid me any money back from the loan yet, but here he was, acting as a father to Serhij and paying for his wedding. I felt like I was back living with Tyotya Valya's judgment, where she would punish me for requesting things that were mine.

I loved my life, and I loved the people in it. I loved my mother and brother, even if they didn't know how to love me in return. I loved my foster brothers and sisters and my many friends and teachers from the orphanage and other schools along the way. I even loved Tyotya Valya and my Dyadya Grisha for taking me into their home and giving me the best life they knew how.

Looking at all the people I considered family in my life, I remembered how they helped me. Though I felt alone and even scared at times, there was always someone to raise my hope again. As hard as it was, I loved my life and my native country, not to be judged but to remember what I learned there. Everything I needed came to me, and I gave credit to God.

EPILOGUE

I often felt I only passed my exams because of God's help. I succeeded through His guidance and with the help of teachers and friends. I created a life free from jail cells and the worst atrocities of poverty because God was there for me, leading the way. God gave me strength.

He guided me through my life, leading me to Tanya, her family, and eventually, the missionaries. We laughed together and supported each other, reading scriptures and always trying to be good people. They were as much a family to me as anyone growing up with me, and I knew I was ready to make my commitment to them to be my eternal family.

I left the wedding thinking of Nadya and how Serhij had abandoned her, the same way she abandoned her child and my mother abandoned me. No one could look beyond their pain to see the pain they were causing others.

I had a good life, better than most orphans. Maybe I wasn't the one who needed anyone else to fill the empty spaces in my heart. Maybe my heart was whole all along, and I was the one who could help others find their way. Nadya was lost and needed help, just as much as her baby. I think my mom needed that too, and she probably never received it. Maybe she didn't have someone like Martha in her life or Slavik. Perhaps life had tossed her to the side, and no one ever found a way for her to be useful. I knew I could be there to give Nadya food when she needed it, but what did my mom need that she never received?

It was time for me to reconcile the one thing I had never reconciled. I needed to be there for the one person who had probably needed my love and support far more than I needed hers. It was time for me to move out of my Uncle Lonya's house and in with my mother.

About the Author

VITALY MAGIDOV earned an MBA degree from the University of Utah, a BS in Computer Science from Utah Valley University, and a BS in Electronics Engineering from Chernivtsi National University. Serving as a Missionary in England, he learned to inspire and assist those in need. His life ambition is to return to Ukraine and offer innovative opportunities for the children now growing up in the same orphanages where he began his journey.

You can connect with me on:

Email: info@vitalybook.com
Website: https://vitalybook.com
Twitter: @vitalybook
Facebook: @readvitalybook
Instagram: @vitalybook

Made in the USA
Middletown, DE
09 March 2022